Welcome

THE EVERYTHING Family Guides®

THESE HANDY, ACCESSIBLE BOOKS are designed to be the perfect travel companions. Whether you're traveling within a restricted budget or feeling the urge to splurge, you will find all you need to know to create the ideal vacation for yourself and your family.

These travel-friendly books present the latest information on hotel accommodations, restaurants, shopping, and transportation, as well as money-saving tips and strategies to beat the crowds and avoid the lines. Also included are detailed descriptions that help you make those tough decisions on which attractions to include in your travel itinerary.

Use these books to help you plan your vacation and then take them along with you for quick and easy reference. You can read them cover to cover or simply pick out the information you need. Let the *Everything® Family Guides* pave the way for your fun-filled and exciting adventures!

📖 TRAVEL TIP

Quick, handy tips

⊕ HOT SPOT

Places not to be missed

≡ FAST FACT

Important sound bytes of information

THE EVERYTHING
— Family Guides —

Dear Reader,

This is the all-new, fourth edition of *The Everything® Family Guide to The Walt Disney World Resort®, Universal Studios®, and Greater Orlando*. This book will help you get the most out of your vacation, by providing you with information about all that there is to see and do, and yes, there's a lot to cover!

If you're planning a return trip to Orlando, during your upcoming visit you'll be able to experience a handful of new rides, shows, parades, attractions, shops and restaurants at virtually all of the various theme parks. Whether this is your first trip to Orlando, or you return to this popular vacation destination every year, some truly amazing experiences await you!

As you're about to discover, the trick to having the most enjoyable and stress-free vacation possible is proper planning. Not only will this book help you plan your trip and choose the activities that are most suitable for you and the people you're traveling with, it'll also help you save money and cut the amount of time you waste standing in lines.

Have a wonderful Orlando vacation! When you get home, please feel free to e-mail me at *jr7777@aol.com*, or visit my Web site at *www.JasonRich.com*, and let me know how you enjoyed your trip!

Sincerely,

THE

EVERYTHING®

FAMILY GUIDE TO
THE WALT DISNEY WORLD RESORT®, UNIVERSAL STUDIOS®, AND GREATER ORLANDO

FOURTH EDITION

A complete guide to the best
hotels, restaurants, parks,
and must-see attractions

Jason Rich

◢

Adams Media
Avon, Massachusetts

Publishing Director: Gary M. Krebs
Managing Editor: Kate McBride
Copy Chief: Laura MacLaughlin
Acquisitions Editor: Eric M. Hall
Development Editor: Christina MacDonald
Production Editor: Jamie Wielgus

Production Director: Susan Beale
Production Manager: Michelle Roy Kelly
Series Designer: Daria Perreault
Cover Design: Paul Beatrice, Matt LeBlanc
Layout and Graphics: Colleen Cunningham,
Rachael Eiben, Michelle Roy Kelly,
John Paulhus, Daria Perreault, Erin Ring

An Everything® Series Book.
Everything® and everything.com® are registered trademarks of F+W Publications, Inc.

Published by Adams Media, an F+W Publications Company
57 Littlefield Street, Avon, MA 02322 U.S.A.
www.adamsmedia.com

ISBN 10: 1-59337-179-9
ISBN 13: 978-1-59337-179-1
Printed in Canada.

J I H G F E D C

Library of Congress Cataloging-in-Publication Data
Rich, Jason.
The everything family guide to the Walt Disney World Resort,
Universal Studios, and Greater Orlando / Jason Rich.—4th ed.
p.   cm.
An everything series book
Rev. ed. of: The everything guide to Walt Disney World, Universal Studios, and Greater Orlando.
ISBN 1-59337-179-9
1. Walt Disney World (Fla.)—Guidebooks. 2. Universal Studios Florida (Orlando, Fla. : Amusement park)—
Guidebooks. 3. Amusement parks—Florida—Orlando—Guidebooks. 4. Orlando Region (Fla.)—Guidebooks.
5. Family recreation—Florida—Orlando Region—Guidebooks. I. Rich, Jason. Everything guide to Walt Disney World,
Universal Studios, and Greater Orlando. II. Title. III. Series: Everything series.
GV1853.3.F62R53 2004
791'.06'875924—dc22
2004009169

Cover illustrations by Barry Littman / Cartography by Creative Force, Inc.

This book is available at quantity discounts for bulk purchases.
For information, call 1-800-289-0963.

Visit the entire Everything® series at www.everything.com

Contents

Top Ten Family Attractions in Orlando

Introduction

WHAT YOU'RE ABOUT TO READ IS THE ALL-NEW fourth edition of *The Everything® Family Guide to The Walt Disney World Resort®, Universal Studios®, and Greater Orlando*. This travel guide was written to help you make the most of your vacation experience. Unless you're planning to spend several weeks and an absolute fortune, there's no possible way that you'll be able to experience everything the Greater Orlando area has to offer. Therefore, you'll have to make decisions about which theme parks you want to visit, which attractions within those theme parks you want to experience, what shows and parades you want to see, and which restaurants you want to dine at.

The Walt Disney World (WDW) Resort, including the theme parks, resort hotels, restaurants, and other activities, offers the world-class service and hospitality that have become legendary. It's this hospitality that helps make everyone's vacation a truly memorable and enjoyable experience, and something that Walt Disney himself believed was so important.

The WDW Resort is a city unto itself, but it's a 30,500-acre (47-square-mile) city unlike any other found on this planet. Yet, with everything that already exists in this ultimate vacation destination, less than one-quarter of the total acreage of the resort complex has been developed. Thus, in the years and decades to come, you can bet that The WDW Resort will continue to evolve and provide many future generations with a taste of Disney magic and the wholesome family vacation experience that Walt Disney himself (along with his brother Roy) intended for all who visit this unique resort.

Located less than a thirty-minute drive from The WDW Resort is another fast-growing tourist destination, which is the second most popular theme park resort complex in the Greater Orlando area. Universal Orlando Resort offers some of the most incredible rides, shows, and attractions found anywhere in the world, yet here you'll find a very different type of vacation experience than at The WDW Resort.

Originally, when Universal Studios Florida opened, it was a single, medium-sized theme park that could be experienced within one day. Now, this park has expanded dramatically, and as you'll read later in this book, it continues to undergo massive construction and development. As a result, vacationers can easily plan on spending two or three full days experiencing everything there is to see and do at Universal Orlando Resort, which now comprises two theme parks, the CityWalk area, plus several resort hotels.

Located near Universal Orlando Resort is the third most popular theme park attraction in Orlando—SeaWorld. This marine park offers an up-close look at marine life, like dolphins and whales, plus it features an assortment of marine-related rides, shows, and attractions.

Inside this book, you will find detailed descriptions of all of the activities and things there are to see and do at The WDW Resort, Universal Orlando Resort, SeaWorld, and other popular tourist attractions. There are also all sorts of tips and suggestions on how you can save time and money while making the most of your vacation.

As you read this book and start thinking about how exactly you want to spend your time, be sure to take notes. Keep track of which rides, shows, attractions, parades, and activities are of interest to you (and the people you'll be traveling with). Once you think you know what you want to experience, start planning out the actual days of your trip. While you're doing this, keep in mind that each of the various theme parks is massive. At The WDW Resort, for example, The Magic Kingdom is 107 acres, Epcot is 300 acres, The Disney/MGM Studios take up about 155 acres, and Disney's Animal

Kingdom is spread across 500 acres, so plan on doing a lot of walking.

This book is "unofficial," which means that it is in no way authorized or sanctioned by The Walt Disney Company, Universal Studios, SeaWorld, or any other Orlando attraction, travel agency, hotel chain, restaurant, or airline. Thus, this book has the freedom to tell it like it is, and to offer you money- and time-saving advice that you won't find in any other travel guide or vacation-planning book.

As you'll read several times throughout this book, the various theme parks and resorts are always evolving. New rides, attractions, shows, parades, shops, restaurants, and activities are always being added, updated, or somehow changed, while outdated attractions are taken out of the various parks. Thus, when you actually visit Orlando, don't be surprised if you encounter something new or different that's not described in this book.

The Magic Kingdom

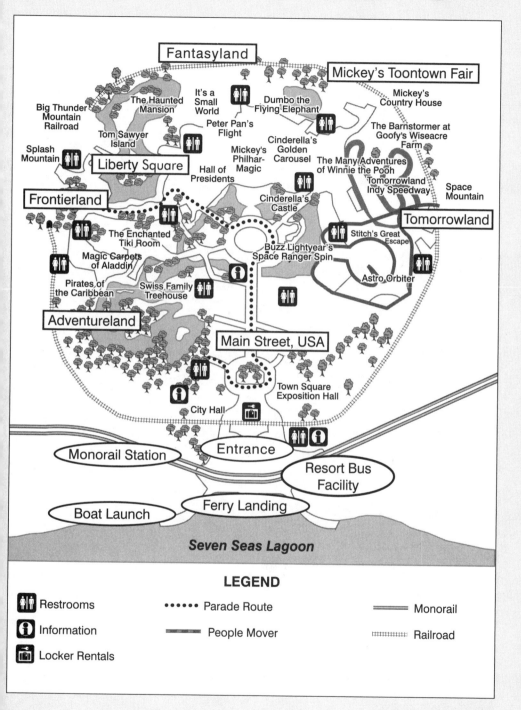

Fantasyland

Mickey's Toontown Fair

Big Thunder Mountain Railroad

The Haunted Mansion

It's a Small World

Dumbo the Flying Elephant

Mickey's Country House

Peter Pan's Flight

Tom Sawyer Island

The Barnstormer at Goofy's Wiseacre Farm

Splash Mountain

Liberty Square

Cinderella's Golden Carousel

Mickey's Philhar-Magic

The Many Adventures of Winnie the Pooh

Hall of Presidents

Tomorrowland Indy Speedway

Space Mountain

Frontierland

Cinderella's Castle

Tomorrowland

The Enchanted Tiki Room

Stitch's Great Escape

Magic Carpets of Aladdin

Buzz Lightyear's Space Ranger Spin

Astro Orbiter

Pirates of the Caribbean

Swiss Family Treehouse

Adventureland

Main Street, USA

Town Square Exposition Hall

City Hall

Entrance

Monorail Station

Resort Bus Facility

Boat Launch

Ferry Landing

Seven Seas Lagoon

LEGEND

- Restrooms
- Information
- Locker Rentals
- •••••• Parade Route
- People Mover
- ═══ Monorail
- ⊞⊞⊞⊞ Railroad

(Major Attractions)

Epcot

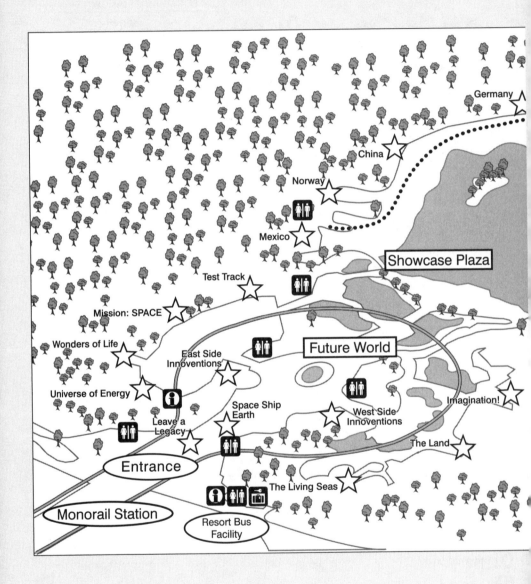

Germany
China
Norway
Mexico
Showcase Plaza
Test Track
Mission: SPACE
Future World
Wonders of Life
East Side Innoventions
Universe of Energy
West Side Innoventions
Imagination!
Leave a Legacy
Space Ship Earth
The Land
Entrance
The Living Seas
Monorail Station
Resort Bus Facility

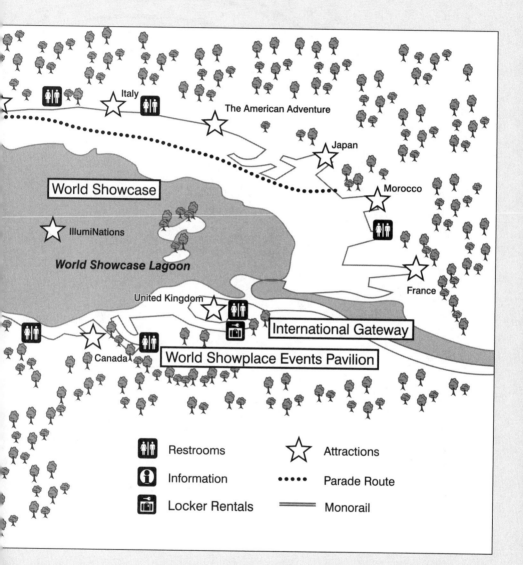

Italy

The American Adventure

Japan

World Showcase

Morocco

IllumiNations

World Showcase Lagoon

France

United Kingdom

International Gateway

Canada

World Showplace Events Pavilion

Restrooms

Attractions

Information

Parade Route

Locker Rentals

Monorail

The Disney-MGM Studios

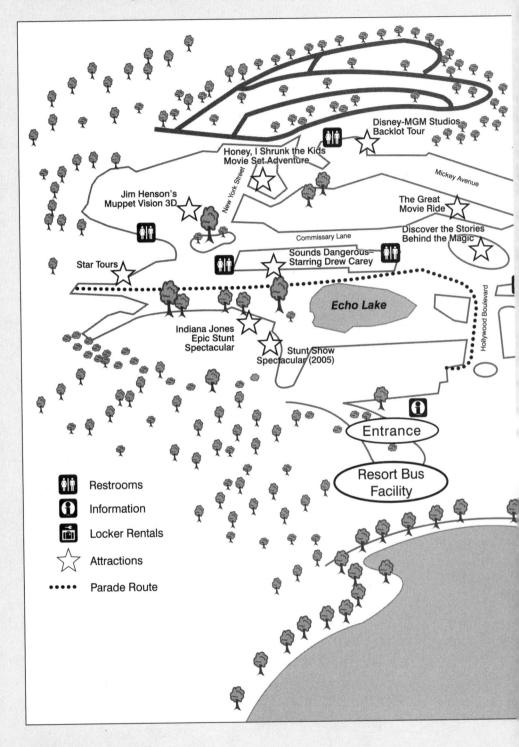

Disney-MGM Studios Backlot Tour

Honey, I Shrunk the Kids Movie Set Adventure

New York Street

Mickey Avenue

Jim Henson's Muppet Vision 3D

The Great Movie Ride

Commissary Lane

Discover the Stories Behind the Magic

Star Tours

Sounds Dangerous— Starring Drew Carey

Echo Lake

Hollywood Boulevard

Indiana Jones Epic Stunt Spectacular

Stunt Show Spectacular (2005)

Entrance

Resort Bus Facility

Restrooms

Information

Locker Rentals

Attractions

•••• Parade Route

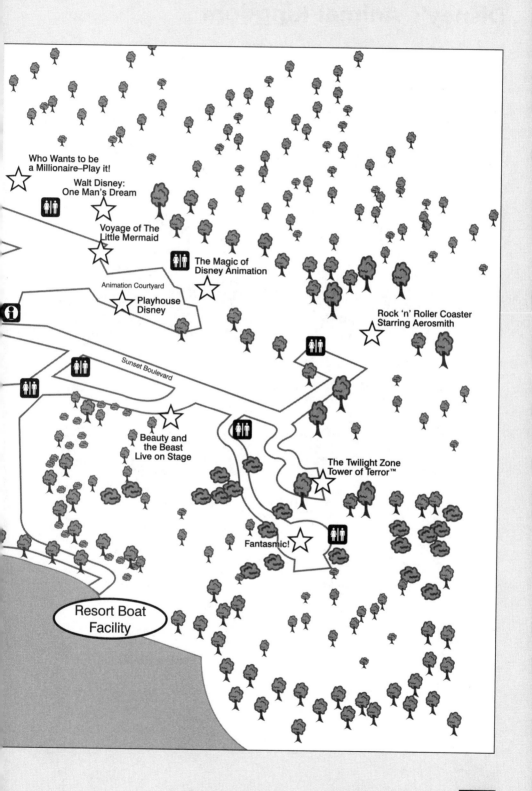

Who Wants to be
a Millionaire–Play it!

Walt Disney:
One Man's Dream

Voyage of The
Little Mermaid

The Magic of
Disney Animation

Animation Courtyard

Playhouse
Disney

Rock 'n' Roller Coaster
Starring Aerosmith

Sunset Boulevard

Beauty and
the Beast
Live on Stage

The Twilight Zone
Tower of Terror™

Fantasmic!

Resort Boat
Facility

Disney's Animal Kingdom

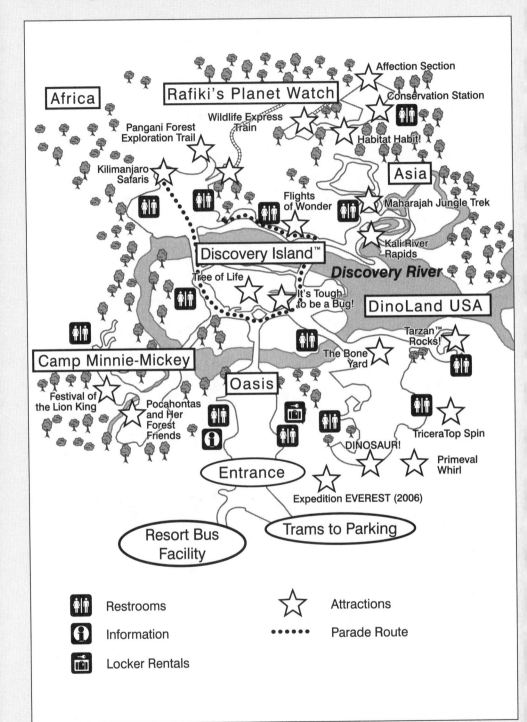

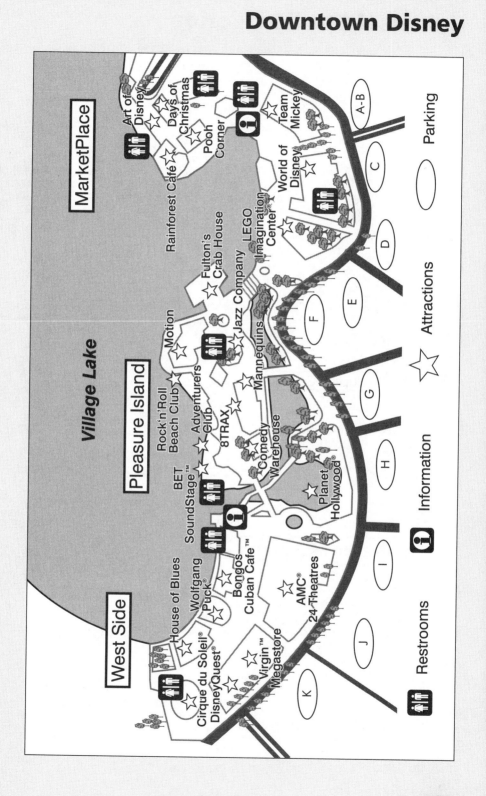

MarketPlace

Art of Disney
Days of Christmas
Pooh Corner
Team Mickey
World of Disney
Rainforest Cafe
Fulton's Crab House
LEGO Imagination Center
Motion
Jazz Company
Mannequins

Village Lake

Pleasure Island

Rock'n'Roll Beach Club
Adventurers Club
8TRAX
BET SoundStage™
Comedy Warehouse
Planet Hollywood®

West Side

House of Blues
Wolfgang Puck®
Bongos Cuban Cafe™
AMC® 24 Theatres
Cirque du Soleil®
DisneyQuest
Virgin™ Megastore

A-B
C
D
E
F
G
H
I
J
K

Parking

Attractions

Information

Restrooms

Universal Studios Florida

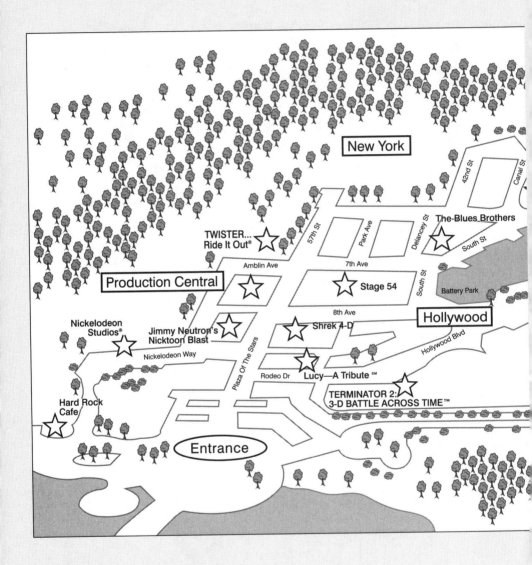

New York

Production Central

Hollywood

TWISTER... Ride It Out®

The Blues Brothers

Stage 54

Nickelodeon Studios®

Jimmy Neutron's Nicktoon Blast

Shrek 4-D

Lucy—A Tribute℠

TERMINATOR 2: 3-D BATTLE ACROSS TIME™

Hard Rock Cafe

Entrance

42nd St

Canal St

57th St

Park Ave

Delancey St

South St

7th Ave

South St

Battery Park

Amblin Ave

8th Ave

Plaza Of The Stars

Nickelodeon Way

Rodeo Dr

Hollywood Blvd

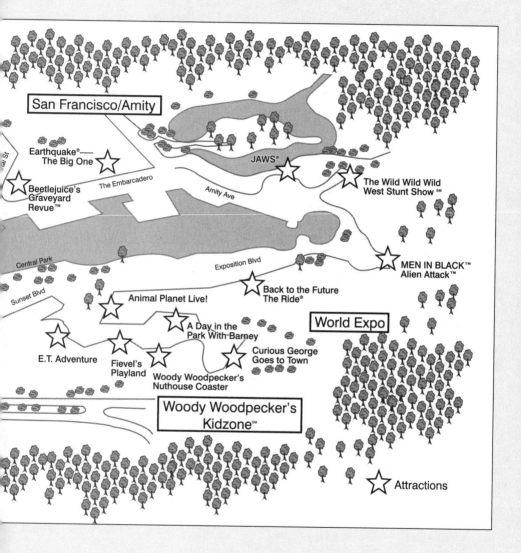

San Francisco/Amity

Earthquake®—
The Big One

Beetlejuice's
Graveyard
Revue™

The Embarcadero

Amity Ave

JAWS®

The Wild Wild Wild
West Stunt Show ℠

Central Park

Sunset Blvd

Exposition Blvd

MEN IN BLACK™
Alien Attack™

Animal Planet Live!

Back to the Future
The Ride®

World Expo

A Day in the
Park With Barney

E.T. Adventure

Fievel's
Playland

Woody Woodpecker's
Nuthouse Coaster

Curious George
Goes to Town

Woody Woodpecker's
Kidzone℠

Attractions

Universal Escape's Islands of Adventure

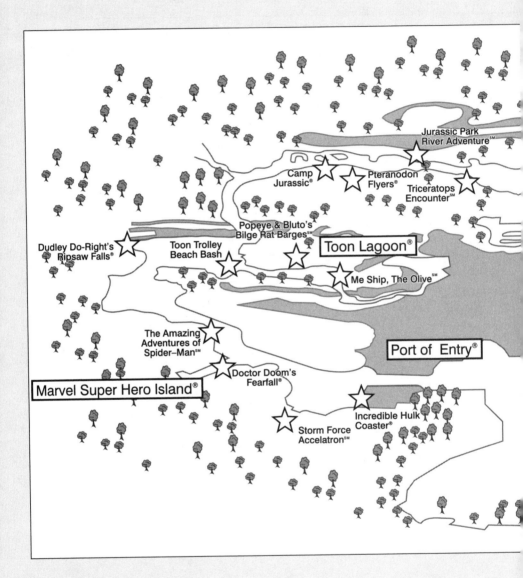

Jurassic Park River Adventure℠

Camp Jurassic®

Pteranodon Flyers®

Triceratops Encounter℠

Popeye & Bluto's Bilge Rat Barges℠

Toon Lagoon®

Dudley Do-Right's Ripsaw Falls®

Toon Trolley Beach Bash

Me Ship, The Olive℠

The Amazing Adventures of Spider–Man℠

Port of Entry®

Doctor Doom's Fearfall®

Marvel Super Hero Island®

Incredible Hulk Coaster®

Storm Force Accelatron℠

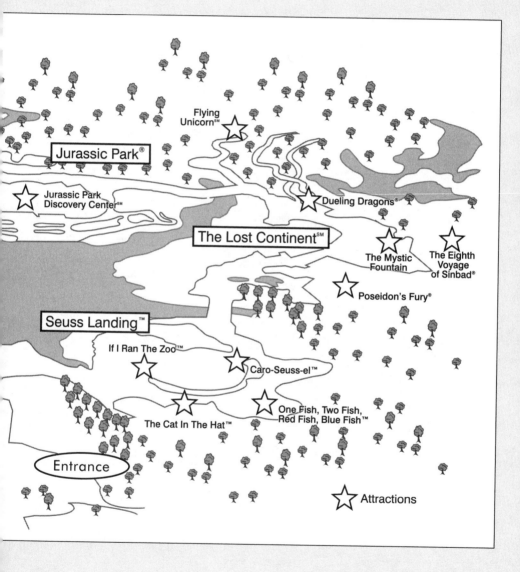

Flying Unicorn℠

Jurassic Park®

Jurassic Park Discovery Center℠

Dueling Dragons®

The Lost Continent℠

The Mystic Fountain

The Eighth Voyage of Sinbad®

Poseidon's Fury®

Seuss Landing™

If I Ran The Zoo™

Caro-Seuss-el™

The Cat In The Hat™

One Fish, Two Fish, Red Fish, Blue Fish™

Entrance

☆ Attractions

Greater Orlando Metro Area

CHAPTER 1

Preparing for Your Vacation

YOUR FIRST STEP IN PLANNING A DISNEY VACATION is to determine how long your vacation is going to last and how much money you have in your travel budget. Next, you'll need to book your airfare and hotel accommodations, and possibly reserve a rental car. This chapter will help you save money and time as you take care of these initial vacation-planning steps.

Inside The WDW Resort

The WDW Resort has become much more than just another theme park. This 30,500-acre resort located near Orlando, Florida, is the single-most popular vacation destination in the world, and one that well over 100 million guests have experienced since the resort opened in 1971. Within The WDW Resort are activities galore. So, no matter where your interests lie, you'll be able to spend your vacation participating in exciting activities or, if you choose, kicking back at your hotel's swimming pool, relaxing, and getting a tan.

Listed in alphabetical order, The WDW Resort consists of:

Blizzard Beach—One of Disney's wettest and wildest water parks.

Championship Golf Courses—If you enjoy playing golf, The WDW Resort offers your choice of award-winning eighteen-hole courses, putting greens, and driving ranges.

Disney-MGM Studios—Get a peek at Disney's motion picture and animation production studios and experience some awesome rides, shows, and attractions, like Tower of Terror 4 and Rock 'n' Roller Coaster Starring Aerosmith.

Disney's Animal Kingdom—Disney's newest and biggest theme park, where the stars are the real-life animals. It's here you'll find awesome rides, shows, and attractions, like *Festival of the Lion King* and Kali River Rapids.

Disney's BoardWalk—A nightspot that's jam-packed with restaurants, clubs, bars, shops, and activities. For dueling piano bar entertainment, Jellyrolls is the place to be after sundown.

Disney's Vacation Club—Disney's timeshare vacation opportunity.

Disney's West Side—Disney comes to life after dark with clubs, restaurants, bars, shops, and activities. Enjoy dining at the theme restaurants, like Planet Hollywood or House of Blues.

Disney's Wide World of Sports Complex—A huge sports facility designed for amateur and professional athletes alike.

Epcot—The Disney theme park that offers both Future World and the World Showcase. It's here you'll find Mission: SPACE, one of the most advanced theme park attractions ever created.

Fort Wilderness Campground—In addition to resort hotels, The WDW Resort complex offers plenty of fully equipped campsites and special activities at this campground area.

The Magic Kingdom—This is the theme park that started it all. Experience the classic Disney attractions and make your own Disney memories. This theme park includes many of the attractions that Walt Disney himself created or helped to develop during his lifetime. Mickey's PhilharMagic is an awesome 3D movie and one of the newest attractions you'll find here.

On-Property Resort Hotels—Each of the award-winning resort hotels has its own special theme, and all offer some of the most incredible customer service and hospitality that you'll find anywhere in the world.

Pleasure Island—For one admission price, guests have a chance to experience a handful of hot clubs. This area of Downtown Disney offers the world's largest street party. The action all starts after the sun goes down.

Restaurants—No matter what type of food you're looking for or how much you have to spend, chances are you'll find it somewhere on Disney property.

Typhoon Lagoon—Another family-oriented water park that offers gallons and gallons of fun and surprises.

⬛ TRAVEL TIP

Planning a family reunion? The WDW Resort makes planning a family get-together (with eight guests or more) fast, fun, and easy, allowing you to create the most memorable vacation experience possible for everyone in your extended family. The program is called "Magical Gatherings." To learn more about this online-based, free downloadable tool, point your Web browser to: *www.disneyworld.com/magicalgatherings*.

Flying to Orlando

All of the airlines listed in this section (and possibly a few others) offer competitive rates and travel packages to the Orlando International Airport, so be sure to shop around for the best airfares and flights. Keep in mind that not all of the airlines will offer service from your home city.

As a general rule, you want to book your airfare as far in advance as possible. Many airlines offer the best prices if you book and pay for your tickets twenty-one days in advance You can, however, also obtain good fares if you make your reservations (and pay for your airline tickets) fourteen or seven days early. When making your travel plans, try to have the most flexible schedule possible. If your schedule permits, you'll almost always get a better airfare if your stay includes a Saturday night.

Keep in mind, with "discounted" or "special" airfares, the tickets will not be refundable, and there will be a fee to change the travel dates the airline ticket is good for. The change fee is usually between $100 and $150, plus the price difference in the airfare itself. To avoid this change fee, most airlines will allow you to fly standby; however, this does not guarantee you a seat on a specific flight, and if you're traveling with a family and the flight you're trying to get onto is close to capacity, your chances of all getting on the same flight are slim, especially during peak travel periods.

📁 TRAVEL TIP

To make your vacation the best it can possibly be, you'll want to invest some time before you depart to properly plan your trip. Especially if you're traveling with children or a group of people, the more preplanning you do now, the more organized and relaxing your trip will be when it actually begins.

If you choose to use your frequent-flier miles to book your airline ticket to Orlando, keep in mind that seats may be difficult to reserve during peak travel periods, so make your reservations early. The advantages of using a frequent-flier ticket are that it's free and most airlines allow you to change your travel plans at the last minute with no penalties or fees.

Always ask the airline reservation representative you speak with for the lowest airfare available. After an airfare is quoted to you, ask again if it is the best deal. Next, ask if there are flights to and from Orlando at around the same times as the ones quoted to you that would make the airfare less expensive. You won't often be quoted the absolute lowest prices the first time you ask. Sometimes, airlines will offer discounted "online-only" fares exclusively from their Web site. For example, US Airways' Web site is at ✍*www.usairways.com.*

Also, check the travel section of your local newspaper for advertised special fares and promotions. You can make a reservation that will be held for twenty-four hours without having to pay for the ticket, so make an unpaid reservation and then shop around by calling additional airlines.

🧳 TRAVEL TIP

If you're traveling cross-country, red-eye (overnight) flights that leave the West Coast between 10:00 P.M. and midnight and arrive in Orlando the following morning are almost always the cheapest flights available. While most people hate flying all night, you can sometimes save up to several hundred dollars when traveling between the West Coast and the East Coast via a red-eye flight on any airline.

Strategies for the Best Airfare

There are several alternatives available to you when it comes to shopping around for the best airfares. You can go to the airport and visit a ticket counter, or book your travel directly with the airline via telephone or its Web site.

You can also surf the Internet and visit the various travel-related Web sites such as Travelocity.com, Hotwire.com, Priceline.com, LastMinuteTravel.com, or Orbitz.com (described later in this chapter).

Another alternative is to call a travel agent and have them do the busywork for you. Travel agents have computer systems that allow them to search for flight availability on all airlines at once. Most travel agents will be happy to work with you over the telephone, so it's not necessary to take time out of your busy schedule during business hours to visit a travel agent's office in person.

When choosing a travel agent, find someone who comes highly recommended by someone you trust. Travel agents can be extremely helpful and save you money, but some will purposely quote you higher-priced airfares since they're receiving a commission from the airline based on the price of the ticket they sell. If you're a member of AAA or have an American Express card, both of these companies offer highly reputable travel agencies that offer their services either in person or by telephone to members.

Finally, you might want to look into package deals offered by the various airlines. Many packages include airfare, hotel, rental car, and perhaps meals or show tickets. Most airlines have a separate "Vacation Package" reservation department that's different from the regular airline reservation department. The Walt Disney Travel Company also offers a handful of discounted packages to The WDW Resort (☎407-939-7675).

📼 TRAVEL TIP

To save money, consider using public transportation to get to the airport in your home city. It'll almost always be cheaper than parking your own car at the airport. The cheapest option is to have a friend or family member drop you off at the airport and pick you up when you return. Another option is to use a door-to-door shuttle bus service, which is almost always cheaper than a taxi, limo, or town car service.

The Orlando International Airport

The Orlando International Airport is the closest major airport to all of the theme parks, resorts, and attractions within the Greater Orlando area. If you'll be flying to Orlando, chances are this is the airport you'll be flying into. While this list is subject to change, the major airlines that service this airport include:

AeroMexico: ☎(800) 237-6639
Air Canada: ☎(800) 247-2262
AirJamaica: ☎(800) 523-5585
AirTran Airways: ☎(800) AIR-TRAN
AirTransat: ☎(877) 872-6728
Alaska Airlines: ☎(800) 252-7522
American Airlines: ☎(800) 433-7300

American Eagle: ☎(800) 422-7300
AmericaWest Airlines: ☎(800) 235-9292
ANA: ☎(800) 235-9262
ATA: ☎(800) 225-2995
Bahamasair: ☎(800) 222-4262
British Airways: ☎(800) AIR-WAYS
Champion Air: ☎(800) 225-5658
ConJet: ☎(800) 809-7777
Continental: ☎(800) 523-3273
Copa Airlines: ☎(800) 359-2672
Delta Airlines/Delta Express: ☎(800) 221-1212
El Al: ☎(800) 223-6700
Frontier: ☎(800) 432-1359
Ibera: ☎(800) 772-4642
Icelander: ☎(800) 223-5500
JetBlue: ☎(800) 538-2583
LTU: ☎(800) 888-0200
Martinair: ☎(800) 627-8462
Mexicana: ☎(800) 531-7921
Midwest Airlines: ☎(800) 452-2022
Northwest Airlines/KLM: ☎(800) 225-2525
Saudia: ☎(800) 472-8342
Song: ☎(800) 359-7664
Southwest Airlines: ☎(800) 435-9792
Spirit Airlines: ☎(800) 772-7117
United: ☎(800) 241-6522
US Airways: ☎(800) 428-4322
US Airways Vacation Packages: ☎(800) 455-0123
Vanguard Airlines: ☎(800) 826-4827
Varig Brazil: ☎(800) 468-2744
Virgin Atlantic: ☎(800) 862-8621
Zoom: ☎(866) 359-9666

Note: A handful of other airlines also operate charter flights to and from Orlando and other major U.S. cities and foreign countries. For more information about The Orlando International Airport, you can call ☎(407) 825-2001 or visit the airport's Web site at ⌨*www.orlandoairports.net*.

💼 TRAVEL TIP

If you're planning to meet people in Orlando, be sure they're provided with the appropriate airline, flight number, and departure time/date. With this information, anyone can contact your airline for arrival information or use one of these Web sites: ✐*http://flighttracker.lycos.com,* ✐*www.travelocity.com,* or ✐*www.flightarrivals.com.*

If you're driving from the airport to The WDW Resort, there are multiple routes that'll get you there. One direct route is to take the North exit from the airport to the Beeline Expressway West (Route 528). Get onto I-4 West and then follow signs to The WDW Resort. You'll want to exit I-4 at either Exit 26B or Exit 25, depending on your final destination within the huge resort complex. The trip is less than 25 miles and should take about thirty minutes (without traffic).

Mears Motor Shuttles offers van service to the various hotels at The WDW Resort (as well as nearby areas) from the Orlando airport (and back). The cost is $16 each way or $28 round trip for adults, $12 one way or $20 round trip for kids (ages four to eleven), and free to kids under age four. These shuttles leave the airport every fifteen minutes or so and can be picked up right outside of the airport terminals. For reservations, call ☎(407) 423-5566 (✐*www.mearstransportation.com*).

Taxi service is available outside of the airport's main terminals, but this is one of the more expensive ways to reach The WDW Resort. Check with the Ground Transportation Information Desk located inside the airport for various other transportation options to get you from the airport to your hotel in the Orlando area. You can also call the Yellow Cab Co. (a fleet of bright orange cars and vans) at ☎(407) 699-9999.

Airport Security Information

Security is extremely tight at all U.S. airports. Be sure to arrive at the airport at least one hour prior to your scheduled departure time and have your driver's license, military ID, or passport ready to show multiple times at various security checkpoints, including the airline ticket counter.

A wide range of items, such as pocket knives, golf clubs, and scissors, cannot be taken aboard any flight as part of a carry-on. For additional security information, point your Web browser to: ✍*www.orlandoairports.net/goaa/security_awareness.htm.*

💼 TRAVEL TIP

If you live in a city with multiple airports, or you live between two cities that both have airports, price your airline tickets going to and from each of the airports closest to you. Airlines often offer special deals and promotions from specific airports.

Taking the Train

Located extremely close to The WDW Resort, there's an **Amtrak** station in Kissimmee, Florida (Amtrak Station Code: KIS). Information about taking an Amtrak train from anywhere in the country to WDW can be obtained by calling ☎(800) USA-RAIL or by visiting the Web site ✍*www.amtrak.com.*

Amtrak offers travel discounts to all students and veterans, as well as to AAA and AARP members who present their membership card when purchasing a train ticket. Amtrak train tickets can be purchased from many travel agents, by visiting any Amtrak ticket office, or by calling Amtrak directly and using a major credit card.

Busing It to Orlando

Greyhound (☎800-229-9424; ✍*www.greyhound.com*) has two bus terminals close to The WDW Resort: one in Orlando (555 North John Young Parkway, Orlando) and the other in Kissimmee (located at 103 East Dakin Avenue, Kissimmee). From these bus terminals, taxi service is available to The WDW Resort, Universal Studios, or any other nearby hotel or destination.

Renting a Car

Just like when making airline reservations, there are several tricks to use when reserving a rental car that will help ensure that you get the lowest rate possible. For starters, reserve your rental car as far in advance as possible (seven days in advance, minimum), and if you can, try to get the weekly rate instead of the daily rate offered by the car rental company. Most rental car companies will apply their weekly rates to five-, six-, or seven-day rentals.

Finding the Best Rate

Especially in tourist areas, like Orlando, the various rental car companies are always running special promotions, so be sure to ask about them, and keep your eyes open for ads from the rental car companies in your local newspaper and in your favorite magazines. In addition, many of the rental car companies provide a discount to AAA members, so after getting the rental car company's best rate, ask for the AAA member discount. The Entertainment Book (described later in this book) also has discount coupons and special offers that apply to many of the popular rental car companies. Finally, visit the various travel-related Web sites (such as *www.travelocity.com*, *www.priceline.com*, or *www.hotwire.com*) for great deals on rental cars.

Some popular credit cards have special promotional deals with the major rental car companies, so call the customer service phone number listed on your credit card and inquire about what deals they offer for renting a car. While you're on the phone with the credit card company, also ask if your credit card automatically provides rental car insurance if you use that credit card to pay for the rental. American Express, Diner's Club, and virtually all Visa and MasterCards (issued as part of an airline's frequent-flier program) automatically offer rental car insurance.

If you think you've found an awesome rental car rate, reserve the car, but continue to shop around. Call three or four other rental car companies and see if they'll beat the deal you've been offered. Many travelers believe that the best-known rental car companies are always the most expensive, but this isn't always the case. You'll often be pleasantly surprised to discover that companies like Hertz, Avis, and National offer highly competitive rates once you take advantage of their special promotional deals, airline frequent-flier discounts, and/or the AAA (or any auto club) member discount.

🧳 TRAVEL TIP

If you're a member of any airline's frequent-flier program, you can often receive a rental car discount from promotional partners of that airline. Check your monthly frequent-flier statement from the airline for information about special rental car offers.

When making a rental car reservation, make sure unlimited mileage is included in the rental price. Some rental car companies charge by the mile, in addition to the daily rental fee, so make sure you understand what's included in the price you're being quoted. Extremely low daily or weekly rental rates often do not include unlimited mileage, and once you travel above the allowed miles, you're charged a hefty fee per mile.

Insurance

No matter what hourly, daily, or weekly rate you're quoted by the rental car companies you call, these rates do not include the various types of optional insurance choices that are offered, nor is tax included in the quoted rate. If you choose to pay for all of the different insurance options, the quoted rate for the rental car often more than doubles. What most travelers don't know, however, is that they do not need all of the optional insurance, because their own regular insurance policies, as well as the travel insurance provided free of charge by some credit card companies, offer more than adequate protection.

Prior to renting a car, call the customer service number for your auto insurance company as well as your homeowner's insurance company. Ask if rental car insurance is automatically offered under your existing policy. If so, you probably don't need any of the insurance offered by the rental car companies. If you rely on your existing insurance, however, and you're forced to make a claim due to an accident in the rental car, your regular insurance rates could go up in the future.

═FAST FACT

One benefit of purchasing the optional insurance from the rental car companies is that your existing policies won't be affected if a claim has to be made (assuming any damage or injury claims are under the limit of the insurance you purchase).

Rental Car Companies

The following are rental car companies in the Orlando area:

Alamo: (800) 327-9633
Avis: (800) 831-2847
Budget: (800) 527-0700
Dollar: (800) 800-4000
Econo Car: (800) 665-9001
Enterprise: (800) RENT-A-CAR
E-Z: (407) 352-3131
Hertz: (800) 654-3131
Hertz Gold Club Reservations: (800) CAR-GOLD
National: (800) 227-7368
Payless Car Rental: (800) PAY-LESS
Thrifty: (800) 367-2277

When reserving your vehicle, make sure the rental car company offers airport service (either a pickup at the airport or a free shuttle to their nearby pickup location). All of the nationally known car rental companies including Hertz, Avis, National, Alamo, and Budget are located within a five-minute free shuttle-bus ride from the Orlando airport.

If you want to enjoy the luxury and novelty of a renting a flashy sports car, such as a Jaguar, Hummer, BMW, Porsche, Mercedes, Viper, Rolls Royce, Ferrari, Lamborghini, or Aston Martin, for example, call **Dream Cars Unlimited** at ☎(866) 624-6396. Rentals are available by the day, week, or month. By visiting the company's Web site at *www.dreamcarsunlimited.com*, you can download and print a discount coupon. Renters must be at least twenty-five years of age, have proof of insurance coverage, and have a major credit card in their name.

Special Services

Most of the rental car companies will provide child safety seats, either free of charge or for a small daily fee. These seats must be reserved in advance. This will save you the hassle of having to bring your own child safety seats with you on your trip. However, you must bring your own if you want your child to sit in one on the airplane.

If you're a nonsmoker, be sure to ask for a nonsmoking vehicle when you make your reservation. Otherwise, you could get stuck with a car that reeks of smoke.

When you pick up your rental car at the airport, computer-generated driving directions and maps are often provided free of charge from the airport to virtually any location in Florida, including all of the popular hotels and attractions.

When you pick up the rental car, ask about the rental car company's policy for additional drivers. Typically, when you rent a car, only the person whose name appears on the rental agreement is legally permitted to drive the car, unless additional paperwork is completed. Some rental car companies charge to add additional names to the rental contract, allowing for multiple drivers. The following are often exempt from additional driver charges (but check with the rental car company): the renter's employer or regular fellow employee when on company business; the renter's spouse; the renter's mate, life companion, significant other, or live-in; and disabled renters who have completed a special form.

💼 TRAVEL TIP

If you're worried about getting lost, Hertz offers an optional feature in some of its rental cars, called NeverLost. The NeverLost unit identifies exactly where you are at any time, and shows and tells you how to get wherever you want to go. The additional daily cost is about $8 per day. NeverLost must be ordered in advance when making your reservation.

Final Suggestions

Before leaving the rental agency, ask if you're required to return the car with a full tank of gas, or if you're paying for the gas in advance. If you're required to return the car with a full tank of gas and you fail to do so (which many people do), you'll be billed up to three times the going rate per gallon of gas needed to fill the tank. Before returning the car, find a low-priced gas station and fill the tank with basic unleaded gasoline (the cheapest stuff you can find). This will fulfill your obligation to return the car with a full tank of gas.

When you pick up the car, ask what time the car must be returned by to ensure that you won't be billed overtime hours, and ask what the overtime rate is. For example, the policy may state that if you pick up the car at 3:00 P.M., you must return the car before 3:00 P.M. on the day your rental agreement ends or you'll automatically be billed for additional hours at a high rate.

As soon as you pick up your car, before leaving the rental car company's parking lot, make sure there is nothing obviously wrong with the vehicle. If there's a problem, report it immediately. Once you leave the rental car company's parking lot, if you notice a problem, call the rental car company and report it. Likewise, if you get stuck on the road, call the rental car company and report your situation. Free assistance, often including towing services, will be provided, and you'll often be given a replacement rental car.

💼 TRAVEL TIP

Before getting behind the wheel, make sure you're totally awake and alert and that you have detailed driving directions. If you're too tired to be driving, take a taxi or shuttle bus to your hotel and pick up your rental car later in the day or the following day. Be sure to call the rental car company and mention your change of plans to avoid being charged.

When returning your car, plan on arriving at the airport about ninety minutes (or even two hours) prior to your scheduled flight time. You will most likely be returning your car several miles from the actual airport, and you'll need to allow ample time to return the car, take the complimentary shuttle bus to your airline terminal, check in at the airline terminal, check your bags, and get to the actual gate. It's a common problem for travelers to miss their flight because they didn't allow enough time to return their rental car, so plan accordingly.

Your Travel Budget

As you begin to plan your trip, it's important to establish a basic travel budget for yourself and to stick to that budget. Once you reach your destination, you'll no doubt be tempted to dine at fancy restaurants, buy extravagant souvenirs, and participate in costly activities. When creating your budget, you'll want to make allowances for these unplanned splurges, but you'll want to maintain control over your spending at all times. Otherwise, you could easily end up with massive credit card bills after your vacation.

The first step in planning a budget is to figure out how much money you have to spend on your upcoming vacation. Next, determine how many people you'll be traveling with (and paying for), how many days you'll be away, and what you want your travel itinerary to be.

Based on this information, start pricing out airfares, hotel/motel accommodations, rental cars, and the cost of various activities (such as admission to the theme parks and dining). The checklist in this chapter will help you predict some of the costs.

Saving Money

Hopefully, once you've priced out everything, the total price of your planned vacation will be within your proposed budget. Before making your reservations, however, invest some time in shopping around for money-saving deals and/or packages. Finding a coupon or utilizing a deal that'll save you $50 on a hotel, for example, is money that can be used for souvenirs or kept in your bank account.

▐ TRAVEL TIP

Unless your budget is unlimited, chances are, once you get to Orlando, you will not be able to afford to do absolutely everything you'd like to during a single trip. Thus, you'll want to use this book (and your firsthand experience) to determine which activities you'd most enjoy, and focus on those to start off with.

Also, you can save money by eating outside of the theme parks. Instead of having the fancy (and sometimes costly) breakfast at your Disney-owned hotel every morning during your trip, consider experiencing that breakfast once, then eating off-property on the rest of the mornings to save some money. Obviously, there's something very special (especially for kids) about eating Mickey Mouse–shaped waffles with the Disney characters roaming the dining room and meeting guests. However, this is something that doesn't need to be experienced every morning.

If this isn't your first trip to The WDW Resort, you can save a lot of money by staying at a non-Disney-owned hotel/motel that's close to the theme parks. While you won't experience the legendary Disney service or the perks associated with staying at a Disney-owned hotel, the financial savings will add up quickly.

Budget Checklist

Use this form to help you approximate the cost of your trip to The WDW Resort/Greater Orlando area in advance. Planning your schedule/itinerary before you leave and setting budgetary spending limits will help you enjoy your vacation without going into unexpected debt or spending outside of your budget.

BUDGET CHECKLIST		
Expense	**Calculation**	**Totals**
Adult airfare	$ _____ per ticket × _____ (# of adults)	$ _____
Child airfare	$ _____ per ticket × _____ (# of children)	$ _____
Rental car	$ _____ per day/week × _____ (# of days/weeks)	$ _____
Insurance/gas	$ _____ per day × _____ (# of days)	$ _____
Transportation	$ _____ per trip × $ _____ (# of people) × $ _____ (# of trips)	$ _____
Hotel/motel	$ _____ per night × _____ (# of rooms) × _____ (# of nights)	$ _____
Adult Disney ticket	$ _____ per ticket × _____ (# of people) × _____ (# of days)	$ _____

(continued)

BUDGET CHECKLIST (continued)

Expense	Calculation	Totals
Child Disney ticket	$ _____ per ticket × _____ (# of people) × _____ (# of days)	$ _____
Adult Universal Studios ticket	$ _____ per ticket × _____ (# of people) × _____ (# of days)	$ _____
Child Universal Studios ticket	$ _____ per ticket × _____ (# of people) × _____ (# of days)	$ _____
Other attraction	$ _____ per ticket × _____ (# of people) × _____ (# of days)	$ _____
Other attraction	$ _____ per ticket × _____ (# of people) × _____ (# of days)	$ _____
Adult nighttime entertainment	$ _____ per person × _____ (# of nights)	$ _____
Child nighttime entertainment	$ _____ per person × _____ (# of nights)	$ _____
Show/movie tickets	$ _____ per person × _____ (# of shows)	$ _____
Total meal budget	$ _____ per person × _____ (# of meals) × _____ (# of days)	$ _____
Snack/drink budget	$ _____ per person × _____ (# of days)	$ _____
Souvenir budget	$ _____ per person	$ _____
Child care	$ _____ per hour × _____ (# of hours) × _____ (# of children)	$ _____
Kennel costs	$ _____ per day × _____ (# of days) × _____ (# of pets)	$ _____

(continued)

BUDGET CHECKLIST *(continued)*		
Expense	**Calculation**	**Totals**
Airport parking	$ _____ per day × _____ (# of days)	$ _____
Other	_____	$ _____
Other	_____	$ _____
Other	_____	$ _____
Approximate Vacation Expenses Total:		$ _____

Using a Travel Agent

Utilizing a full-service travel agency to plan your trip and make your travel reservations will typically save you a lot of time, but not necessarily a lot of money. Most travel agents these days specialize in corporate travel or high-priced vacations and earn their income by taking a commission of the total price of the trip they coordinate for you. Thus, unless you have an established relationship with a travel agent, they're not always apt to find you the lowest possible rates. Of course, there are plenty of exceptions.

If you don't already have a reliable travel agent that you use, consider seeking out a favorable recommendation from a friend or relative as opposed to opening the telephone book. When choosing a travel agent, make sure he or she specializes in planning family vacations and is familiar with Orlando.

Hotel room brokers, discount travel agents, and hotel reservation services in the Orlando area include:

Central Reservation Service: ✆(800) 548-3311
Check-In Reservation Services: ✆(800) 237-1033
Destinations Travel Service: ✆(407) 859-3501
Eventures Unlimited, Inc.: ✆(800) 356-7891 (This service offers special package deals designed specifically for senior citizens interested in vacationing at The WDW Resort.)

Booking Your Vacation Online

If you have some time to invest when planning your vacation, and you have access to the Internet, you can save an absolute fortune by planning and booking your travel arrangements online. Airfares, hotels, and rental cars can all be reserved and paid for using the Web and a major credit card.

When using the Internet to plan and book your own travel, you have three primary options:

1. Visit the Web site of the specific airline, hotel chain, and/or rental car company. For example, if you're booking your airfare on **US Airways**, you'd visit *www.usairways.com*. Often, each individual airline offers discounted online-only fares and specials that cannot be obtained anywhere else. The drawback to using an airline's Web site is that to shop around for the best fares, you'll need to visit the Web sites of multiple airlines.

2. Utilize the services of an online travel-related Web site, such as **Travelocity** (*www.travelocity.com*), **Hotwire.com** (*www.hotwire.com*), **Expedia** (*www.expedia.com*), **Orbitz** (*www.orbitz.com*), or **Yahoo! Travel** (*http://travel.yahoo.com*). These services allow you to quickly search all of the major airlines for the best flights and fares. You'll also find great deals on hotels, rental cars, and travel packages. When using one of these services, the more time you spend exploring them, the better your chances of saving a lot of money will be. Once you know when you want to travel, try searching for better fares by altering your travel dates slightly. Sometimes, leaving a day earlier or later, for example, can save you money. You can also try looking up various airport combinations. For example, if you're flying from New York's LaGuardia Airport to Orlando International Airport, you can also look up departing flights from Newark Airport and New York's Kennedy Airport. Checking each

variable takes only seconds using one of these online travel services.

3. If you have a somewhat flexible travel schedule, you can save between 30 and 70 percent on airfares, hotels, and rental cars using a service such as **Priceline.com** (✍*www.priceline. com*), **Last Minute Travel** (✍*www.lastminutetravel.com*), or **Travel Hub** (✍*www.travelhub.com/airfares*). Many of these online services now offer even greater package deal savings if you book your airfare along with your hotel and/or rental car.

Vacation Packages and When to Visit

There are a variety of organizations that offer various types of discounts and travel packages to The WDW Resort, Universal Studios, and other Orlando-area destinations. A travel package might consist of any or all of the following: airfare, hotel accommodations, meals, rental car, and admission to one or more theme parks. Using the budget checklist in this chapter, calculate what it will cost you to plan your own vacation, then compare those rates with those offered by comparable travel packages from an airline or one of the following travel organizations.

≡FAST FACT

The Hotel Reservations Network in Orlando advertises up to 60 percent off hotel rates at more than 300 hotels and motels in the Orlando area. This company will also help you find available hotel rooms during peak travel periods. For more information, call ✆(800) 511-5321. Also, be sure to check out the Web site Hotels.com (✍*www.hotels.com*) for discounts of up to 60 percent on hotels, motels, and resorts.

In addition to contacting the various airlines directly about individual airfares or travel packages, contact organizations such as the

AAA, which has a travel department (✆ 800-222-7448, ✎ *www.aaa.com*), or the **AARP** (✆ 800-424-3410, ✎ *www.aarp.org*).

Two travel agencies that offer an assortment of different travel packages for people interested in The WDW Resort include:

> American Express Travel: ✆ (800) 346-3607, ✎ *www.itn.net*
> Walt Disney Travel Company: ✆ (800) 225-2024

The Disney Credit Card

BankOne offers an official Disney Visa card. Using this credit card to make your everyday purchases allows you to earn "Disney Dream Reward Dollars" that can be used toward discounts on Disney vacation packages and Disney merchandise. Paying for your Disney vacation (airfares, hotel, rental car, theme park tickets, souvenirs, meals, etc.) with this credit card entitles you to additional discounts. To apply for the card, call ✆ (877) 252-6576.

The Entertainment Book

Entertainment Books (✆ 800-933-2605, ✎ *www.entertainment.com*) offer 50 percent off and two-for-one discounts at your favorite places for dining and shopping, at attractions, for sports, and for services like dry cleaning and movie rentals. Entertainment Books also include discounts for hotels and other travel services.

≡FAST FACT

> The 2004 Entertainment Book for the Orlando area offers discounts and money-saving coupons for 276 local area restaurants, more than 5,000 hotels (nationwide), and special deals from rental car companies and various retail stores and tourist attractions. The Orlando edition of the Entertainment Book is priced at $25.

The Entertainment Book is an extremely useful resource for finding restaurants in the Orlando area that are not located on

Disney property. The book typically offers sample menus as well as money-saving offers. People with access to a rental car who can travel freely around the Orlando area will get the most out of this discount book.

The Best Times to Visit

During The WDW Resort's peak summer season (and during major holidays), you could be sharing your vacation with 40,000 to 65,000 other visitors in each theme park. Throughout the year, Saturday is each theme park's busiest day of the week. Around noon, the park is usually the most crowded. On Sundays and during the week, the park is less crowded. The drawback to visiting The WDW Resort on a weekday is that the parades and shows happen less frequently, and sometimes not at all.

As soon as you arrive at the Disney theme park of your choice (Magic Kingdom, Epcot, Disney-MGM Studios, or Disney's Animal Kingdom), pick up a copy of the free guide-map booklet given out at the main entrances of each park. These colorful booklets contain the times for all parades and shows, describe the times and places to meet the Disney characters, and offer a detailed map of the park that lists all of the major attractions, restaurants, and amenities (restrooms, public phones, ATM machines, etc.).

Anytime during the year, if it's raining, you can count on much smaller crowds than usual. Bring along rain gear (avoid umbrellas), or pick up one of the plastic Mickey Mouse rain ponchos sold throughout the park on rainy days. Expect all parades, outdoor shows, and a few outdoor rides to be cancelled or closed on rainy days. Much of the park (including most of the attractions) will, however, be open, and the lines will be far shorter.

For the shortest lines, visit the Disney theme parks during any weekday in the off-season. If you happen to visit on a busy day, go against the crowds. For example, you'll notice that in the morning, most people race toward the most popular rides and attractions, and these same people stake out a prime viewing spot for a parade up to two or three hours before show time. Most of the park's most popular parades happen twice each afternoon or evening. During the first parade presentation is the best time to visit all of the most popular attractions. You can catch the second showing of the parade when the crowds are greatly reduced. Likewise, when most people break for lunch or dinner, many of the lines for attractions are shorter.

⊕ HOT SPOT

Within The Magic Kingdom, you can find out exactly what the lines are like for every attraction by visiting the Information Desk/Wait Board. Similar Information Desks/Wait Boards can be found at each of the Disney theme parks and at other popular theme parks (including Universal Studios and Islands of Adventure).

The very best times of year to visit The WDW Resort, due to lack of crowds, are:

- The week after Thanksgiving through the week before Christmas
- The week after Labor Day until Thanksgiving week
- The second week of January through the beginning of February

Attendance is considered "average" during the following times of year. If you're planning to travel during one of these times, expect to experience lines for the most popular WDW theme park attractions between thirty minutes and ninety minutes long.

- The first week of January
- Early February until Presidents' week
- Late February until mid-March
- Late April until early June
- Late August until Labor Day
- Thanksgiving week

Busiest Times of Year

The WDW Resort and all of the Orlando-area theme parks are the busiest during the following times of year. These times are considered "peak" travel periods. The good news is that the theme parks are open longer hours and more parades and shows are held per day, but you can expect long waits for the major theme park attractions, and you'll have to deal with relatively large crowds, even if the weather is bad. These "peak" travel periods are:

- Presidents' week
- Late March until late April
- Mid-June until late August (the summer season)
- Christmas through New Year's Day

Hours of Operation

Prior to choosing the exact dates for your trip (if you have flexibility), call The WDW Resort's main reservations number (✆407-W-DISNEY) and inquire about each theme park's hours of operation during the dates of your proposed visit. During the "off peak" times, the parks tend to close around 7:00 P.M. or 9:00 P.M. as opposed to 11:00 P.M. or midnight during "peak" periods. The hours of operation for each theme park are also posted at the official Disney World Web site (⌨*www.disneyworld.com*).

🧳 TRAVEL TIP

When you attempt to make your hotel reservation, if your first choice for accommodations is already booked solid, make alternate reservations, but keep checking back with your first-choice hotel. Even during the busy times of year, last-minute cancellations are common.

Even if the parks will be closing early during off-peak times, you probably won't have to wait in any really long lines to experience attractions, so you'll get to experience a lot more each day. You will, however, have to plan evening and nighttime activities that don't include the theme parks. If you want to stay on Disney property, spending evenings and nights at Pleasure Island and/or Disney's BoardWalk will provide plenty of dining and entertainment options until as late as 2:00 A.M. (throughout the year).

If you're planning your Disney vacation during one of the busy periods, book your reservations as early as possible, especially if you hope to stay at one of the more popular Disney-owned hotels.

CHAPTER 2

Choosing Your Accommodations

WHILE YOU PROBABLY WON'T BE SPENDING TOO much time in your hotel or motel room while on vacation, you'll definitely want accommodations that are comfortable and that offer the amenities you need and want, at a price that's within your budget. This chapter will help you select the accommodations that are most suited to your needs within the Orlando area.

Getting to the Theme Parks

From any of the hotels and resorts on Disney property, reaching any of the Disney theme parks is as easy as catching a bus that stops in front of the hotel. The complimentary Disney Bus Service transports guests from the various hotels to the Disney theme parks and attractions (including the water parks and Downtown Disney areas). The buses typically run every fifteen to twenty minutes.

In some cases, a Disney hotel may be within walking distance to one or more of the Disney theme parks. Monorail, boat, or other transportation may also be available. When using the bus service, allow approximately thirty to forty-five minutes (including wait time) to reach your destination. All of the buses are handicap accessible and air conditioned. You'll also find that the drivers are extremely knowledgeable about the theme parks and events happening at The WDW Resort.

Defining Your Needs

To experience the ultimate Disney vacation and the superior service and hospitality Disney is known for, you'll probably want to stay at one of The WDW Resort's hotels. If, however, you're looking for a clean, fully functional hotel room or suite, or even a less expensive motel, either of which will save you a lot of money, staying at a non-Disney hotel is an excellent idea, especially if you're planning on renting a car to get around.

💼 TRAVEL TIP

For hotels, motels, and resorts located off-property, contact the hotel's front desk or concierge to determine if complimentary shuttle service is available to the parks.

As you make your hotel reservation, shop around for the best room rates. Non-Disney hotel rates are often negotiable, plus most will honor some type of discount program (AAA, the Entertainment Book, etc.). Before mentioning that you're a member of any discount program, ask the hotel for its best rate and negotiate the best deal you can, then mention that you'd like the added discount.

To ensure that you'll get the best selection and rates, make your hotel reservations as far in advance as possible and be prepared to guarantee your reservation using a major credit card. (Be sure to write down your reservation's confirmation number.) If you're having trouble locating a hotel that offers the accommodations you're looking for, consider using the services of a travel agent.

If you need help finding accommodations and making a reservation, especially during peak travel times, consider contacting one of these organizations:

The Kissimmee–St. Cloud Convention & Visitors Bureau:
  📞(407) 847-5000
Official Visitor Center: 📞(407) 363-5872, 🖎*www.orlandoinfo.com*

🧳 TRAVEL TIP

In addition to the hotel room's nightly charge, determine in advance any extra charges you'll incur, such as phone surcharges, parking charges, shuttle bus charges, an extra fee for a roll-away bed, and so on. All of these charges can easily add up.

The WDW Resort Hotels

As you'll discover, there are several advantages to staying at one of The WDW Resort's on-property resort hotels (accounting for more than 33,000 guest rooms); however, you'll pay a premium for these privileges.

If you stay at one of the Disney-owned and -operated resort hotels, you'll be staying on Disney property and you'll be treated to the world-class service and hospitality that Disney is known for. Guests of The WDW Resort hotels have full access to the WDW Transportation bus service to travel around the resort complex. Some of the Disney resort hotels also offer their own special attractions and activities for guests that add to the overall Disney vacation experience.

Prices

The WDW Resort hotels are divided into price-based categories. The following ranges are based on 2004 prices:

- Campground facilities (located on property) range from $35 to $80 per night.
- Value hotel rooms range from $77 to $124 per night.
- Moderate hotel rooms range from $133 to $219 per night.
- Home Away From Home hotel rooms range from $289 to over $1,800 per night.
- Deluxe hotels range from $329 to $920 (and up) per night.

Resort Perks

The following are some of the perks you'll receive by staying on Disney property, at a WDW Resort hotel:

- **Easy access to the theme parks.** No need to deal with parking your car at the theme parks—complimentary transportation via boats, buses, and monorails carries Disney's resort guests directly to any area in the entire WDW Resort.
- **Advance dining reservations.** Resort guests can make advance dining reservations for priority seating up to sixty days before their arrival at many of the more than 200 restaurants throughout The WDW Resort. Call ☎(407) WDW-DINE to make reservations.
- **Character dining opportunities.** Here's your chance to meet and dine with Mickey and his friends. Disney's famous character breakfasts are held daily at Disney's Grand Floridian Resort & Spa, Disney's Beach Club Resort, Disney's Polynesian Resort and Disney's Contemporary Resort.
- **Preferred tee times.** If you're visiting The WDW Resort to play golf, you'll receive preferred tee times at Disney's six courses, which total ninety-nine holes of championship golf.
- **Childcare services.** Enjoy a break away from your kids! Resort guests can drop off the kids at one of Disney's childcare facilities, available to resort guests for a nominal fee.
- **On-property sports and recreation.** A variety of playtime activities, including tennis, swimming, and golf, are available to resort guests. Several WDW hotels offer workout facilities and full-service day spas. Additional activities available to resort guests include canoeing, fishing, sailing, horseback riding, playgrounds, croquet, and shuffleboard.
- **Free movies.** Complimentary Disney cartoons and full-length Disney films are shown nightly at Fort Wilderness to all resort guests.
- **Guaranteed entry into the theme parks.** Even on the busiest days, when the parking lots are full, resort guests

using Disney transportation are guaranteed entry to all Walt Disney World theme parks and water parks.

- **Central billing.** The WDW Resort identification cards, which can be used to charge food and merchandise, now also have guests' ticketing options encoded on the back. The resort ID cards are issued upon check-in, and all purchases are charged to guests' resort hotel accounts.

- **Extra Magic Hours.** Each day, one of the four WDW theme parks opens for Disney resort guests one hour early, providing exclusive time in the parks to experience select attractions and meet and greet Disney characters. During this hour, the parks are less crowded, allowing people to experience the most popular attractions in less time.

═FAST FACT

To make reservations to stay within "the heart of the magic" or to request color brochures for WDW Resort properties, a free Disney vacation video, or other information about any of The WDW Resort hotels, call ✆ (407) W-DISNEY or visit ✎ *www.disneyworld.com*.

All-Star Resorts
Hotel Rate Classification: Value

The All-Star Music Resort, All-Star Sports Resort, All-Star Movies Resort, and Pop Century Resort are the least expensive on Disney property. These resorts have thousands of rooms starting at $77 per night. Each of these complexes has at least 1,920 nice but no-frills rooms, consisting of two double beds, a color TV, a small amount of furniture, and a bathroom. The rooms aren't large (260 square feet), but if you're looking to stay on Disney property and don't want to spend a fortune, these no-frills hotels are your best bet.

Transportation to all theme parks and attractions is available via the WDW Transportation buses. Expect to spend between thirty and forty-five minutes (each way) traveling from these WDW hotels to most of the Disney attractions via the WDW Transportation Bus service.

The newest and largest Disney All-Star Resort, which opened in December 2003, is called Disney's Pop Century Resort. This themed resort sends guests on a trip back through American popular culture, with oversized icons representing each decade of the twentieth century. For example, to represent the 1950s, you'll see a larger-than-life jukebox.

To reach guests staying at the **All-Star Music Resort**, call ✆(407) 939-6000. Guests staying at the **All-Star Sports Resort** can be reached by calling ✆(407) 939-5000. To reach guests at the **Pop Century Resort**, call ✆(407) 938-4000. You can reach people at the **All-Star Movies Resort** by calling ✆(407) 939-7000, or ask the Disney operator to connect you if you're calling from a courtesy phone or WDW Resort hotel room phone.

═FAST FACT

One of the benefits of staying at a WDW Resort is that as a guest, you can take advantage of the amenities at other WDW Resorts. For example, if you're staying at the All-Star Movies Resort, you can spend an afternoon at Disney's Yacht and Beach Club's pool area. You can use The WDW Resort bus transportation system (free) to travel from location to location within Disney property.

Beach Club and Yacht Club
Hotel Rate Classification: Deluxe

Located along a lovely 25-acre lake, these are two of the nicest Disney resort hotels, both inside and out. The Beach Club and the Yacht Club are modeled after New England seashore hotels from the 1880s. Both are full-service hotels that are within walking distance from Epcot.

The Beach Club offers 583 guest rooms, while the Yacht Club offers 630 guest rooms. Both have a nautical theme and absolutely fabulous outdoor pool/beach areas. Whether or not you're staying at one of these two hotels, checking out these hotels' joint 750,000-gallon pool area is worthwhile. Both hotels also offer a variety of indoor and outdoor activities such as boat rentals, tennis, a video arcade, a playground, and a full-service health club.

The **Beach Club** resort's phone number is ✆(407) 934-8000. The phone number for the **Yacht Club** is ✆(407) 934-7000. To reach a guest at one of these hotels, call the number directly or ask the Disney operator to connect you if you're calling from a courtesy phone or another WDW Resort hotel room phone.

Disney's Beach Club Villas opened in July 2002 and feature an ambiance of casual elegance. This property is part of The Disney Vacation Club (timeshare) and is situated next to Disney's Beach Club Resort. It's a 205-room property offering studio, one-, and two-bedroom vacation villas. While you typically need to be a Disney timeshare member to stay here, some rooms and suites on this property are made available to the general public during off-peak seasons. To reach guests staying here, call the Beach Club Resort at ✆(407) 934-8000 or ask the Disney operator to connect you if you're calling from a courtesy phone or WDW Resort hotel room phone.

BoardWalk Inn
Hotel Rate Classification: Deluxe

This hotel offers 378 rooms, all decorated with cherry wood furniture. All rooms have two double beds or one king-size bed and a daybed. Room rates are based on the view offered. If you want the best view, be sure to request a room overlooking the Seven Seas Lagoon.

The hotel offers several restaurants, plus the restaurants at Disney's BoardWalk, a full health club facility, day care and children's programs, tennis courts, swimming pool, and all sorts of other amenities that you'd expect from one of Disney's full-service resorts.

To reach guests staying at this resort, call ☎(407) 939-5100 or ask the Disney operator to connect you if you're calling from a courtesy phone or WDW Resort hotel room phone.

≡FAST FACT

One of the nicest features of this hotel is that all rooms also have a private balcony or patio. This hotel is located in the heart of Disney's BoardWalk, so it overlooks the Seven Seas Lagoon and is within walking distance of Epcot.

BoardWalk Villas
Hotel Rate Classification: Home Away From Home

While The BoardWalk Villas are part of Disney's Vacation Club timeshare program and are typically available only to members, when vacancies exist (especially during off-peak times), these villas are offered as hotel rooms to the general public. Studio, one-, two-, and three-bedroom villas include kitchenettes or kitchens are available, with amenities that typical hotel rooms don't offer. The BoardWalk Grand Villas offer the ultimate in comfort and luxury for families (up to twelve people). These Grand Villas are also among the most expensive accommodations you'll find anywhere within The WDW Resort complex.

To reach guests staying at this hotel, call ☎(407) 939-6200 or ask the Disney operator to connect you if you're calling from a courtesy phone or WDW Resort hotel room phone.

Caribbean Beach
Hotel Rate Classification: Moderate

Located within The WDW Resort complex, the Caribbean Beach Resort is a 200-acre resort unto itself, complete with its own indoor and outdoor activities. The 2,000-plus rooms offered here, however, are pretty basic. Most rooms contain two double beds and are designed to sleep four people. The entire resort consists of two-story buildings that are divided into clusters. Each group of buildings has its own pool and beach area, named after an island in the Caribbean. The resort has a central check-in area and food court. Everything has a tropical island feel.

This is one of The WDW Resort's moderately priced hotels. If you're staying here, however, you'll save time each day by renting a car. You won't want to rely on WDW Transportation buses to get you to and from the various theme parks, or you'll wind up spending a considerable amount of time each day commuting.

To reach guests staying at this hotel, call ☎(407) 934-3400 or ask the Disney operator to connect you if you're calling from a courtesy phone or WDW Resort hotel room phone.

💼 TRAVEL TIP

One of the biggest problems with the massive Caribbean Beach Resort is that all of the buildings look identical, so it's easy to get lost. If you're staying here, make sure you don't forget what section you're in as well as your room number.

Contemporary Resort
Hotel Rate Classification: Deluxe

This was the very first WDW Resort hotel and is the only one that the Disney monorail system passes directly through. This fifteen-story A-frame tower has 1,041 rooms, six shops, three restaurants, two snack shops, two lounges, its own marina, a manmade beach, a full health club, a pool (complete with water slide), two hot tubs, and an arcade. It's one of the most centrally located hotels to most of the resort's attractions, plus it's been recently renovated to offer the very latest amenities, including a new décor, new family-style restaurants, and additional swimming pools, tennis courts, and other activity areas.

To reach guests staying at this hotel, call ☎(407) 824-1000 or ask the Disney operator to connect you if you're calling from a courtesy phone or WDW Resort hotel room phone.

Coronado Springs Resort
Hotel Rate Classification: Moderate

The Coronado Springs Resort features 1,967 moderately priced guest rooms that encircle a fifteen-acre lagoon. This resort is divided into three two-story guest buildings, each with its own pool. The hotel also features a food court area, a lounge, a salon, and a health club. In addition to the basic rooms, which are equipped with two double beds (designed to sleep four people), a coffee maker, and ironing equipment, the hotel also has a limited number of executive suites, VIP suites, and junior suites.

To reach guests staying at this hotel, call ☏(407) 939-1000 or ask the Disney operator to connect you if you're calling from a courtesy phone or WDW Resort hotel room phone.

Port Orleans Riverside
Hotel Rate Classification: Moderate

Disney's Port Orleans Riverside is divided into two primary sections, the Mansion area and the Bayou. In all, there are 2,048 rooms within this property. Most of the rooms have two double beds; however, some are furnished with a king-size bed and have space for portable twin beds that can be brought into the room for children (for a small extra fee).

To reach guests staying at this hotel, call ☏(407) 934-6000 or ask the Disney operator to connect you if you're calling from a courtesy phone or WDW Resort hotel room phone.

≡FAST FACT

Transportation via the WDW Transportation bus system is provided to all of the theme parks and attractions throughout the resort complex. The Downtown Disney area, however, can be reached via a shuttle boat.

Walt Disney Dolphin and Swan Resorts
Hotel Rate Classification: Moderate/Deluxe

Unlike many of the other official WDW Resort hotels that are owned and operated by Disney, the Swan is operated by Westin Hotels, while the Dolphin is operated by ITT Sheraton. Each room at the Swan offers one king-size bed or two queen-size beds, although special suites are available. The Dolphin rooms are furnished with two double beds or one king-size bed, and suites are available.

Both hotels have full-service restaurants and a wide range of activities and amenities, including a full-service health club, a salon, tennis, swimming pools, children's programs, and shopping. These hotels also have a special Web site: ✒*www.swandolphin.com.*

To reach guests staying at the **Swan** or **Dolphin**, call ✆(407) 934-4000, or ask the Disney operator to connect you if you're calling from a courtesy phone or WDW Resort hotel room phone.

Fort Wilderness Resort & Campground
Hotel Rate Classification: Campground Facilities/
Home Away from Home

In addition to providing 784 campsites (between 25 and 65 feet in length), Fort Wilderness offers 408 Wilderness Homes and Cabins (which have air conditioning and full amenities).

Many of the sites offer cable TV connections (for RVs), electricity and water hookups, and sanitary disposal. The sites also feature a picnic table, a paved driveway pad, and a charcoal grill. Restrooms, showers, ice machines, telephones, and a laundry room are available at the campsites.

The Wilderness Homes are designed to hold up to six people (four adults and two children). The log cabins are more rustic in design than other Disney Resort hotel accommodations, but each has a private deck.

Transportation to and from the other theme parks is available via the WDW Transportation bus system or water shuttle (which is faster). Golf carts can also be rented for use around the campground facility.

To reach guests staying at this hotel, call ☏(407) 824-2900 or ask the Disney operator to connect you if you're calling from a courtesy phone or WDW Resort hotel room phone.

⊕ HOT SPOT

The campsites at Fort Wilderness offer the cheapest way to stay on Disney property. Campsites with partial hookup start at around $35 per night.

Grand Floridian Resort and Spa
Hotel Rate Classification: Deluxe

Located along the Seven Seas Lagoon, the Grand Floridian is a 900-room resort with a Victorian theme that truly defines the word "elegance." In addition to offering elegant décor, full-service restaurants, and top-quality Disney service, this resort also offers business services for guests, a health club, a luxurious full-service day spa, and plenty of on-site activities. The Grand Floridian is located along the Disney monorail system, so getting to and from The Magic Kingdom, Epcot, and the Ticket and Transportation Center is easy and fun.

To reach guests staying at this hotel, call ☏(407) 824-3000 or ask the Disney operator to connect you if you're calling from a courtesy phone or WDW Resort hotel room phone.

Old Key West Resort
Hotel Rate Classification: Home Away from Home

This resort complex is also part of Disney's Vacation Club time-share. While membership is normally required, when vacancies are available, especially during the off-peak season, villas can be rented by nonmembers. Studios as well as one-, two-, and three-bedroom villas are available. All offer a kitchenette, a living room, and a bathroom in addition to the bedroom(s). Guests also enjoy the villas' whirlpool tubs and oversize showers.

If you're not a member of Disney's Vacation Club, call the regular reservation number (☏407-W-Disney) for room availability. To reach guests staying at this hotel, call ☎(407) 827-7700 or ask the Disney operator to connect you if you're calling from a courtesy phone or WDW Resort hotel room phone.

Polynesian Resort
Hotel Rate Classification: Deluxe

This hotel offers guest rooms and has a monorail stop right outside the door, providing easy access to The Magic Kingdom, Epcot, and the Ticket and Transportation Center. The Polynesian also has multiple restaurants, two swimming pools, an arcade, and a playground.

To reach guests staying at this hotel, call ☎(407) 824-2000 or ask the Disney operator to connect you if you're calling from a courtesy phone or WDW Resort hotel room phone.

≡FAST FACT

One of the classic nighttime attractions offered at this resort is the Polynesian Luau, presented nightly at 5:15 P.M. and 8:00 P.M. (times may vary based on season). This dinner show is open to everyone and is priced at $49.01 per adult and $24.81 per child. Reservations are required.

Port Orleans Resort—French Quarter
Hotel Rate Classification: Moderate

Modeled after the historic French Quarter of New Orleans, the Port Orleans resort offers 1,008 rooms located in seven three-story buildings. Most of the rooms offer two double beds and are designed to accommodate families of four. Adjoining rooms are available but can't be guaranteed when you make your reservation. WDW Transportation buses take guests to and from all of the Disney theme parks and attractions; however, water shuttle service is available to the Downtown Disney area.

To reach guests staying at this hotel, call ☎(407) 934-5000 or ask the Disney operator to connect you if you're calling from a courtesy phone or WDW Resort hotel room phone.

Disney's Saratoga Springs Resort & Spa

Hotel Rate Classification: Home Away From Home / Deluxe

Formally called The Villas at the Disney Institute, the new Disney's Saratoga Springs Resort & Spa (which opened in Spring 2004) is part of the Disney Vacation Club. Designed around a late-1800s theme, the new resort occupies a 65-acre site overlooking the lakefront district of Downtown Disney and the Lake Buena Vista Golf Course. Upon completion of all phases in 2005, this will become the largest Disney Vacation Club resort to date, complete with 552 units, including studio, one-, and two-bedroom villas and Grand Villa units that sleep up to twelve guests. For information or to make a reservation, call ✆(407) W-DISNEY.

Disney's Wilderness Lodge

Hotel Rate Classification: Deluxe

This hotel looks like a giant log cabin with two authentic totem poles in the front and offers 728 rooms, many of which are equipped with queen-size beds and bunk beds, or two sets of bunk beds, which are a favorite among kids and teens.

The Villas at Disney's Wilderness Lodge offer more family-oriented Home Away From Home accommodations.

To reach guests staying at this hotel, call ✆(407) 824-3200 or ask the Disney operator to connect you if you're calling from a courtesy phone or WDW Resort hotel room phone.

🧳 TRAVEL TIP

You'll probably want to have a rental car available if you're staying at the Wilderness Lodge, in order to avoid the daily commute time associated with riding the WDW Transportation buses from the hotel to the various theme parks and back. This rustic-looking hotel with a full complement of modern amenities is truly in the woods, so it isn't within walking distance of any of the theme parks.

Shades of Green on Walt Disney World Resort

Formally known as the Disney Inn, this 288-room complex is located along one of Disney's popular PGA championship eighteen-hole golf courses. Golf, tennis, swimming, a fitness center, and a game room are among the activities offered.

This resort is operated as an Armed Forces Recreation Center for the exclusive use of military members and their families. For reservations, call ☎(407) 824-3600 (reservations for this property cannot be booked through ☎407-W-DISNEY).

Animal Kingdom Lodge
Hotel Rate Classification: Deluxe

This is a 1,307-room, African themed (and decorated) resort featuring deluxe guest rooms and luxury suites. Rates start at just over $200 per night, but the atmosphere alone makes these accommodations worth every penny. What make this resort so special are the wild animals that coexist with the guests. To reach guests staying at this unique hotel, call ☎(407) 934-7639.

⊕ HOT SPOT

Over 1,000 exotic animals live at Disney's Animal Kingdom, and guests of this resort will find themselves overlooking a 33-acre African savanna. So, instead of looking out the window or off the balcony and seeing a parking lot, swimming pool, or golf course, what guests see are incredible views of real-life giraffes, zebras, antelopes, and other wild animals.

The Celebration Hotel

While not located on The WDW Resort's property, the Celebration Hotel is in the heart of Celebration, Florida—the town that Disney built. This independently owned, 150-room hotel reflects the charm of historic America's small-town inns, yet offers top-notch amenities. Room rates begin at around $100 per night for this quiet and elegant resort hotel. It's about a ten-minute drive (5 miles) to the various Disney theme parks and transportation is provided.

The Celebration Hotel is located at 700 Bloom Street, Celebration, Florida. The hotel's main number is ✆(407) 566-6000; for reservations call ✆(888) 499-3800, or check out the Web site at ✍*www.celebrationhotel.com.*

Universal Orlando Accommodations

If you choose to stay near Universal Orlando Resort (where you'll find Universal Studios Florida, Islands of Adventure, and CityWalk), this area also contains several conveniently located, on-property hotels. In conjunction with your stay at any of these properties, special theme park admission deals and travel packages are available. To make reservations for any of the following hotels on Universal Orlando Resort's property, call ✆(888) 322-5541 or visit ✍*www.uescape.com.*

The Portofino Bay Hotel

The Portofino Bay Hotel (owned and operated by Loews Hotels) is within walking distance from the theme parks and CityWalk (however, complimentary transportation is provided). This resort offers Mediterranean architecture and landscaping. The buildings surround a beautiful manmade bay.

In addition to offering all of the amenities you'd expect from a prestigious resort, the Portofino Bay Hotel offers several advantages to Universal Orlando Resort guests. For example, guests of the hotel are invited to enter the theme parks one hour before the general public. This means that for the first hour, there are virtually no lines for the most popular rides and attractions offered within either theme park.

The Portofino Bay Hotel is an upscale, family-oriented resort with eight restaurants (with many more dining options available at CityWalk). There's also a 10,600-square-foot, fully equipped spa (offering Swedish massage, wraps, aromatherapy tubs, and a full-service salon). Outdoor activities include a Roman aqueduct-styled pool with a water slide, a private villa pool, three whirlpools, and a children's pool. In addition, you'll find an outdoor jogging, walking, and bicycle path and two bocce ball courts.

═FAST FACT

A wide range of room rates are available at Portofino Bay, based on season, type of guest room (or suite), and the room's view. Room rates begin around $250 per night and go up to over $2,500 per night for a multibedroom suite.

The Hard Rock Hotel

Rock legends and families alike will receive superstar treatment at the Hard Rock Hotel. Designed in the architectural style of a California mission, this resort caters to a hip crowd, offering 654 guestrooms, suites, and bungalows. The resort also offers two restaurants and bars, a music-filled pool area, a fitness center, retail shops, and a children's activity center.

Guests of this resort receive early admission to the theme parks, priority seating at certain restaurants, plus the ability to purchase length-of-stay theme park tickets. This is definitely a more adult-oriented hotel and will appeal to guests looking for an upbeat party atmosphere. It's ideal for spring breakers, young business travelers, honeymooners, and adults traveling alone.

Royal Pacific Resort

This 1,000-guest room property offers elaborate landscaping, waterfalls, and lagoons, plus it provides a unique design that will make guests feel as if they've been transported to the enchanted isles of the South Pacific. The resort offers world-class Loews Hotel service and accommodations, plus a wide range of amenities. A variety of dining options includes a restaurant, a pool snack bar, and the Village Bazaar featuring a medley of fast-food options. There are retail shops, a business center, fitness and children's activity centers, plus meeting and function facilities including a 28,000-square-foot ballroom.

Orlando-Area Accommodations

In the Orlando area, there are literally more than 1,000 motels, resorts, and hotels, as well as luxury suites where you can stay. These facilities are located outside of Disney property, but some offer free shuttle service to and from Disney and other nearby attractions.

For about the same price as a "value" or "moderate" room at a WDW Resort hotel, you could enjoy a stay at a top-rated and often luxury hotel or resort that's located outside of Disney property but only a few minutes' drive away via a complimentary shuttle bus that's provided by the hotel or via rental car.

===FAST FACT

Many non-Disney hotels are often substantially cheaper than the Disney resort hotels, or at the very least offer a better value. If you're a AAA member, be sure to check out the TourBook for Florida (available free of charge at any AAA office or by calling ☎800-AAA-HELP). The TourBook lists Orlando-area hotels rated by AAA, many of which offer discounts to members. Be sure to inquire about additional AAA discounts when renting a car or visiting any Orlando-area attraction.

The independent hotels located outside of Disney property are so competitive that basic rooms are available for as little as $50 per night. A deluxe two-bedroom suite that's complete with a kitchen, living room, and plenty of amenities and hotel services can be found starting as low as $150 per night (less if you receive a discount using the Entertainment Book or another discount hotel program).

Benefits for Families

By staying at an independent or chain hotel outside of The WDW Resort, you'll get more for your money (or save money). You can have a full apartment-style suite for the same price as a "moderately" priced room at a WDW Resort hotel. These suites and apartment-style accommodations offer multiple bedrooms, giving the people you're traveling with some added privacy and more personal space. (This will result in a more stress-free vacation for everyone and could reduce the arguments that are common when family members travel together.) Plus, with a fully equipped kitchen or kitchenette, you can make your own breakfasts and/or lunches and save on meal expenses. For families with children or teens, staying in an apartment-style, multibedroom suite offers comfort, added privacy, convenience, and a money-saving opportunity. If you're looking for a clean, fully functional hotel room or suite that'll save you a lot of money, staying at a non-Disney hotel is an excellent idea.

☰FAST FACT

The Orlando/Orange County Convention & Visitors Bureau (✆407-363-5871, ✑www.orlandoinfo.com) reports that in the Orlando area, there are more than 109,784 hotel rooms available. In 2003, the average per-night rate among hotels in the Orlando area was $86.16. Call this visitors bureau for a complete listing of area hotels.

Apartment-Style Accommodations Close to WDW

If you're looking for multibedroom, apartment-style accommodations (complete with kitchen and living room), several top-notch properties include: The Sheraton Safari Hotel (✆407-239-0444, ✆888-625-4988, ✑www.sheraton.com), The Caribe Royale All-Suites Resort & Convention Center (✆800-823-8300, ✑www.cariberoyale.com), and The Staybridge Suites (✆407-238-0777, ✑www.ichotelsgroup.com). These resort properties are midpriced and ideal for families traveling with kids or teens. They're also very close to The WDW Resort and offer free shuttle transportation to and from Orlando's major attractions.

Five-Star Resorts Outside of WDW

The Orlando area offers several five-star resorts close to WDW that offer the ultimate in comfort, luxury, and fun. Located less than two minutes from the Downtown Disney area at WDW is the Hyatt Regency Grand Cypress (✆800-835-7377, *www.hyattgrand cypress.com*), one of the nicest resorts you'll find in Orlando. This resort offers so much in the way of activities and amenities, you could easily enjoy a multiday vacation without ever leaving the property. For example, there's horseback riding, several swimming pools and spas, a game room, an award-winning golf course, tennis, racquetball, pitch 'n putt golf, bike rentals, a fully equipped health club and day spa, jogging trails, several restaurants, and a daycare center (plus private babysitting service for young kids). If you choose to visit one of the nearby theme parks, a free shuttle service is available. In addition to the incredible hospitality offered by the staff, what sets this resort apart from others is its beauty and immaculate landscaping. This is a 1,500-acre property with more than 750 rooms and 74 suites that are all ultramodern, clean, spacious, and well-equipped. Rates start around $250 per night and go up considerably. Adjoining rooms and multibedroom suites are available to families.

A similar, family-oriented resort, located about one mile from The WDW Resort, is the new Gaylord Palms Resort (✆407-586-2000, *www.gaylordhotels.com/gaylordpalms*). It, too, offers a wide range of amenities and activities you can experience without ever leaving the property. This resort is also the home of the Canyon Ranch Spa, an award-winning world-class day spa. For kids, the **La Petite Kids' Academy Kids Station** offers a camplike experience, complete with supervised activities every day of the year.

≡FAST FACT

For a more complete Yellow Pages listing of hotels, motels, and resorts, visit *www.switchboard.com* and do a search for "Hotel & Motel Reservations" in Orlando and surrounding areas.

Area Hotels

There are more than 1,000 hotels, resorts, and motels located in the Orlando, Lake Buena Vista, or Kissimmee areas that are close to The WDW Resort, Universal Orlando Resort, SeaWorld, and/or other popular attractions. The following is a sampling of what's available. The rates for these hotels vary based on season and room availability, so contact each hotel directly for exact rates and availability for the dates you plan on visiting. All rates listed are approximations (subject to change) and are based on double occupancy.

ORLANDO AREA HOTELS	
Hotel Name **Phone Number**	**Distance to WDW by Car** **Price Range per Night**
Adam's Mark of Orlando ☎(407) 859-1500	25 minutes $90–$150
Arnold Palmer's Bay Hill Club & Lodge ☎(407) 876-2429 or ☎(800) 523-5999	15 minutes $90–$150
Baymont Inn ☎(407) 240-0500 or ☎(800) 428-3438	5 minutes $50–$100
Best Western Lake Buena Vista Hotel ☎(407) 828-2424 or ☎(800) 348-3765	On WDW Resort property $100–$300
Best Western Orlando West ☎(407) 841-8600 or ☎(800) 645-6386	25 minutes Under $50
Best Western Plaza International ☎(407) 345-8195	10 minutes $50–$100
Buena Vista Suites ☎(407) 239-8588 or ☎(800) 537-7737	5 minutes $100–$150
Caribe Royale Resort Suites ☎(407) 238-8000 or ☎(800) 823-8300	5 minutes $100–$150
The Castle Doubletree Hotel ☎(800) 952-2785	10 minutes $110 and up
Clarion Maingate ☎(407) 396-4000 or ☎(800) 568-3352	3 minutes $60–$110
The Clarion Universal of Orlando ☎(407) 351-5009 or ☎(800) 445-7299	15 minutes $50–$100

(continued)

ORLANDO AREA HOTELS *(continued)*

Hotel Name Phone Number	Distance to WDW by Car Price Range per Night
Comfort Inn – Universal Studios ☎(407) 363-7886	10 minutes $50–$100
Comfort Suites Orlando ☎(407) 351-5050	10 minutes $50–$100
Courtyard By Marriott ☎(800) 223-9930	On WDW Resort property $110–$175
Courtyard By Marriott ☎(407) 239-6900 or ☎(800) 635-8684	10 minutes $75–$150
Crowne Plaza Universal ☎(407) 355-0550	10 minutes $100–$200
Days Inn Convention Center/SeaWorld ☎(407) 352-8700	15 minutes $50–$100
Days Inn East of Universal Studios ☎(407) 351-3800	20 minutes $50–$100
Days Inn Lake Buena Vista ☎(407) 239-4441 or ☎(800) 224-5058	3 minutes $50–$100
Doubletree Guest Suites ☎(407) 934-1000 or ☎(800) 222-8733	On WDW Resort property $130–$250
Doubletree Hotel ☎(407) 239-4646 or ☎(800) 521-3297	3 minutes $100–$150
Econo Lodge Maingate Hawaiian Resort ☎(407) 396-2000 or ☎(800) 365-6935	3 minutes $50–$100
Embassy Suites International Drive/ Jamaican Court ☎(407) 345-8250 or ☎(800) 327-9797	10 minutes $100–$150
Embassy Suites International Drive South ☎(407) 352-1400 or ☎(800) 433-7275	20 minutes $120–$180
Embassy Suites Lake Buena Vista Resort ☎(800) 257-8483	5 minutes $100–$150
Fairfield Inn By Marriott ☎(407) 363-1944	10 minutes $50–$100

(continued)

ORLANDO AREA HOTELS *(continued)*

Hotel Name / Phone Number	Distance to WDW by Car / Price Range per Night
Gaylord Palms Resort	5 minutes
☎(407) 586-2000	$250–$500
Grosvenor Resort	On WDW Resort property
☎(407) 828-4444 or ☎(800) 624-4109	$115–$500
Hampton Inn at Universal Studios	15 minutes
☎(407) 351-6716 or ☎(800) 231-8395	$50–$100
Hampton Inn Maingate Hotel	5 minutes
☎(407) 396-8484	$50–$100
Hampton Inn South of Universal Studios	15 minutes
☎(407) 345-1112 or ☎(800) 763-1100	$50–$100
Hilton	On WDW Resort property
☎(407) 827-4000 or ☎(800) 782-4414	$200–$800
Holiday Inn Express International Drive	15 minutes
☎(800) 365-6935	$50–$100
Holiday Inn Family Suites	10 minutes
☎(407) 387-5437	$129–$300
Holiday Inn International Drive Resort	15 minutes
☎(407) 351-3500 or ☎(800) 206-2747	$50–$100
Holiday Inn Main Gate East	5 minutes
☎(407) 396-4488 or ☎(800) 366-5437	$65–$130
Holiday Inn Sunspree	5 minutes
☎(407) 239-4500 or ☎(800) 366-6299	$90–$130
Holiday Inn Universal Studios	15 minutes
☎(407) 351-3333 or ☎(800) 327-1364	$50–$100
Homewood Suites Maingate at the Parkway	5 minutes
☎(407) 396-2229	$100–$150
Howard Johnson Inn Maingate East	5 minutes
☎(407) 396-1748 or ☎(800) 288-4678	$50–$100
Howard Johnson's Plaza Resort	20 minutes
☎(407) 351-2000 or ☎(800) 327-3808	$50–$150

(continued)

ORLANDO AREA HOTELS (continued)

Hotel Name / Phone Number	Distance to WDW by Car / Price Range per Night
Hyatt Regency Grand Cypress Hotel ☎(407) 239-1234 or ☎(800) 233-1234	3 minutes $195–$850
Knights Inn Maingate ☎(407) 396-4200 or ☎(800) 944-0062	5 minutes $35–$70
LaQuinta Inn Lakeside ☎(407) 396-2222 or ☎(800) 848-0801	5 minutes $50–$100
Leisure Resorts at Orlando ☎(407) 239-0707 or ☎(800) 633-1405	10 minutes $100–$150
Magic Castle Inn ☎(407) 396-1212 or ☎(800) 446-5669	10 minutes $50–$100
Rosen Centre Hotel ☎(407) 354-9840 or ☎(800) 204-7234	15 minutes $150 and up
Parc Corniche Resort ☎(407) 239-7100 or ☎(800) 446-2721	6 minutes $69 and up
Peabody Orlando ☎(407) 352-4000 or ☎(800) 732-2639	20 minutes $240–$1,400
Quality Inn Plaza ☎(407) 345-8585 or ☎(800) 999-8585	15 minutes $50–$100
Radisson Barcelo Hotel Orlando ☎(407) 345-0505 or ☎(800) 333-3333	15 minutes $100–$150
Radisson Inn Lake Buena Vista ☎(407) 239-8400 or ☎(800) 333-3333	5 minutes $100–$150
Ramada Plaza Gateway ☎(407) 396-4400 or ☎(800) 327-9170	3 minutes $60–$300+
Rosenpleza Hotel ☎(407) 352-9700 or ☎(800) 627-8258	15 minutes $135–$700
Royal Plaza Hotel ☎(407) 828-2828 or ☎(800) 248-7890	On WDW Resort property $110–$300
Sheraton Universal Resort Hotel ☎(407) 351-2100 or ☎(800) 327-1366	20 minutes $100–$150
Sheraton Vistana Resort ☎(407) 239-3100 or☎(877) 668-9330	15 minutes $160–$350

(continued)

ORLANDO AREA HOTELS *(continued)*	
Hotel Name Phone Number	Distance to WDW by Car Price Range per Night
Sheraton World Resort ☎(407) 352-1100 or ☎(800) 325-3535	12 minutes $100–$150
Summerfield Suites Hotel ☎(407) 352-2400 or ☎(800) 830-4964	20 minutes $150 and up
Summerfield Suites Lake Buena Vista ☎(407) 238-0777 or ☎(800) 830-4964	6 minutes $170–$275
Travelodge Maingate Hotel ☎(407) 396-0100 or ☎(800) 327-9151	5 minutes Under $50
Travelodge Orlando Convention Center ☎(407) 345-8000 or ☎(800) 346-1551	20 minutes $70–$100

Travel times, as reported by each hotel, motel, or resort, are approximate and will vary based on traffic and weather conditions.

Timeshares

No matter where you go in Orlando, various companies, including the Walt Disney Company, will try hard to get you interested in purchasing timeshare vacation packages. If you're interested in learning more about some of the timeshare vacation opportunities available in the Orlando area, contact these companies:

A Time Share Resale Broker: ☎(407) 273-0559

Disney Vacation Club: ☎(800) 500-3990, ✍*www.disneyvacationclub.com*

Hilton Grand Vacations Club: ☎(407) 238-2600

Sheraton/Vistana Resort: ☎(407) 239-3100

Time Share Resales of America: ☎(800) 789-2718

≡FAST FACT

Just for sitting through a sales presentation, you'll be offered all sorts of incentives, ranging from free (or discounted) admission to popular attractions, free (or discounted) hotel accommodations, free meals, and/or other incentives.

Packing for Your Vacation

In addition to carefully planning out an itinerary and prebooking all of your travel arrangements (airfares, hotel, rental car, etc.), you'll also want to ensure that you pack all of the belongings and wardrobe items you'll need while traveling. This section will help you actually put together the ultimate packing list.

The Orlando Climate

To find out the current weather in Orlando, be sure to watch The Weather Channel, check the weather map in *USA Today,* or visit the WDW Web site at *www.disneyworld.com* for an up-to-date weather report. You can also call (407) 824-4104 for Walt Disney Resort weather. Another option is to visit one of these Web sites:

MSNBC Weather: *www.msnbc.com*

USA Today: *www.usatoday.com/weather*

Weather Channel Online: *www.weather.com*

Yahoo! Weather: *http://weather.yahoo.com*

AVERAGE TEMPERATURES AT THE WDW RESORT			
Month	Average High Temperature (°F)	Average Low Temperature (°F)	Average Rainfall
January	70	50	2.2"
February	72	51	2.9"
March	77	56	3.3"
April	82	61	2.2"
May	88	66	4.0"
June	90	71	7.4"
July	92	73	7.8"
August	92	73	6.3"
September	90	73	5.6"
October	84	65	2.8"
November	78	57	1.8"
December	71	54	1.8"

Theme Park Attire

The trick to dressing appropriately at any theme park is not to wear the trendiest or most stylish outfits. Comfort and protection from the sun are the keys! On hot days, wear light and comfortable clothing. On cooler days, wear layers that can be removed and that aren't too bulky. (You can always store clothing items in the lockers available at the theme parks.)

Finally, comfortable shoes should round out your theme park attire. If you're traveling with kids, or plan to experience rides where you get wet, bring along an extra change of clothes for everyone and store it in a locker (or in your car) until it is needed. Ideally, you'll want to keep your hands as free as possible, so try to avoid heavy purses, backpacks, and shoulder bags. Waist packs are an excellent solution for carrying smaller items such as wallets, glasses, keys, and small cameras.

On rainy days, many people are inclined to bring an umbrella to the theme parks. This is a bad idea. Navigating around within the theme parks (among the crowds) is difficult with an open umbrella. You're better off wearing a waterproof hat, raincoat, or one of the plastic rain ponchos sold at the theme parks for about $6 each.

Before getting dressed in the morning, find out what the weather will be like for the day and dress accordingly, keeping in mind that at night the temperature may drop.

≡FAST FACT

Due to heightened security measures, all bags you carry into a theme park will be hand-searched by security personnel at the park, so plan accordingly.

Rain or Shine: Always Wear a Hat

You'll want to protect your head and neck area from Florida's intense sun while you're exploring the various theme parks or spending time by the pool. Even on overcast days, the Florida sun can cause a serious burn relatively quickly if you're not protected, so make sure that you use powerful sunblock on all exposed skin. This is particularly important with kids.

A hat and sunglasses are virtually always a must. Wearing a hat will protect you from the sun (or the rain), and help keep you comfortable throughout the day. You can pack your own hat or cap, or purchase a Disney-themed hat at almost any souvenir or gift shop at The WDW Resort.

Packing Carry-On Luggage

All of the airlines have changed their policies regarding carry-on luggage—the bags you physically carry onto the airplane with you and store either under the seat or in the overhead compartment. Virtually all of the airlines are now strict about allowing only one or two carry-on bags (including a purse or laptop case) per passenger, and the size requirements for each bag continue to change. Be sure to bring along a book or magazine to keep you entertained, as well as a snack or meal. Many airlines have discontinued in-flight meals and video entertainment. Also, within your carry-on, pack any electronics (cameras, video equipment, etc.), jewelry, prescription medications, and valuables that you wouldn't want lost or stolen.

Leaving Home

Due to the increased security within airports, make sure to arrive at the airport at least one hour (or even ninety minutes) prior to your flight's scheduled departure. For international flights, arrive at the airport at least two hours early. With this in mind, plan your schedule accordingly. As you get ready to leave your home and depart on your vacation, here's a quick checklist of things you might want to do prior to leaving.

❒ Arrange for someone to care for your pets and plants.
❒ Ask a friend, relative, or neighbor to check on your home or apartment while you're gone.

❑ Ask the post office to hold your mail (and fill out the appropriate form).

❑ Clean all dirty dishes.

❑ Close and lock all windows and close the blinds/curtains.

❑ Contact your child's teacher if he/she will be missing classes.

❑ Empty your refrigerator of perishable items.

❑ Empty your trash.

❑ Get a haircut, manicure, etc.

❑ Give a copy of your house keys to a nearby friend or relative.

❑ Leave your contact information with coworkers, friends, relatives, or anyone who might need to reach you in case of an emergency.

❑ Pay your mortgage, rent, credit card bills, and other bills.

❑ Refill all prescription medications.

❑ Stop daily newspaper delivery or arrange for newspapers to be placed in an area that's out of sight. You don't want to make it obvious that you're on vacation.

❑ Turn down the heat or air conditioning.

❑ Unplug electrical appliances.

❑ Visit a bank to get cash and traveler's checks.

CHAPTER 3

Admission to the Disney Theme Parks

ONCE YOU DEVELOP A PRELIMINARY ITINERARY FOR your trip, decide how many days you'll spend exploring the various Disney theme parks. There are one-park/one-day tickets that provide unlimited admission to one of Disney's theme parks for a single day. Other options include multiday/multipark passes (called "Park Hopper" or "Park Hopper Plus" passes), and annual passes.

Admission Prices and Passes

Admission to the various theme parks at WDW can be purchased per park, by the day. If you're staying at WDW for multiple days, however, you'll save money by purchasing multiday Park Hopper passes that give you full access to all of the WDW theme parks.

An alternative to purchasing single-day/single-park passes or multiday Park Hopper passes is to purchase a complete vacation package from the Walt Disney Travel Company, any travel agent, or most major airlines. Package prices and what the packages include vary greatly.

The primary Disney theme parks include:

- The Magic Kingdom
- Epcot
- The Disney-MGM Studios
- Disney's Animal Kingdom

Unless you purchase a 5-Day Park Hopper Plus Pass or Premium Annual Pass, separate admission is required for:

- Blizzard Beach
- DisneyQuest
- Disney's Wide World of Sports complex
- Pleasure Island
- Typhoon Lagoon

The following are some of the admission prices for the WDW theme parks. (All prices are subject to change.) For more information about park admission prices or to prepurchase your passes, call ☎(407) W-DISNEY, visit Disney World's Web site (⊘*www. disneyworld.com*), or visit any Disney Store.

💼 TRAVEL TIP

Utilize Disney's "Advance Purchase Savings Program" and save up to $22 on each multiday theme park ticket. You can save time when you visit the theme parks (and avoid lines) by purchasing your admission tickets in advance through any Disney Store, by calling ☎(407) W-DISNEY, or from the ⊘*www.disneyworld.com* Web site. For example, a 4-Day Park Hopper pass purchased in advance is priced at $192 (versus $208 at the gate).

1 Day/1 Park Ticket

These tickets are good for one day's admission to any one of the primary WDW theme parks (listed on page 69).

ANY PRIMARY WDW THEME PARK		
Duration	Adult Pass	Child Pass (Ages 3 to 9)
1 Day	$54.75	$43.75

Water Park One-Day Admission

Admission to Typhoon Lagoon or Blizzard Beach is included with this ticket. To avoid standing in line to enter a Disney water park, you can now purchase your admission tickets from automated ticket vending machines located at the front gates. All major credit cards and your Disney Resort room key (with charge privileges activated) are accepted.

TYPHOON LAGOON OR BLIZZARD BEACH		
Duration	Adult Pass	Child Pass (Ages 3 to 9)
1 Day	$31	$25
Annual Pass (both water parks)	$106.45	$85.74

Pleasure Island Admission

During the day, Pleasure Island, which is located between the Downtown Disney shopping area and Disney's West Side, is open to the public. There is no admission fee. In the evenings and at night, however, when the Pleasure Island clubs open, there is a separate admission fee that includes admission to all of the clubs and attractions within this area. (Drinks and food, however, are sold separately.)

Note that for special events at Pleasure Island (such as New Year's Eve), an additional admission fee and advance reservations may be required.

PLEASURE ISLAND		
Duration	Adult Pass (18+ Only)	Child Pass
1 Night	$19.95	Not Available
Annual Pass	$54.95	Not Available

▣ TRAVEL TIP

When you purchase a one-night admission ticket to Pleasure Island, you can upgrade to a six-consecutive-night ticket for just $5 more. This offer is subject to end at any time, however.

Disney's Wide World of Sports

For sports fans of all ages who wish to explore Disney's Wide World of Sports complex, there is a separate admission fee.

DISNEY'S WIDE WORLD OF SPORTS		
Duration	Adult Pass	Child Pass (Ages 3 to 9)
1 Day	$9.81	$7.24

DisneyQuest

Within Disney's West Side area is an indoor, high-tech interactive attraction called DisneyQuest, which combines video arcade games with state-of-the-art virtual reality rides and attractions. While DisneyQuest will appeal primarily to boys between the ages of ten and twenty-one, there is plenty to do here for everyone. The all-inclusive, one-day pass includes unlimited use of all rides and attractions within DisneyQuest.

DISNEYQUEST		
Duration	Adult Pass	Child Pass (Ages 3 to 9)
1 Day	$31	$25
Annual Pass	$84.14	$67.10

4-Day Park Hopper Pass

This pass allows you to visit The Magic Kingdom, Epcot, the Disney-MGM Studios, and Disney's Animal Kingdom only. You enter and exit these parks as often as you'd like during any four days. In most cases, unused days do not expire and the days do not have to be consecutive. Five-day Park Hopper passes are also available, however, you'll probably want the benefits of a Park Hopper Plus pass if you'll be staying at The WDW Resort for more than four days.

PARK HOPPER PASS		
Duration	Adult Pass	Child Pass (Ages 3 to 9)
4 Days	$219	$176
4 Days (advance purchase)	$202	$162

5-Day Park Hopper Plus Pass

This pass allows you to visit The Magic Kingdom, Epcot, the Disney-MGM Studios, and Disney's Animal Kingdom, and enter and exit these parks as often as you'd like during any five days. In addition to the primary theme parks, this type of ticket also grants the holder the choice of admission to two of the following: Blizzard Beach, Typhoon Lagoon, or Pleasure Island. Unused days do not expire. Six- and seven-day Park Hopper Plus passes are also available, as are Length-of-Stay passes with these benefits.

PARK HOPPER PLUS PASS		
Duration	Adult Pass	Child Pass (Ages 3 to 9)
5 Days	$282	$226
5 Days (advance purchase)	$259	$208

Length of Stay Pass

If you're staying at The WDW Resort for a number of days that isn't included in one of the pass options, you can purchase a special Length of Stay Pass that offers you unlimited access to all of the theme parks during your entire stay. These passes are good from the moment you check in at your WDW Resort hotel until midnight of the day you check out of the hotel. These passes give guests total freedom to go from park to park at will, and use all WDW Transportation. The price for this type of pass varies based on the length of your stay. For more information, call ✆(407) W-DISNEY.

💼 TRAVEL TIP

Ultimate Park Hopper Tickets are available to guests staying at a Walt Disney World resort and provide unlimited admission from the time of check-in through the day of check-out to all four theme parks, two water parks, Downtown Disney, Pleasure Island, and DisneyQuest. When making your Disney resort reservation, inquire about this type of pass and pricing, which is based upon your length of stay.

Annual Pass

If you plan on visiting The WDW Resort multiple times in any twelve-month period, consider purchasing an annual pass. These passes provide unlimited admission to The Magic Kingdom, Epcot, the Disney-MGM Studios, and Disney's Animal Kingdom during normal operating hours. Parking and unlimited use of WDW Transportation is included. Special discounts are also offered for food and merchandise. The twelve-month period begins on the first day the pass is used to enter a theme park (not when it's issued).

ANNUAL PASS		
Type of Pass	Adult Pass	Child Pass (Ages 3 to 9)
Annual Pass	$379	$322
Florida Resident Annual Pass	$299	$254

Premium Annual Pass

These twelve-month passes offer unlimited admission to The Magic Kingdom, Epcot, the Disney-MGM Studios, and Disney's Animal Kingdom, plus Pleasure Island, Typhoon Lagoon, Blizzard Beach, Disney's Wide World of Sports complex, and DisneyQuest during normal operating hours. Parking and unlimited use of WDW

Transportation is included. Special discounts are also offered for food and merchandise.

PREMIUM ANNUAL PASS		
Type of Pass	Adult Pass	Child Pass (Ages 3 to 9)
Premium Annual Pass	$499	$424
Florida Resident Premium Annual Pass	$399	$339

Beware of Counterfeit Passes and Scams

Up until recently, non-Disney tourist centers made a lot of money buying and selling unused passes for The WDW Resort. If a family purchased 5-Day Park Hopper Passes, but used only three of the days on each pass, independent ticket agencies would purchase the unused days at a fraction of the true value, and then resell those passes to other tourists to earn a profit.

Recently, however, the Walt Disney Company began using new technology to print and issue passes for the Disney theme parks that prevents counterfeiting, unauthorized ticket brokering, or illegal ticket scalping. As a result, to protect yourself, do not purchase any admission passes to any Disney theme park (for any price) from any unauthorized ticket agent.

≡FAST FACT

Some unofficial tourist information centers will offer legitimate discount tickets to the Disney theme parks; however, you must first sit through a long sales presentation for local timeshare vacation/investment opportunities.

The safest places to purchase your admission passes for the Disney theme parks are from your own travel agent, directly from any WDW Resort ticket counter (on Disney property), from a Disney Store, or from Disney Online. American Express Travel Services and AAA Travel Services are among the agencies that are allowed to sell admission tickets to the Disney theme parks. If someone tries to sell you highly discounted admission tickets to the Disney theme parks, or asks to purchase your used or unused passes, walk away.

Avoid Long Lines with FASTPASS

It's everyone's dream to visit one of the Disney World theme parks and discover the place is absolutely empty—with none of those dreaded lines to wait in, even for the most popular rides. Well, the chances of that dream coming true, no matter how much pixie dust you use, are slim. Thanks to WDW's FASTPASS, however, visitors don't have to wait hours at a time to experience the most popular rides within the various Disney theme parks.

Combine careful planning with the FASTPASS system, and you'll be able to enjoy most or all of each park's most popular rides, without having to wait for hours at a time in line to experience each of them. FASTPASS use is free of charge to all theme park visitors.

⊕ HOT SPOT

Mission: SPACE and Test Track are two of Epcot's newest and most popular attractions; therefore, there's almost always a long wait. If you don't want to take advantage of FASTPASS, consider experiencing these rides as a single person and getting into the special singles' line located near the ride's entrance—the wait will typically be considerably shorter.

When you approach a ride that supports FASTPASS, you'll see two clocks located near the ride's entrance. One clock displays the estimated wait time in the regular line. (For a popular ride during a peak vacation period, the wait could be sixty to ninety minutes or more.) The second clock displays the current return time for people using FASTPASS.

If you choose to use FASTPASS, simply insert your theme park admission ticket (passport or annual pass) into the special kiosk located near the ride's entrance. A special pass will be printed explaining what time to return to the ride. For example, if it's 1:00 P.M. when you approach the ride for the first time, and you insert your ticket into the FASTPASS turnstile, you may be told to return to the ride at 2:30 P.M., at which time you can proceed directly to the ride's preshow or boarding area. There will then be little or no wait.

📁 TRAVEL TIP

Guests are given a one-hour window during which they can return to experience the ride once they take advantage of FASTPASS. So if the printed FASTPASS ticket you receive indicates you should return at 2:00 P.M., for example, you can arrive at the ride's entrance anywhere between 2:00 P.M. and 3:00 P.M.

Using FASTPASS is like making a reservation to experience a ride, without having to wait in line. While guests can't specify a specific time they'd like to experience a ride, it is possible to save considerable time and avoid waiting in long lines. While you're waiting for your designated FASTPASS time, you're free to experience other rides, shows, and attractions within the theme park.

Guests can activate FASTPASS for only one ride at a time. So, if you're waiting to experience Splash Mountain, for example, and you have ninety minutes until your designated boarding time, you can't race over to Space Mountain and also take advantage of FASTPASS until after you've experienced Splash Mountain.

Using FASTPASS within any of the Disney theme parks is easy. It all starts by purchasing an admission ticket for The Magic Kingdom, Epcot, the Disney-MGM Studios, or Disney's Animal Kingdom. Once you're in one of the parks, follow these steps:

1. Proceed to the ride of your choice that supports FASTPASS.
2. Check the clocks located near the ride's entrance to determine the wait time without using FASTPASS and what time you could experience the ride if you obtain a FASTPASS ticket.
3. Based on your schedule, if you choose to request a FAST-PASS ticket, insert your theme park admission ticket into the ride's special turnstile. You will then receive a printed ticket indicating what time you should return to the ride. (Keep in mind, you have a one-hour window from the time printed on the ticket.)
4. When the designated time to return to the ride arrives, proceed directly to the ride's preshow or boarding area. At this point, you can expect little or no wait.

Since FASTPASS works with many of the most popular rides within each of Disney's theme parks, you can use this free feature to help plan your day and ensure that you're able to experience everything you'd like to during your visit to each park. FASTPASS is particularly useful if you're traveling with young kids, who are typically impatient and hate waiting in lines, especially on a hot day.

TRAVEL TIP

If used correctly, FASTPASS can save you up to two hours each day. This gives you up to 25 percent more time to experience rides and attractions, as opposed to waiting in long lines for the popular attractions.

Travel Tips

As you read this book and start thinking about how exactly you want to spend your time, be sure to take notes and keep track of which rides, shows, attractions, parades, and activities are of interest to you and the people you'll be traveling with. Once you think you know what you want to experience, start planning out the actual days of your trip. While you're doing this, keep in mind that each of the various theme parks is massive, so plan on doing a lot of walking.

Make sure everyone you're traveling with gets to experience activities that he or she is most excited about. This may mean making compromises or separating at various times. There's no reason why every family member should be dragged to activities that others aren't interested in. While you'll definitely want to plan some "quality family time," that time together will be more thoroughly enjoyed if everyone you're traveling with is happy and excited about the activities he or she has experienced during the vacation.

▣ TRAVEL TIP

To save yourself a considerable amount of time traveling between theme parks and activities, plan out your itinerary in half-day chunks. Also, when making up your schedule, don't forget to leave time to eat, rest, experience the popular rides and attractions, and also wait in line to experience those attractions.

Tips for Traveling with Small Kids

The Disney theme parks offer plenty to do for people of all ages, including young children. When traveling with young kids, however, it's important to plan your day to accommodate their needs. For example, plan on arriving at any of the theme parks early in the day, then take a break in the middle of the day for lunch and a nap. Head back to the theme park again later in the day when everyone is rested. Also, be sure to take advantage of stroller rentals at each of the parks. Visiting a theme park requires a lot of walking and kids tire easily. (See the "Guest Services" section of this chapter for more information on renting a stroller.)

For two adults who are traveling with younger kids, take advantage of the "Kid Switch" program described in Chapter 5 to save time waiting in lines for rides. Also, if you're traveling with young kids, plan on spending extra time within The Magic Kingdom. Here, you'll find the majority of young-kid–oriented rides, shows, and attractions.

Finally, when dining on Disney property, be sure to ask about the money-saving kids' menus and special meal deals. To keep your kids entertained during a meal, consider participating in one of the Disney character dining experiences offered at restaurants throughout The Walt Disney World Resort.

Tips for Seniors

Senior citizens should consider pacing themselves when visiting any of the theme parks, since a lot of walking is required. Anyone who tires easily or doesn't enjoy a lot of walking should seriously consider renting a wheelchair or electronic convenience vehicle. You might also consider arriving at a park early in the morning, exploring for three or four hours, taking several hours to relax in the afternoon, and then venturing back out in the late afternoon or evening for several more hours. Epcot offers the most attractions designed for older guests.

In addition to a lot of walking, one of the biggest concerns older people should have when visiting The WDW Resort is dealing with the heat and sun. Overexposure to the sun can cause health problems. Be sure to wear plenty of sunblock, a hat, sunglasses, and light clothing that covers your entire body. Also, drink plenty of fluids and take rests often. During the afternoon hours (when the weather is the hottest), plan to visit the indoor, air-conditioned attractions. At Epcot, these include Innoventions, The Living Seas,

Wonders of Life, and Universe of Energy. You can easily plan on spending between one and three hours at each of these indoor attractions.

🧳 TRAVEL TIP

If you're traveling with a large family, or your group includes very small children or elderly adults, consider planning your vacation to The WDW Resort during the off-peak season, so you won't have to deal with large crowds and long lines for the attractions.

Guest Services

Within each of the Disney theme parks (The Magic Kingdom, Epcot, the Disney-MGM Studios, Disney's Animal Kingdom, the water parks, etc.), you'll find the following guest services designed to make your visit to the parks more comfortable and enjoyable.

Automated Teller Machines

Within the Disney theme parks, as well as within Downtown Disney, you'll find multiple automated teller machines (ATMs). Ask any Disney cast member for directions to the closest machine, or check the map located within the souvenir guide map and daily schedule brochures. Your bank may charge a transaction/ withdrawal fee for using an ATM that's outside of your bank's own network.

Throughout The WDW Resort, cash (U.S. currency), traveler's checks, Disney Dollars, personal checks, Visa, MasterCard, American Express, JCB, the Disney Credit Card, and Discover Card are accepted. Credit cards are not accepted at the various food and merchandise kiosks located throughout the parks. If you're staying within a Disney hotel/resort, your room key can also be used as a charge card within the parks. Your purchases will be billed directly to your hotel room.

Within The WDW Resort, there's a full-service SunTrust bank that's located across the street from Downtown Disney. The branch is open on weekdays between 9:00 A.M. and 4:00 P.M. (6:00 P.M. on Thursdays). Call ✆(407) 237-4141 or ✆(800) 432-4760 for details. At this branch, you can obtain a cash advance from a major credit card, receive a wire transfer, and perform many other banking functions.

Child Care

Baby Service areas can be found within each of the primary Disney theme parks. Private rooms are available for nursing and feeding. Highchairs, bibs, plastic spoons, and diaper changing rooms are provided. Additional baby care products (disposable diapers, formula, etc.) can be purchased. Baby-changing tables are available in all public restrooms throughout the theme parks.

In-room babysitting service is available twenty-four hours a day by calling your hotel's front desk or concierge. There is an hourly (per child) charge. In addition, there are childcare programs available at several of the Disney hotels. Call Disney's Kids' Nite Out at ✆(407) 828-0920 for details and fees.

≡FAST FACT

Several Disney resorts, including Disney's Polynesian Resort, Disney's Beach Club Resort, Disney's Contemporary Resort, Disney's Grand Floridian Resort & Spa, Disney's BoardWalk, and the Disney Animal Kingdom Lodge offer child care facilities for toilet-trained kids between the ages of four and twelve. There is a per-child/per-hour fee for this service. Contact your Disney hotel's front desk for details.

Emergency Services

No matter what type of emergency you experience, medical or otherwise, contact the nearest Disney cast member immediately. Those who work at The WDW Resort and the theme parks are highly trained to deal with virtually any type of emergency, such as lost children, medical-related problems, and lost or stolen items.

Within all of the Disney theme parks, you'll find fully equipped first aid stations. Various amenities such as pain relievers, sunblock, and bandages can be purchased at many of gift shops, including those along Main Street, U.S.A. (within The Magic Kingdom) or D-TV (within Pleasure Island).

When adults get separated, messages can be left at the Guest Relations desk (typically located near the entrance to each park). It's highly recommended, however, that you predetermine a location and time to meet if you get separated within the theme parks. Many travelers also resort to cell phones and/or walkie-talkies to stay in contact with one another.

Health-Related Services

Aside from the first aid stations located within each of the theme parks, there are walk-in medical facilities (operated by Florida Hospital) located just outside of The WDW Resort area. For information about these medical facilities, call ☎(407) 238-2000 or ☎(407) 239-6463. Complimentary transportation to these walk-in medical centers is available.

To receive an in-room visit from a doctor (at your Disney hotel), call the Doctors-On-Call service at ☎(407) 399-3627. This service is available twenty-four hours per day. Two of the closest hospitals to The WDW Resort are Sandlake Hospital (☎407-351-8500) and Celebration Health (☎407-303-4000).

To arrange to have a prescription delivered to your hotel room, call Centra Care at ☎(407) 239-7777. There are also three Walgreens pharmacies (☎800-289-2273) located near The WDW Resort (near the Downtown Disney area).

Refrigeration facilities for prescription medications (such as insulin or antibiotics) are available, free of charge, within the theme parks and Disney hotels. Contact the First Aid office or Guest Relations for more information.

💼 TRAVEL TIP

Before leaving on your vacation, make sure to obtain a copy of your prescription to take with you, along with contact information for your doctor and medical insurance company. Thus, if you need to have your prescription refilled, it will be much less of a hassle.

Religious Services

To find a house of worship or nearby religious services, check any local Orlando-area telephone book or ask the front desk (or concierge) at your hotel. In many cases, free shuttle service is available from The WDW Resort to the house of worship of your choice.

Lockers

Lockers are available for rent within all of the Disney theme parks. These are excellent for storing an extra change of clothing, jackets, or camera equipment during the day until they're needed. While visiting the parks, you'll want to keep your hands as free as possible. Storing items you bring into the park or that you purchase (souvenirs) is an excellent strategy. Renting a locker is a lot more convenient than running back and forth to your parked car or hotel room, which will typically require a long walk and/or a tram ride. The daily charge for unlimited use of a locker within each of the Disney theme parks is $7 (plus a $1 refundable deposit).

Lost and Found

There's a Lost and Found office located within each theme park. If you lose an item, report it missing as quickly as possible. If someone returns the item quickly, you can pick it up at the Lost and Found office. If the item is found after your departure from the park, the Walt Disney Company will mail the item to you at whatever address you provide.

If you find someone else's lost item, bring it to one of the park's Lost and Found offices. If the item is not claimed within sixty days, you have the option of keeping it. Ask any Disney cast member for the location of the Lost and Found desk within the Disney theme park or Disney resort you're visiting.

Package Express Service

If you're staying at one of the Disney hotels, one of the perks is that whenever you make a purchase (of a souvenir, for example), you can have the purchased item delivered directly to your hotel room, free of charge. This means you won't have to carry around your purchases or store them in lockers.

For those who aren't staying at one of the Disney hotels, you can arrange to have your purchases delivered and held at the Package Express Pickup Window, located just outside the main entrance to the theme parks. You can pick up your items at the end of the day. This is a complimentary service.

■ TRAVEL TIP

Looking for extra-special VIP treatment when you visit the various Disney theme parks? For guests who'd like the ultimate customized experience, there's a private guided tour service that can plan and lead a personalized itinerary. This service isn't cheap, but it's certainly memorable. To plan a custom guided tour, call Disney Special Activities at ✆ (407) 560-4033.

Pet Care

The WDW Kennels can be found adjacent to the Transportation and Ticket Center, at the entrance to Epcot, at the entrances to the Disney-MGM Studios and Disney's Animal Kingdom Park, and near the entrance to Disney's Fort Wilderness Resort & Campground.

The daily fee is $6 per day (per pet) and/or $11 per night (per pet). When you leave your pet within the kennels, you will be required to drop in for a visit at least once per day. Dog owners, for example, are required to walk their own dogs at least twice daily (or three times daily for puppies). The Epcot location offers an extra dog walking service for $2.50 per walk.

Kennel space is somewhat limited, especially during peak travel times, so be sure to reserve space in advance. Making a hotel reservation is separate from reserving space for your pet within one of the kennels. In addition to housing dogs, the kennels will also accept cats, birds, ferrets, small rodents, and nonvenomous snakes (if in their own carriers).

≡FAST FACT

Keep in mind that all dogs and cats are required to have a certificate of vaccination signed by a licensed veterinarian (rabies, parvo, DHLP, Bordetella for dogs; rabies, FPRC for cats).

Public Telephones

Throughout The WDW Resort (in public areas of the hotels, as well as within the theme parks and in the Downtown Disney area), you'll find an abundance of public telephones. The majority of the pay telephones accept coins, credit cards, or prepaid phone cards.

You'll find that virtually all of the nationwide cellular services work within the Orlando area; however, depending on your cellular service or digital PCS contract, you may be charged per-minute roaming fees, so contact your cellular service provider for details.

Long-distance rates vary. If you can find a good deal on a calling card (with no per-call surcharge and only a per-minute rate), this will probably be the least expensive option when using a pay phone or making calls from a hotel room.

Before making calls from your hotel room, determine what the surcharges will be. Some hotels charge $1 or more every time you pick up the phone to make an outgoing call, even if you're calling locally or using a toll-free phone number.

Restaurant Priority Seating/Reservations

Many of the upscale, sit-down restaurants within the Disney theme parks, the Disney hotels, and in the Downtown Disney area accept reservations. You can call ✆(407) WDW-DINE to make a restaurant reservation, drop into the restaurant in person, visit the guest relations desk within the theme parks, or ask the concierge at your hotel to make the reservation for you.

For those restaurants that do accept lunch and dinner reservations (especially those within the parks), space fills up quickly, so make your reservations early. Group reservations (or plans for a special event or private party) should be made well in advance.

Services for the Disabled

The WDW Resort offers a wide range of services for physically disabled guests. Manually operated wheelchairs and electric convenience vehicles both can be rented (for a small daily fee) near the entrance of each theme park. If you're staying at a Disney hotel, complimentary wheelchairs are available from the hotel. See the front desk for details. The buses that transport guests throughout The WDW Resort are all wheelchair accessible.

For guests with visual disabilities, a special Braille guidebook is available, free of charge, from Guest Relations at any of the theme parks. For those with hearing impairments, closed captioning is available on many of the movie/video-based attractions, written storylines are available for virtually all of the rides and attractions, and some of the rides and attractions utilize Assistive Listening Systems. (The receiver is available from Guest Relations within the theme parks.)

For additional information about all of the various services available for disabled guests, call Guest Relations at ✆(407) 824-4321. A free publication, called *The Guidebook for Guests with Disabilities,* offers information about accessibility to the various rides, shows, attractions, shops, and restaurants within the theme parks. This guide is available from Guest Relations.

If you have special dietary needs, speak with the chef at any of the sit-down (full-service) restaurants within The WDW Resort. Whenever possible, your special needs will be met.

All of the Disney hotels also offer special accommodations for the disabled. These accommodations must be reserved in advance, when making your actual reservation.

═══FAST FACT

Throughout your visit to The WDW Resort, guests with almost any type of disability will find that their needs will be met. In some cases, however, preplanning is required to ensure the proper accommodations and/or services will be available.

Stroller Rentals

Within the theme parks, stroller rentals are available for $8 per day (plus a $1 refundable deposit). A two-passenger stroller can be rented for $15 per day (plus a $1 refundable deposit). The rental locations are near the entrances of The Magic Kingdom, at the base of Spaceship Earth within Epcot, within Oscar's Super Service at the Disney-MGM Studios, and at the entrance to Disney's Animal Kingdom.

When renting a stroller, be sure to keep the receipt with you at all times. If you park your stroller in order to experience an attraction, and your stroller is gone when you return, simply go to a stroller replacement center or the main rental area for a replacement. Ask any Disney cast member for the location of the nearest replacement center.

Because you'll be leaving the stroller unattended (parked outside of each attraction you experience), it's an excellent idea to rent a stroller when you get to one of the theme parks. Do not plan on bringing your own. Also, never leave anything valuable within the storage compartments of the stroller.

Gathering More Information

If you still have questions regarding your travel plans and making reservations at The Walt Disney World Resort, call the appropriate telephone number listed here:

Disney Cruise Lines: ☎(888) DCL-2500

Disney Restaurant Advance "Priority Seating" Reservations: ☎(800) WDW-DINE

Disney Tour Information: ☎(407) 939-8687

Walt Disney World Resort Reservation and Information Line: ☎(407) W-DISNEY

Walt Disney Travel Company: ☎(800) 828-0228

Walt Disney World Guest Information: ☎(407) 824-4321

CHAPTER 4

Orlando-Area Dining

CHANCES ARE, VISITING THE VARIOUS ORLANDO-area theme parks and tourist attractions is going to make you hungry. Well, when it comes to dining out, your choices in the Orlando area are extensive! No matter what type of food you enjoy, chances are you'll find it within The WDW Resort or in a nearby area.

Dining at Disney

In addition to the many fast-food and sit-down (full-service) eating establishments within each of the theme parks (described in Chapters 6, 8, 9, and 10), there is also a handful of excellent restaurants within the Downtown Disney, Disney's West Side, and Disney's BoardWalk areas (see Chapter 12), plus each of the Disney resorts offers at least several dining options for breakfast, lunch, dinner, and snacks. When you head over to Universal Orlando Resort, you'll also find a handful of excellent restaurants within the CityWalk area (described in Chapter 17).

You'll find that the various dining establishments offer diverse menus and cater to different needs. For example, there are fast-food dining options, moderately priced full-service restaurants, fine-dining (expensive) restaurants, and family-oriented theme dining options available—all on WDW property and easily accessible using the Disney bus system, monorails, boats, or other forms of transportation.

On WDW Resort property alone, there are dozens upon dozens of restaurants. For dining suggestions, contact the front desk (or concierge) of your hotel, or call ☎(407) WDW-DINE. Keep in mind, many of the full-service restaurants, especially those within the theme parks, tend to be crowded during peak mealtimes. To avoid long waits, it's best to make reservations.

International Dining Options

While not cheap, the various fine-dining restaurants located within the World Showcase at Epcot offer a wide range of international, authentic, and delicious dining options, whether you're in the mood for Japanese, Chinese, Italian, German, Moroccan, French, English, or Mexican cuisine. See Chapter 8 for details.

Theme Dining

When it comes to theme dining, people of all ages will enjoy Planet Hollywood, located within the West Side area of Downtown Disney. Just look for the giant globe. This is the world's largest Planet Hollywood restaurant. It's jam-packed with all kinds of Hollywood memorabilia, plus it features an extensive menu.

⊕ HOT SPOT

If you're in the mood for an elegant dining experience without leaving the park, the place to visit is the Brown Derby. This restaurant is a re-creation of the original Brown Derby restaurant, located in Hollywood, California, where the Cobb Salad (the house specialty) was originally created. All of the food here is top-notch, whether you enjoy a full lunch or dinner.

There's also the Rainforest Café at Downtown Disney and Disney's Animal Kingdom, The House of Blues at Disney's West

Side, the ESPN Café at the Disney Wide World of Sports, The Cheesecake Factory Express (within DisneyQuest), the Hard Rock Café within Universal's CityWalk, and many other exciting themed dining experiences waiting for you.

Dining Outside of Disney Property

If you have access to a rental car, you'll be able to save a lot of money on all of your meals by dining outside of Disney property. You can leave The WDW Resort and check out the literally dozens of fast-food franchise options (including McDonald's, Wendy's, International House of Pancakes, Subway, Blimpie, Popeye's, Domino's, Little Caesars Pizza, Hardee's, Burger King, Waffle House, etc.) and family-oriented restaurants just a few blocks away from the Downtown Disney area.

Within minutes of The WDW Resort (and even closer to Universal Orlando and SeaWorld), there are countless dining options along International Drive. You can enjoy top-quality food at many of these restaurants, without having to pay a premium for eating at a theme park.

For dining suggestions, visit the icFlorida/WFTV Web site (*www.wftv.com/restaurants/*). Restaurant reviews and listings can also be obtained at the *Orlando Weekly* Web site (*www.orlando weekly.com/dining*).

TRAVEL TIP

To save money when dining at participating non-Disney restaurants, take advantage of the Entertainment Book for the Orlando area (800-374-4464, *www.entertainment.com*), or the Dining-A-La-Card program offered free with the Diner's Club credit card (800-2-DINERS).

The following franchise and independently owned restaurants are located within 2 miles of The WDW Resort.

RESTAURANTS WITHIN 2 MILES OF WDW RESORT

Restaurant Name	Address (in Orlando)	Phone Number
Arthur's 27	1900 Buena Vista Drive	☎(407) 827-2727
Bahama Breeze	8615 Vineland Avenue	☎(407) 938-9010
Baskervilles	1850 Hotel Plaza Blvd.	☎(407) 828-4444
Bennigan's	13520 SR 525	☎(407) 938-0909
Black Swan	One North Jacaranda	☎(407) 239-4700
Bongos Cuban Café	Downtown Disney West Side	☎(407) 828-0999
Cabana Bar & Grill	1500 Epcot Resorts Blvd.	☎(407) 934-4335
Cascade Restaurant	1 Grand Cypress Blvd.	☎(407) 239-1234
The Cheesecake Factory	1486 E. Buena Vista Drive	☎(407) 828-8066
La Coquina Restaurant	1 Grand Cypress Blvd.	☎(407) 239-1234
Crab House	8496 Palm Parkway	☎(407) 239-1888
Denny's Restaurant	12375 State Road 525	☎(407) 239-7900
Domino's Pizza	8542 Palm Parkway	☎(407) 239-1221
Finn's Grill	1751 Hotel Plaza Blvd.	☎(407) 827-3838
Fortune Court	8607 Palm Parkway	☎(407) 239-4999
Giraffe Café	1905 Hotel Plaza Blvd.	☎(407) 828-2828
Havana Café	8544 Palm Parkway	☎(407) 238-5333
Hemingway's Restaurant	1 Grand Cypress Blvd.	☎(407) 239-1234
House of Blues	Downtown Disney West Side	☎(407) 934-BLUE
Jungle Jim's	12501 State Road	☎(407) 827-1257
Landry's Seafood House	8800 Vineland Avenue	☎(407) 827-6466
Lone Star Steakhouse	8850 Vineland Avenue	☎(407) 827-8225
Max Orient	8200 Vineland Avenue	☎(407) 239-4139
McDonald's	12549 State Road 525	☎(407) 827-1030
McDonald's	1674 E. Buena Vista Drive	☎(407) 828-0224
Olive Garden Restaurant	12361 Apopka Vineland	☎(407) 239-6708
Outback Restaurant	1900 Buena Vista Drive	☎(407) 827-2727
Perkins Family Restaurant	12559 State Road 535	☎(407) 827-1060
Pizzeria Uno	12553 State Road 535	☎(407) 827-0022
Planet Hollywood	Downtown Disney West Side	☎(407) 827-7827
Ponderosa Steakhouse	14407 International Drive	☎(407) 238-2526
The Rainforest Café	Disney's Animal Kingdom	☎(407) 938-9100

(continued)

RESTAURANTS WITHIN 2 MILES OF WDW RESORT *(continued)*

Restaurant Name	Address (in Orlando)	Phone Number
The Rainforest Café	Downtown Disney	☎(407) 827-8500
Red Lobster Restaurant	12557 State Road 535	☎(407) 827-1045
Sizzler	12195 S. Apoka-Vineland Road	☎(407) 238-1551
Shoney's Restaurants	12204 S. Apopka-Vineland Road	☎(407) 239-5416
Subway	8127 Vineland Avenue	☎(407) 239-1296
Taco Bell	12555 State Road 535	☎(407) 827-8226
TGI Friday's	12543 State Road 535	☎(407) 827-1020
Waffle House	12805 State Road 535	☎(407) 239-6444
Watercress Café	1900 N. Buena Vista Drive	☎(407) 827-3440
Wolfgang Puck	Downtown Disney West Side	☎(407) 938-9653

The following are other nearby upscale restaurants, many of which offer a family-oriented dining experience in addition to full bar service. Reservations should be made for any of these restaurants, which are ideal for celebrating special occasions.

ORLANDO RESTAURANTS

Restaurant Name	Address (in Orlando)	Phone Number
Arthur's 27	1900 Buena Vista Drive	☎(407) 827-3450
Benihana Japanese Steak House	1751 Hotel Plaza Blvd.	☎(407) 827-4865
The Butcher Shop Steakhouse at the Mercado	8445 International Drive	☎(407) 363-9727
Charley's Steakhouse	8255 International Drive	☎(407) 363-0228
Charlie's Lobster House at The Mercado	8445 International Drive	☎(407) 352-6929
Christini's Ristorante Italiano	7600 Dr. Phillips Blvd.	☎(407) 345-8770
Del Frisco's Prime Steak & Lobster	729 Lee Road	☎(407) 645-4443
DiVino's Italian Restaurant at The Mercado	8445 International Drive	☎(407) 345-0883
Dux	9801 International Drive	☎(407) 345-4550

(continued)

ORLANDO RESTAURANTS (continued)

Restaurant Name	Address (in Orlando)	Phone Number
FishBones	6707 Sand Lake Road	☎(407) 352-0135
Kobe Japanese Steakhouse	8350 International Drive	☎(407) 352-1811
Kobe Japanese Steakhouse	5606 Kirkman Road	☎(407) 248-1978
Palm Restaurant of Orlando	5800 Universal Blvd.	☎(407) 503-7256
Ruth's Chris Steak House	7501 Sand Lake Drive	☎(407) 226-3900

Restaurants in Celebration

Celebration, Florida, is the city conceived and designed by Walt Disney. It was built about ten minutes away from The WDW Resort and is an absolutely charming area to shop, dine in, and explore. For additional information, visit ✑*www.celebrationfl.com*.

⊕ HOT SPOT

The main street area of Celebration, called Market Street, features several upscale, fine-dining restaurants well worth experiencing. Make sure, however, that you leave ample time to explore the nearby shops when you visit Celebration.

Some of the dining options within Celebration, Florida, include:

Bostonian: ☎(407) 566-2526

Café D'Antonio: ☎(407) 566-2233

Celebration Town Tavern: Seafood, Steaks & More: ☎(407) 566-2526

Columbia Restaurant: ☎(407) 566-1505

Herman's Ice Cream Shoppe: ☎(407) 566-1300

Market Street Café: ☎(407) 566-1144

Seito Japanese Restaurant: ☎(407) 566-1889

Upper Crust Pizza: ☎(407) 566-1221

Calculating the Tip

At any full-service restaurant, you're expected to leave a tip for your server. The customary amount to leave is 15 percent of the total bill;

however, you may choose to leave slightly more or less depending on the quality of service you receive.

Many restaurants automatically add a gratuity to the bill for groups, so be sure to determine if a gratuity has already been added to your meal bill if you're dining with a group of people. The following table will help you quickly calculate the appropriate tip amount (based on 15 or 20 percent):

SUGGESTED TIP AMOUNTS		
Meal Price	15% Tip	20% Tip
$5.00	$.75	$1.00
$10.00	$1.50	$2.00
$12.00	$1.80	$2.40
$14.00	$2.10	$2.80
$16.00	$2.40	$3.20
$18.00	$2.70	$3.60
$20.00	$3.00	$4.00
$25.00	$3.75	$5.00
$30.00	$4.50	$6.00
$35.00	$5.25	$7.00
$40.00	$6.00	$8.00
$45.00	$6.75	$9.00
$50.00	$7.50	$10.00
$55.00	$8.25	$11.00
$60.00	$9.00	$12.00
$65.00	$9.75	$13.00
$70.00	$10.50	$14.00
$75.00	$11.25	$15.00
$80.00	$12.00	$16.00
$85.00	$12.75	$17.00
$90.00	$13.50	$18.00
$95.00	$14.25	$19.00
$100.00	$15.00	$20.00
$125.00	$18.75	$25.00
$150.00	$22.50	$30.00

The Ultimate Fine-Dining Experience

Located less than thirty minutes away from The WDW Resort is what could easily be called the very best restaurant in Orlando. While this fine-dining establishment isn't cheap, it offers the best steak and lobster entrees that you can imagine. Del Frisco's Prime Steak & Lobster is the perfect restaurant if you're looking to add an extremely memorable dining experience to your vacation. It's the ideal place to celebrate a birthday, anniversary, or any special occasion, and is where many of Orlando's residents choose to dine.

Owned and operated by Russ and Carole Christner, the secret of this restaurant's incredible success is that Russ, Carole, or one of their sons or sons-in-law can always be found in the kitchen whenever food is being prepared. This is to ensure that the restaurant's award-winning recipes are being followed to the letter, and that the food is being prepared with the freshest ingredients and with absolute quality consistency.

⊕ HOT SPOT

Del Frisco's does no advertising, yet it's crowded virtually every night of the week due to word of mouth and frequent returns by Orlando-area residents. From the moment you step into this restaurant, you'll quickly discover why it has won several awards and has been rated one of the country's top-ten steak houses. Great food, an upbeat and friendly atmosphere, and top-notch service—what more could anyone ask for?

While everything served at Del Frisco's Prime Steak & Lobster is delicious, the specialties of the house are the 8-ounce and 12-ounce filet mignons, the prime porterhouse steak, and the lobster. Entrees range in price from $19.95 to $32.95. Appetizers, vegetables, soups, and salads range from $4.50 to $12.95 each.

In addition to serving some of the best food you'll experience anywhere, the service at Del Frisco's is prompt and friendly. The décor of the restaurant is elegant, featuring fine wood paneling and antiques. There's also a full bar, which features a wine cellar that's extensive and the biggest selection of single malt Scotch in the country, including a bottle that sells for $6,000. The newest addition to this restaurant is a piano bar area, which offers live musical entertainment nightly.

Del Frisco's is open for dinner only, Monday through Thursday, between 5:00 P.M. and 10:00 P.M., and on Friday and Saturday, between 5:00 P.M. and 11:00 P.M. Reservations are definitely recommended, and valet parking is available. Private rooms are available for parties, business meetings, and banquets of up to fifty people.

Del Frisco's Prime Steak & Lobster is located at 729 Lee Road, Orlando, FL 32810. The phone number is ✆(407) 645-4443, and the Web site is ✍*www.delfriscosorlando.com.*

CHAPTER 5

Introduction to The Magic Kingdom

IF THIS ISN'T YOUR FIRST TRIP TO THE MAGIC Kingdom, but you haven't been to this park in years (or decades), what awaits you is a combination of nostalgic rides, shows, and attractions and a whole new set of entertaining experiences. This chapter provides information that will help you get ready to visit The Magic Kingdom.

Getting to and from The Magic Kingdom

Getting to The Magic Kingdom is easy, especially if you're staying at one of The WDW Resort hotels. Ferryboats and other types of ships cross the Seven Seas Lagoon and take guests to and from nearby hotels and the Ticket and Transportation Center (TTC). The resort's famous monorail system stops right in front of The Magic Kingdom and also picks up and drops off guests at several Disney hotels, as well as the Ticket and Transportation Center. After you arrive at the TTC (either by car or by WDW Transportation bus), the ride to The Magic Kingdom will take about four to six minutes once you board a ferryboat or the monorail. A monorail departs from the Ticket and Transportation Center to The Magic Kingdom every three minutes or so.

When attempting to take the monorail service or ferryboat to The Magic Kingdom, if there's a long wait, get yourself to Disney's

Contemporary Resort, then walk to The Magic Kingdom (it's about a ten- to fifteen-minute walk). At the end of the day, you can avoid long exit lines by walking to Disney's Contemporary Resort and then hopping in your car or taking the WDW Transportation bus to your own hotel or back to the TTC.

The WDW Transportation bus system takes guests to and from all of the Disney hotels as well as the various other theme parks and attractions located in the entire resort. While the bus system will, in fact, take you anywhere within the resort complex that you need to go, it's not a terribly fast service, so plan on spending at least thirty minutes to one hour traveling each time you need to use this free bus service.

Having a rental car to get around the resort is a much faster (and less crowded) mode of transportation, but there are parking fees if you want to park at The Magic Kingdom or any of the theme parks. Independent taxi service is available (for a fee, of course). Taking taxis eliminates the wait times involved with taking a WDW Transportation bus, plus eliminates parking hassles, but is very expensive compared to other options.

≡FAST FACT

No matter where you need to get to within The WDW Resort, the WDW bus system will get you there. This complimentary service features over 230 buses that operate continuously in order to transport guests between theme parks, the Disney hotels/resorts, and around the resort property.

Especially during holiday and peak seasons, those traveling by car should plan on arriving at the Ticket and Transportation Center (the parking area for The Magic Kingdom) early to ensure you'll get a parking spot before the lot gets too jammed. Daily parking fees are $7 per car. (It's free if you're staying at a WDW Resort hotel; however, you'll have to pay a daily parking fee at the hotel.)

If you're being dropped off by someone (in a car), you'll need to go to the parking lot of the Ticket and Transportation Center, and then take the monorail or ferry boat to The Magic Kingdom. The driver will have to pay the daily parking fee; however, this fee will be refunded if the driver stops at the Exxon gas station near the exit of the parking lot and presents the parking receipt to the attendant within one hour.

First Things First

Admission to The Magic Kingdom (or any theme park) requires a ticket. For details about the various ticket and pricing options for visiting The Magic Kingdom and all of the theme parks within The WDW Resort, see Chapter 3.

Whenever you leave The Magic Kingdom, be sure to have your hand stamped as you exit in order to be granted re-admission into the park later that day or evening. In addition to the hand stamp, be sure to retain your ticket stub. The hand stamps are designed to be water-resistant, so don't worry if your hand gets wet if you choose to return to your hotel in the middle of the day to go swimming, and then want to return to The Magic Kingdom later that evening. Try to refrain, however, from scrubbing your hands clean with soap until your day's visit to The Magic Kingdom is totally complete.

What to Bring

Make sure you wear comfortable shoes! Depending on the weather, you might want to take along a jacket (you can always store it in a locker). Try to avoid carrying too much stuff with you. You'll enjoy your visit more if your hands are as free as possible. Don't forget to bring your camera, along with plenty of film and batteries. Avoid having to purchase high-priced film, batteries, or camera supplies in the park.

In case of rain, plan on getting a bit wet. Wear a raincoat or plan to purchase a bright yellow Mickey Mouse poncho (for about $6). Avoid bringing an umbrella into the park. You'll find it frustrating trying to walk around the crowded park with an open umbrella. During a rainstorm, crowds will be less; however, some outdoor rides and attractions will be closed, and some parades and shows might be cancelled. Planning for bad weather is important, but when it's sunny (or even slightly overcast), make sure you protect yourself and those you're traveling with by applying plenty of sunscreen. Also, wear a hat to protect your face from the sun.

🧳 TRAVEL TIP

One good rule is to always travel against the crowds. For example, many rides and attractions will have two lines. Most people automatically head to the right. You'll probably find that the line to the left will be shorter.

Choose a Place to Meet

As soon as you arrive at The Magic Kingdom, choose a place where you'll meet up with the other people in your group if you get separated. Two ideal meeting places are in front of City Hall or at the Hub (in front of the Walt Disney and Mickey Mouse statue). Decide to meet on the half-hour if you become separated. Adults can leave written messages for each other at City Hall.

If you're traveling with children, upon arriving at The Magic Kingdom, set some ground rules. Instruct the kids to stay close to you (the parent or adult) at all times. They should know that if they get lost, they should immediately contact any Disney cast member.

The Rating System

To help you choose which rides, shows, and attractions are most worth experiencing while visiting The Magic Kingdom (and all of the theme parks at The WDW Resort), this book offers a star-based ratings system. The ratings are based on the age group each attraction will most appeal to. For each ride, you'll see a chart listing several age groups, plus a one- to three-star rating for that attraction.

Thus, if a rating chart for an attraction has three stars under each age group (as depicted below), this ride, show, or attraction is suitable for the entire family and should not be missed.

Ages 2–4:	★★★
Ages 5–10:	★★★
Ages 11–15:	★★★
Ages 16–Adult:	★★★
Senior Citizens:	★★★

If a specific ride, show, or attraction receives two or three stars, but only under one age-group category, that's who will enjoy it the most. In some cases, it may not be suitable for other age groups. In the case of a thrill ride, such as Magic Mountain, it may be a "must-see" ride for the Ages 11–15 and Ages 16–Adult age groups, but it's not suitable for young kids, senior citizens, or anyone else who doesn't enjoy thrill rides. An "N.S." rating indicates that a specific ride, show, or attraction is not suitable for a specific age group. This is what a rating chart might look like for a highly turbulent thrill ride:

Ages 2–4:	N.S.
Ages 5–10:	N.S.
Ages 11–15:	★★★
Ages 16–Adult:	★★★
Senior Citizens:	N.S.

Here's a brief summary of how each ride, show, and attraction is rated within this book, and what the difference is between one, two, and three stars. These ratings are only recommendations. If you have a mature nine-year-old, he or she may very well enjoy a ride, show, or attraction that's more suitable for an eleven- to fifteen-year-old. As a parent, that's a judgment call you'll need to make based on the information provided within this book and after seeing the ride, show, or attraction for yourself once you get to the theme park.

★ = Rides and attractions that earned just one star aren't worth waiting for and could be skipped, especially if your time within the theme park is limited.

★★ = Rides and attractions that earned two stars are good, but they don't fall into the "must-see" category.

★★★ = The rides and attractions that earned three stars are definitely worth seeing and should not be missed.

N.S. = This denotes rides and attractions that are "Not Suitable" for a specific age group.

🧳 TRAVEL TIP

The very best time to visit the park and not have to deal with huge crowds is on Sunday morning.

Kid Switch Policy

Not all of the rides and attractions within The Magic Kingdom are suitable for young children. If two adults are traveling with young kids, but both adults want to experience a ride that's not suitable for the kids, they can take advantage of the Kid Switch policy offered at all of the Disney theme parks.

The Kid Switch policy gives both adults (Mom and Dad, for example) the opportunity to enjoy the various thrill ride attractions that aren't suitable for kids, without the double wait. To take advantage of this policy, one parent waits in line with a small child while the other parent rides the attraction. When the first adult exits the attraction and returns to the loading area, he/she takes custody of the child while the second parent rides—without having to wait in line.

Dining in The Magic Kingdom

If you're looking for a fine-dining experience, you'll find fancy restaurants located in many of The WDW Resort hotels, as well as in Epcot, the Disney-MGM Studios, Pleasure Island, Downtown Disney, and Disney's BoardWalk. This isn't really the park to visit for a very special meal. However, for a basic, family-oriented dining experience, The Magic Kingdom offers a variety of restaurants and snack shops. Smoking is not permitted in any of the park's eating establishments.

The restaurants in The Magic Kingdom will be the most crowded every day between 11:00 A.M. and 2:00 P.M. (for lunch) and between 5:00 P.M. and 7:00 P.M. (for dinner). If you don't mind having a flexible eating schedule and you want to avoid the crowds, your best bet is to hit The Magic Kingdom's most popular attractions during these times, and eat during the nonbusy periods. It's always a good idea to experience the more turbulent rides (Magic Mountain, Big Thunder Mountain Railroad, Splash Mountain, etc.) before eating a big meal.

⊕ HOT SPOT

Kids love meeting the Disney characters and no vacation photo album is complete without a shot of Mickey hugging your child. You're guaranteed to meet Mickey and his friends within Mickey's Toontown Fair (an area of The Magic Kingdom) or at any of the character dining experiences offered at certain restaurants throughout.

For additional information about the dining options available in The Magic Kingdom, call ✆(407) WDW-DINE. At some of these restaurants, special meals can be ordered to accommodate most dietary restrictions. If you need special meals prepared, however, you're better off eating at one of the restaurants located elsewhere in The WDW Resort. Salads as well as low-salt, vegetarian, and low-cholesterol meals are available at many of the following snack shops and full-service restaurants in The Magic Kingdom.

💼 TRAVEL TIP

At all of the full-service snack shops and restaurants, be sure to ask about children's portions or discounted children's menus. Full table service is available at Cinderella's Royal Table, The Crystal Palace, Liberty Tree Tavern, The Plaza Restaurant, and Tony's Town Square Restaurant.

Fast Food/Snack Shops

These eating establishments are considerably cheaper than the full-service restaurants in The Magic Kingdom. With a few exceptions, hamburgers, hot dogs, chicken strips/nuggets, salads, soft drinks, bottled water, and ice cream are the typical menu offerings at the following fast-food snack shops.

Aloha Isle (Adventureland)—Dole pineapple "whips" are the snack food available from this kiosk. Plan on spending under $7 per person for a snack.

Auntie Gravity's Galactic Goodies (Tomorrowland)—If you're looking for frozen yogurt and fruit juices that are out of this world, park your rockets here for a snack. Plan on spending under $7 per person for a snack.

Aunt Polly's Dockside Inn (Frontierland)—This is the only place on Tom Sawyer's Island where you can purchase food, including "picnic lunches" featuring a ham-and-cheese sandwich. Plan on spending under $12 per person for a meal.

Casey's Corner (Main Street U.S.A.)—Hot dogs (with many different toppings), French fries, soft drinks, and a wide range of desserts are available for lunch and dinner. Plan on spending under $12 per person for a meal.

Columbia Harbor House (Liberty Square)—Fried chicken strips and fried fish, clam chowder, sandwiches, and other fast-food items are on the menu. Plan on spending under $12 per person for a meal.

Cool Ship (Tomorrowland)—This is a drink-only kiosk. Coca-Cola and other sodas are served. Plan on spending under $4 per person for a drink. Because this is a kiosk and not a restaurant, only cash is accepted here.

Cosmic Ray's Starlight Café (Tomorrowland)—Traditional burgers; vegetarian burgers; chicken entrees; soups; tossed, chef, and Caesar salads; and sandwiches are available at this cafeteria-style dining location. On the stage in this indoor (air-conditioned) café is an Audio-Animatronic alien (Sonny Eclipse) who performs an ongoing musical act that kids will enjoy watching while they eat. Plan on spending under $12 per person for a meal.

Enchanted Grove (Fantasyland)—Slushes and soft-serve ice cream may be the perfect snack on a hot day. Plan on spending under $7 per person for a snack.

Frontierland Fries (Frontierland)—In addition to a variety of cold drinks, this is one of the few places within The WDW Resort where McDonald's French fries are available. They're a favorite snack among kids. Plan on spending under $7 per person for a snack.

Launching Pad at Rockettower Plaza (Tomorrowland)—Various snack-food items, beverages, and smoked turkey legs are available. Plan on spending under $7 per person for a snack.

Main Street Bakery (Main Street U.S.A.)—Freshly baked goods, including cookies and pastries; various flavored gourmet coffees; and cold beverages are available here. If you choose to order a bagel and cream cheese, you'll be given an extremely small amount of cream cheese. Additional cream cheese costs extra, and you'll quickly discover that while the baked goods are fresh, the bagels aren't made on-site. Plan on spending under $7 per person for a snack.

Mrs. Potts' Cupboard (Fantasyland)—Slushes, soft-serve ice cream, and sundaes are served here. Plan on spending under $7 per person for a snack.

Pecos Bill Café (Frontierland)—Burgers, BBQ chicken, hot dogs, wrap sandwiches, and salads are the main entrees available. Plan on spending under $12 per person for a meal.

Pinocchio Village Haus (Fantasyland)—Hamburgers, cheeseburgers, hot dogs, and salads are among this snack shop's most popular selections. Plan on spending under $12 per person for a meal.

El Pirata Y El Perico (Adventureland)—It's not Taco Bell, but if you're in the mood for tacos, nachos, hot dogs, and the like, this is the place to stop for a quick Mexican lunch or dinner. Plan on spending under $12 per person for a meal.

Plaza Ice Cream Parlor (Main Street U.S.A.)—Carnation ice cream is the most popular item here. Plan on spending under $7 per person for a snack.

The Plaza Pavilion (Tomorrowland)—Individual pan pizzas, fried chicken strips, and salads are among the main entrees served at this location. Plan on spending under $12 per person for a meal.

Scuttle's Landing (Fantasyland)—Shaved ice and drinks are sold here. Plan on spending under $5 per person for a snack. This is a favorite snack stop among kids with a sweet tooth looking to cool down on a hot day.

Sleepy Hollow (Liberty Square)—Various types of snacks and beverages can be consumed here if a light, informal snack or meal is what you're looking for. Cappuccino, espresso, and gourmet coffee are served. Plan on spending under $7 per person for a snack.

Sunshine Tree Terrace (Frontierland)—Nonfat frozen yogurt, cappuccino, espresso, and various citrus drinks and snacks are available. Plan on spending under $7 per person for a snack.

Toontown Farmer's Market (Toontown)—Fresh fruit, snacks, and drinks are served. This is one of the few places where truly healthy snacks can be purchased within The Magic Kingdom. Plan on spending under $6 per person for a snack.

Also located throughout the park are wagons and snack kiosks that serve a variety of specialty items, including sodas, bottled water, juices, popcorn, ice cream, turkey legs, eggrolls, pretzels, and fresh fruit. The turkey legs are extremely popular. Genuine McDonald's french fries can also be purchased from a kiosk across from Pecos Bill Café in Frontierland.

Restaurants

If you're looking for a complete meal in a full-service, sit-down restaurant, the following eating establishments are offered within The Magic Kingdom. Plan on spending between $15 and $25 per person when eating at any of these restaurants. To make a same-day lunch or dinner "Preferred Seating" reservation, call ✆(407) WDW-DINE, visit City Hall, or drop by the individual restaurants as early in the day as possible.

Cinderella's Royal Table at King Stefan's Banquet Hall (Fantasyland, inside the castle)—Chicken, prime rib, salads, and a few different seafood dishes are the primary dinner entrees at this restaurant. There's also a "Once Upon A Time" character breakfast, served every morning between 8:00 A.M. and 10:00 A.M. that allows you and your family to dine with popular Disney characters. Reservations are suggested.

The Crystal Palace (Main Street U.S.A.)—You'll probably run into several popular Disney characters as you dine at this all-you-can-eat buffet. The menu at this restaurant changes throughout the year; however, American cuisine and seafood are served. Reservations are suggested. Breakfast, lunch, and dinner are served.

Liberty Tree Tavern (Liberty Square)—If you have about an hour to spend eating, this full-service restaurant offers a large menu of American favorites. You'll often find Disney characters wandering around this restaurant mingling with guests. Reservations are suggested. It's open only for dinner.

Plaza Restaurant (Main Street U.S.A.)—An ideal place to stop for lunch, this restaurant offers a large selection of salads, grilled deli-style sandwiches, gourmet burgers, and other light entrees. For dessert, ice cream sundaes, milkshakes, and old-fashioned ice cream sodas are served. A full dinner menu is available. The service is fast, so you can get back into The Magic Kingdom quickly and continue enjoying your day. Reservations are suggested.

Tony's Town Square (Main Street U.S.A.)—Italian lunch and dinner entrees are what you'll find at this "old New York"–style restaurant. Reservations are suggested.

Just outside of The Magic Kingdom, picnic facilities are available (free of charge) if you bring your own food to the park. Guests, however, are not encouraged to bring their own food or drinks into The Magic Kingdom. If you happen to hide a sandwich, piece of fruit, or a candy bar in your jacket pocket or purse, you're not going to be arrested by the Disney Police. If you get caught trying to smuggle a picnic basket of goodies into the park, you'll be asked to store it in a locker or return it to your car.

Chewing gum is not sold anywhere in The Magic Kingdom. If you choose to bring your own chewing gum, please be considerate of other guests and dispose of it in a trash can when you're done chewing it.

⊕ HOT SPOT

For breakfast, head over to Cinderella's Royal Table. This breakfast with the Disney characters fills up fast, so make reservations! For lunch, join Winnie the Pooh and other characters at the Crystal Palace: A Buffet with Character. For dinner with the characters, the Liberty Tree Tavern is the place to dine, starting at 4:00 P.M.

The Magic Kingdom and WDW Resort Tours

For guests who have been to Disney in the past, or who are looking for something to make their vacation even more memorable, Disney's Adult Discoveries program offers more than fourteen themed tours that offer a unique behind-the-scenes look at the entire WDW Resort. For more information, call ✆(407) 939-8687.

For example, The Keys to the Kingdom tour is offered every day and provides a four-hour behind-the-scenes look at The Magic Kingdom. Tour guides explain the history of the park and offer guests a special look at the underground tunnel system. This tour begins promptly at 8:30 A.M., 9:00 A.M., and 9:30 A.M. from The Magic Kingdom's City Hall and costs $58 per person (minimum age is sixteen), plus the cost of admission to the park. If you're looking for a more personalized, private VIP tour, call ☎(407) 560-4033.

⊕ HOT SPOT

In addition to being able to meet the various Disney characters in Mickey's Toontown Fair and at other predetermined locations within the park, "Cinderella's Surprise Celebration" offers a musical show and a chance to meet over twenty of your favorite Disney characters afterward. This musical celebration takes place daily in the Castle forecourt.

CHAPTER 6

Exploring The Magic Kingdom

THE HEART AND SOUL OF THE WALT DISNEY WORLD
Resort is the place that probably most resembles Walt Disney's original dream for a theme park—The Magic Kingdom. This chapter will provide you with an attraction-by-attraction tour of the family-oriented rides, shows, and attractions within The Magic Kingdom, plus explain how you can make the most of your time visiting this popular theme park.

Park Overview

This area of the resort is modeled after Disneyland (in Anaheim, California), and while it's only one of several theme parks that now make up the entire WDW resort, this theme park can easily provide at least one or two full days (and evenings) of fun-filled entertainment, especially if you're traveling with kids. Out of all the theme parks and activities available at The WDW Resort, The Magic Kingdom is most likely what kids will enjoy the most, since most of the rides and attractions, especially in Fantasyland and Mickey's Toontown Fair, are designed with kids in mind.

Like Disneyland, Walt Disney considered The Magic Kingdom to be a giant stage, in which guests participate in every aspect of their entertainment. Many of the rides, shows, and attractions in

The Magic Kingdom are based on classic Disney stories and movies, and like Disneyland (which was built first), The Magic Kingdom is divided up into distinctly themed lands—Adventureland, Liberty Square, Frontierland, Fantasyland, Mickey's Toontown Fair, Tomorrowland, and Main Street U.S.A. These lands are composed of rides, shows, attractions, restaurants, snack shops, gift shops, outdoor entertainers, and specially designed architecture that make you feel totally immersed in the theme park experience.

≡FAST FACT

This park opened on October 1, 1971; however, the official grand-opening ceremony took place October 22 through 24 and was televised nationally on NBC. At the time, The Magic Kingdom comprised twenty-two major attractions.

Guests enter through the Main Entrance, pass under the Walt Disney World Railroad, and find themselves on Main Street U.S.A. This street, which is The Magic Kingdom's parade route, is lined with shops, restaurants, and plenty of delightful surprises, like the Main Street vehicles, street performers, and musicians.

As guests wander down Main Street U.S.A., the sight ahead is Cinderella's Castle—the most famous landmark in The WDW Resort. This 180-foot-tall castle is the entrance to Fantasyland and is located just past the Hub, where an almost life-size statue of Walt Disney and Mickey Mouse is displayed. This circular park (complete with benches and beautiful landscaping) is known as the Hub because it's located in the center of The Magic Kingdom. From this location, guests can easily locate the entrances to each of The Magic Kingdom's themed lands (with the exception of Mickey's Toontown Fair).

Main Street U.S.A.

Located along Main Street U.S.A. are all sorts of interesting shops that offer a wide selection of souvenirs, gifts, and memorabilia, along with film and various other necessities. These shops are most crowded first thing in the morning and just before the park closes. Don't forget, anything you purchase can be held at a pickup location near the exit of The Magic Kingdom, stored in a locker, or delivered to your WDW Resort hotel. You probably don't want to carry around your purchases throughout the day.

Many of these shops are fully air-conditioned, so if the sun and heat outside become too overwhelming, come inside, browse, and cool off. For your convenience, the shops along Main Street U.S.A. tend to stay open up to one hour later than the rest of the park.

Boulevard Entertainment

Throughout the day, guests are entertained by sidewalk performers, including Dapper Dan's Barbershop Quartet, Rhythm Rascals Band, Casey's Corner Piano, and other talented performers who all add ambiance to Main Street U.S.A. and surrounding areas.

══FAST FACT

City Hall is The Magic Kingdom's main information and reservation center as well as the Lost and Found. Tickets to the walking tour of The Magic Kingdom can also be purchased here. For adults who get separated during their visit to this park, messages can be left at City Hall.

Wishes Fireworks Show

Ages 2–4:	★★
Ages 5–10:	★★★
Ages 11–15:	★★★
Ages 16–Adult:	★★★
Senior Citizens:	★★★

For as long as The Magic Kingdom has been open, a nightly fireworks show has been offered. The Wishes show (which debuted in late 2003), however, is the best fireworks display ever offered in the park. It takes place almost every night high above Cinderella's Castle. The fireworks are choreographed and synchronized to popular Disney tunes, particularly the song *When You Wish upon a Star*. With its unique star-shaped fireworks, Wishes is truly breathtaking, so don't miss it! The best viewing locations can be found along Main Street U.S.A., toward (and around) the Hub. Basically, if you have a good view of the top of the castle, you'll see the entire fireworks show clearly. If you're traveling with kids, the fireworks will be less noisy if you watch the show from along Main Street U.S.A., but stand closer to the train station near the park's entrance (as opposed to near the castle). This is a twelve-minute show featuring more than 655 pyrotechnics.

✔ This is a must-see attraction.

Main Street Cinema

Ages 2–4:	★
Ages 5–10:	★
Ages 11–15:	★★
Ages 16–Adult:	★★
Senior Citizens:	★★★

If you're in the mood to catch Mickey Mouse in his very first animated features, drop in to this old-fashioned cinema located along Main Street U.S.A. Mickey's movies are shown continuously, so you're free to come and go as you please. There's seldom a crowd at this attraction, and since the theater is air-conditioned, dropping in for a few minutes is a great way to cool off and experience some of Walt Disney's classic animation. There are no seats in this small theater, but there is an area where kids can sit on the floor.

Main Street Railroad Depot

Ages 2–4:	★★
Ages 5–10:	★★
Ages 11–15:	★★
Ages 16–Adult:	★★
Senior Citizens:	★★

This is the main station for the Walt Disney World Railroad, which follows a circular track around the perimeter of The Magic Kingdom. Here's your chance to ride in an authentic 1920s steam train and get a tour of The Magic Kingdom at the same time. You can get on and off at any of the train stations, or take a ride completely around the park. (It takes about twenty minutes to complete the 1.5-mile journey.)

⊕ HOT SPOT

Take a ride on a horseless carriage, an old-fashioned fire engine, trolleys drawn by beautiful Belgian and Percheron horses, and other vehicles that provide free transportation from one end of Main Street U.S.A. to the other.

SpectroMagic Parade

Ages 2–4:	★★★
Ages 5–10:	★★★
Ages 11–15:	★★★
Ages 16–Adult:	★★★
Senior Citizens:	★★★

In 1991, the Main Street Electrical Parade was replaced by the SpectroMagic Parade. Floats and popular Disney characters are covered with thousands of fiber-optic lights that flash in a rainbow of colors as this parade travels down Main Street U.S.A. accompanied by popular Disney music.

This is a family-oriented parade that's presented in the evenings and shouldn't be missed. One good viewing location is from the porch of the Visitor's Center, located near the train station, opposite City Hall. Otherwise, you can catch this parade from anywhere along Main Street U.S.A. Be sure to arrive early to stake out your viewing location, especially if the park is crowded. If two shows are presented the evening of your visit, the crowd for the second performance will be much smaller.

✔ This is a must-see attraction.

Share a Dream Come True Parade

Ages 2–4:	★★
Ages 5–10:	★★★
Ages 11–15:	★★★
Ages 16–Adult:	★★
Senior Citizens:	★★

Each day, there's a parade that features some of your all-time favorite Disney characters riding on colorful floats and dancing to popular Disney tunes. This parade is more kid-oriented, although it'll appeal to people of all ages and help get you into the Disney spirit as you spend your day in The Magic Kingdom.

The best viewing spots are anywhere along Main Street U.S.A., such as in front of the Plaza Ice Cream Parlor. As with any parade or show, you'll want to arrive early to stake out the best viewing location.

Performed daily, typically at 3:00 P.M., this parade lasts about fifteen minutes and features more than 110 cast members, including many of your favorite Disney characters.

══FAST FACT

Every day, you'll see concerts presented by the official Walt Disney World Marching Band as it travels up and down Main Street U.S.A. and also performs live in Town Square.

Town Square Exposition Hall

Located on the right side of Main Street U.S.A., just after you pass under the train tracks, you'll find the Town Square Exposition Hall. What's offered within this attraction changes periodically. The movie theater inside (which typically offers a behind-the-scenes look at Walt Disney and/or Disney animation) is fully air-conditioned and comfortable seating is provided. There's also the AAA Travel Center/Information Desk inside this building along with a camera shop. It's here you can purchase the photos taken of you and your family by Disney cast members when you enter the park.

Adventureland

As you already know, The Magic Kingdom is divided into various themed areas. Starting with Adventureland, here's a rundown of the rides, shows, and attractions you'll find in this area of the theme park. Anything that's specifically targeted to young kids (and not necessarily teens or adults), however, is described in the next chapter.

The Jungle Cruise

Ages 2–4:	★
Ages 5–10:	★★
Ages 11–15:	★★
Ages 16–Adult:	★★
Senior Citizens:	★★

This is one of The Magic Kingdom's original rides that opened in 1971. Safari boats carry guests down a manmade river that resembles a scene right out of Africa. You'll see life-size Animatronic animals as you embark on a ten-minute journey. Don't worry, this ride is pretty mellow (you won't get wet, and the boat travels slowly). You should definitely experience the Jungle Cruise during daylight hours. Be prepared to hear corny jokes from your tour guide.

Pirates of the Caribbean

Ages 2–4:	★
Ages 5–10:	★★★
Ages 11–15:	★★★
Ages 16–Adult:	★★★
Senior Citizens:	★★★

Since 1973, this boat ride has taken guests on a magical journey to a port on the Spanish Main. You'll be singing "Yo ho, yo ho; a pirate's life for me" along with the life-size Audio-Animatronic pirates as you experience this enjoyable ten-minute cruise. While it's no longer state-of-the-art and isn't a thrill ride, Pirates of the Caribbean is one of The Magic Kingdom's most popular rides.

✔ This is a must-see attraction.

⊕ HOT SPOT

As with many of the rides located throughout WDW, this one has several hidden Mickey ears that are visible if you're looking for them during the cruise, so keep your eyes peeled for the ears.

Swiss Family Treehouse

Ages 2–4:	N.S.
Ages 5–10:	★★★
Ages 11–15:	★★★
Ages 16–Adult:	★★
Senior Citizens:	N.S.

Inspired by the 1960 Disney film *Swiss Family Robinson*, this is a giant tree house that guests of all ages are welcome to climb and explore. This tree contains over 300,000 lifelike polyethylene leaves that appear to grow on 1,400 man-made branches. Children in particular will enjoy exploring the hidden areas located in this tree house.

The Enchanted Tiki Room—Under New Management

Ages 2–4:	★
Ages 5–10:	★★★
Ages 11–15:	★★★
Ages 16–Adult:	★★★
Senior Citizens:	★★★

Originally, this was one of the first Disney attractions ever to utilize Audio-Animatronics (robotic characters that seem lifelike). A version of this show was first introduced at Disneyland back in 1963. It featured 225 Audio-Animatronic birds that sang and entertained guests during a seventeen-minute performance that was extremely cute.

Back in 1998, however, this attraction was reworked. While the concept is pretty much the same, this attraction is now "hosted" by Audio-Animatronic adaptations of Iago (from Disney's *Aladdin)* and Zazu (from *The Lion King*). The music that's performed has also been updated. So, if you haven't visited The Magic Kingdom in the past few years, seeing this new show will provide a new entertainment experience, yet rekindle a touch of Disney nostalgia.

The Magic Carpets of Aladdin

Ages 2–4:	N.S.
Ages 5–10:	★★★
Ages 11–15:	★★
Ages 16–Adult:	★
Senior Citizens:	★

Here's your chance to hop aboard a magic carpet and see Agrabah in style. Based on Disney's *Aladdin,* guests climb aboard moving vehicles (four people per carpet), which they then control. Carpets can move up and down, plus pitch forward and backward. During the ride, water gets shot at guests by spitting camels. (Don't worry, you'll hardly get wet.) This ride is very similar to Dumbo the Flying Elephant, but has a different theme.

⊕ HOT SPOT

Throughout the day, at specific times that are listed within the *Guide Map: Magic Kingdom,* Disney characters will make appearances throughout the park. Look for the white-gloved Mickey Mouse hand icons on the map. These indicate where you're apt to find Disney characters to meet.

Frontierland

Here's a rundown of what you'll experience in this area of The Magic Kingdom, which was inspired by America's early days of exploration and expansion.

Big Thunder Mountain Railroad

Ages 2–4:	N.S.
Ages 5–10:	★★
Ages 11–15:	★★★
Ages 16–Adult:	★★★
Senior Citizens:	N.S.

Don't confuse this fast and furious runaway train ride with the Walt Disney Railroad. This is a four-minute, high-speed, fast-turning thrill ride up, down, and around a manmade mountain. Along this ride's 2,780 feet of roller coaster track, over twenty Audio-Animatronic characters and over $300,000 worth of genuine mining antiques help to add a sense of authenticity. To truly experience this ride, check it out after dark. Guests must be at least 40 inches tall to experience Big Thunder Mountain Railroad, and anyone who suffers from heart or back problems or is pregnant should skip it. This is one of the attractions in The Magic Kingdom that teens and adults won't want to miss.

✔ This is a must-see attraction.

Frontierland Shootin' Arcade

Ages 2–4:	N.S.
Ages 5–10:	★
Ages 11–15:	★
Ages 16–Adult:	★
Senior Citizens:	★

Replica rifles that use infrared bullets are used in this old-Western-style shooting gallery. Get ready for the unexpected if you hit your targets. (If you want to test your aim, it'll cost you fifty cents. Like all of the arcades, shooting costs aren't included in the price of your admission to The Magic Kingdom.)

Country Bear Jamboree

Ages 2–4:	★★
Ages 5–10:	★★★
Ages 11–15:	★★★
Ages 16–Adult:	★
Senior Citizens:	★

Country music is performed by a group of about twenty life-size Audio-Animatronic bears and creatures. Young kids and adults will find this show charming, while the teen set will probably find it a bit hokey. This seventeen-minute show will have you singing and clapping along. Shows are continuous, and there's excellent visibility from all seats in the theater, so don't worry about trying to get preferred seating in the front or center of the auditorium.

Splash Mountain

Ages 2–4:	N.S.
Ages 5–10:	N.S.
Ages 11–15:	★★★
Ages 16–Adult:	★★★
Senior Citizens:	N.S.

This light-hearted flumelike boat ride starts out totally calm and mellow, as guests are entertained by dozens of singing Audio-Animatronic characters from Disney's animated classic *Song of the South.* "Zip-A-Dee-Doo-Dah" is the theme song of this ride, which tells the story of Brer Rabbit as he tries to locate his "laughing place."

Brer Rabbit gets the last laugh, however. At the end of this ride, you'll be sent cruising down a 52-foot drop at a 45-degree angle, traveling in excess of 40 miles per hour. In all, this is a rather calm eleven-minute boat ride. It's only the very last few seconds that constitute the thrill-ride element. Splash Mountain is definitely one of The Magic Kingdom's very best attractions, from both an entertainment and a thrill-providing standpoint. It's not suitable for young children (under 44 inches tall), nor should it be experienced by anyone with back or heart problems or who can't endure the final drop at the end of the ride.

✔ This is a must-see attraction.

══FAST FACT

Chances are, you will get a bit wet at the end of this ride, so be sure that you cover up your camera equipment and snugly stow your belongings. As you're taking the final plummet, be sure to smile! Color 8" × 10" photos of your plunge are available as you exit this ride, for an additional fee.

Tom Sawyer Island

Ages 2–4:	★
Ages 5–10:	★★
Ages 11–15:	★★★
Ages 16–Adult:	★★
Senior Citizens:	★

This manmade island is located in the center of the Rivers of America. To reach this island, you'll need to hop aboard one of the Tom Sawyer log rafts, which depart regularly. The island is open during daylight hours only. Kids especially will love exploring Injun Joe's Cave, Harper's Mill, and Ft. Sam Clemens. The island is filled with dirt paths to follow, bridges to cross, and lots of places to explore. Kids who know the story of Tom Sawyer and Huck Finn will enjoy this attraction the most.

Liberty Square

Give me liberty or give me Mickey! Patriotic tourists, thrill seekers, and fun-loving vacationers alike will find a lot to experience in this area of The Magic Kingdom.

Goofy's Country Dancin' Jamboree

Ages 2–4:	★★
Ages 5–10:	★★★
Ages 11–15:	★★★
Ages 16–Adult:	★★
Senior Citizens:	★★

Goofy and his pals host a fun and upbeat musical show for young guests several times a day in the world-famous Diamond Horseshoe Saloon. Check the *Guide Map: Magic Kingdom* for show times.

Davy Crockett Keel Boats

Ages 2–4:	N.S.
Ages 5–10:	★
Ages 11–15:	★★
Ages 16–Adult:	★★
Senior Citizens:	★

Head for the dock near the Haunted Mansion and climb aboard one of these keel boats for a ride around Tom Sawyer's Island (along the Rivers of America).

Liberty Square Riverboat

Ages 2–4:	★★
Ages 5–10:	★★
Ages 11–15:	★★
Ages 16–Adult:	★★
Senior Citizens:	★★★

The Richard F. Irvine is a real stern-wheeler steamboat that was built at Disney World and named after one of its designers. This boat picks up passengers and takes them for a fifteen-minute ride around the Rivers of America (a one-half-mile-long cruise), giving a great view of Tom Sawyer's Island and many other sites in The Magic Kingdom.

For the best view of the park, climb to the upper deck during the cruise. This is a great way to get off your feet for a while, and at the same time, experience the ambiance of The Magic Kingdom.

═FAST FACT

This ship has been cruising since 1971 and makes trips regularly throughout the day. Since this ship holds a huge number of passengers, you're almost always guaranteed to get aboard on the cruise of your choice with a minimal wait.

The Hall of Presidents

Ages 2–4:	N.S.
Ages 5–10:	★
Ages 11–15:	★★
Ages 16–Adult:	★★★
Senior Citizens:	★★★

This attraction is sort of like visiting a high-tech museum in which Audio-Animatronic re-creations of America's presidents actually teach guests history. Kids will most likely get bored by this twenty-minute presentation; however, adults will find it both highly patriotic and extremely interesting. Advanced Audio-Animatronic technology is used to make several of the presidents, including George W. Bush (the newest addition to this attraction), come to life on the stage. President George W. Bush makes an inspirational ninety-second speech (which he actually recorded for this attraction) about freedom to create, to prosper, and to dream.

This presentation is shown in an air-conditioned theater. In fact, even the waiting room is air-conditioned. As you're spending time in the waiting room, browse around and check out the historical paintings on the walls. Take a look back at American history in this educational and inspirational attraction.

The Haunted Mansion

Ages 2–4:	N.S.
Ages 5–10:	★★
Ages 11–15:	★★★
Ages 16–Adult:	★★★
Senior Citizens:	★★★

Yes, this is a haunted house that's jam-packed with all sorts of awesome special effects, but this ride is designed to provide family-oriented entertainment, so don't expect anything too scary. During much of your eight-minute tour of this mansion, you'll be riding in a moving love seat. This is definitely one of The Magic Kingdom's most technologically advanced rides in terms of the special effects. As you enter the house, be sure to read the rather bizarre inscriptions on the tombstones.

As you wait outside of the mansion for your tour, you'll be covered by an awning, so you won't be exposed to direct sun or rain. Be sure to notice the somber costumes worn by Disney cast members working at this attraction. When you're escorted into a small room that appears to stretch, be sure to look upward, especially just after the lights go out. The ride portion of this attraction begins as you exit the small room (which is really an elevator). You'll be loaded into two-person love-seat-like vehicles.

When your tour begins, check out the "animated" statues in the library. Other awesome effects to be on the lookout for are the woman's head in a crystal ball and the ghosts in the ballroom (be sure to look all around this room, including near the floor and ceiling). Near the very end of your tour, look into the mirror to see who (or what) is sitting between you and the living person you're sitting next to in this final haunting special effect.

✔ This is a must-see attraction.

═FAST FACT

This is another one of The Magic Kingdom's classic attractions that has been entertaining guests since the park first opened.

Tomorrowland

When The Magic Kingdom first opened in 1971, this land was designed to offer guests a peek into the future. As the years have gone by, Tomorrowland has evolved, with older (outdated) rides and attractions being replaced by newer, more state-of-the-art rides and attractions that continue to offer a futuristic theme.

Stitch's Great Escape

Ages 2–4:	★★★
Ages 5–10:	★★★
Ages 11–15:	★★★
Ages 16–Adult:	★★
Senior Citizens:	★★

In late 2004, Stitch's Great Escape will replace The ExtraTERRORestrial Alien Encounter attraction (which closed in late 2003). This all-new attraction is based loosely on the animated film *Lilo & Stitch* and will feature the most sophisticated Audio-Animatronic characters ever created by Walt Disney Imagineering (the folks who create all of the rides, shows, and attractions at WDW). Stitch's Great Escape will invite guests to join The Galactic Federation's security division. Your mission is to help capture Stitch after Experiment 626 goes haywire. Stitch's Great Escape will be a funny, entertaining, and colorful experience.

✔ This is a must-see attraction.

The Timekeeper

Ages 2–4:	★
Ages 5–10:	★★
Ages 11–15:	★★
Ages 16–Adult:	★★
Senior Citizens:	★★

Are you ready to take a twenty-minute tour through time? That's the theme of this attraction, which combines Audio-Animatronic characters with an impressive 360-degree movie experience. Jules Verne and H. G. Wells are just two of the "people" you'll meet as you trek through time and around the world.

This is an exciting attraction that's suitable for people of all ages. Even with your feet planted firmly on the ground, the 360-degree movie makes you feel like you're actually moving. If this experience gets too real or too intense, simply shut your eyes to re-establish your equilibrium. This attraction operates on a seasonal basis. Consult the *Guide Map: Magic Kingdom* for details.

▮ TRAVEL TIP

Guide Map: Magic Kingdom is a full-color map and brochure provided free of charge when you enter that park. It lists all of the rides, shows, and attractions; times of parades; and other information about your visit to the park. The red dotted line on the map indicates the parade route. You can pick up a free *Guide Map* for each of the Disney theme parks.

Space Mountain

Ages 2–4:	N.S.
Ages 5–10:	★★
Ages 11–15:	★★★
Ages 16–Adult:	★★★
Senior Citizens:	N.S.

Since 1975, this has been one of the most popular rides in all of WDW, and with good reason. Space Mountain is a high-speed roller coaster that uses some special effects to make you feel like you're seated in a rocket that's racing through space. In reality, you'll be traveling about 28 miles per hour.

This entire ride is experienced in almost total darkness, so you won't see what's coming. This is an awesome thrill ride. For those who don't normally enjoy roller coasters, this one offers a lot of high-speed sharp turns, but very few drops, making it exciting, but a bit tamer than a typical roller coaster. The ride itself lasts under three minutes, but the wait is usually about one hour (or more). Space Mountain is one of those rides you don't want to miss, so plan your time in The Magic Kingdom accordingly.

The best times to experience this ride are during one of the parades, or during peak lunch or dinner hours. Space Mountain is not suitable for very young children (there is a height restriction of 44 inches and children under the age of seven need an adult to ride with them) or anyone with heart, back, or other medical problems. Pregnant women should also sit this one out. As soon as the park opens, race to this ride for the shortest wait.

✔ This is a must-see attraction.

═FAST FACT

While experiencing Space Mountain, and all of the other rides at WDW, guests are under constant video surveillance. The Walt Disney Company is extremely safety conscious. Guests who act in a manner that endangers themselves or others will be dealt with accordingly.

Astro Orbiter

Ages 2–4:	N.S.
Ages 5–10:	★★
Ages 11–15:	★★
Ages 16–Adult:	★
Senior Citizens:	N.S.

Here's one way to get a great view of Tomorrowland and at the same time enjoy a mild thrill ride. Guests sit in rocket-shaped cars that go up and down as they travel around in circles high above ground level. The line for this ride moves very slowly. If there's a long wait, either return later in the day or skip this ride.

Walt Disney's Carousel of Progress

Ages 2–4:	★
Ages 5–10:	★★
Ages 11–15:	★★★
Ages 16–Adult:	★★★
Senior Citizens:	★★★

This classic WDW attraction was revamped in 1996 but is still as charming as when it first began entertaining guests in 1975. Guests are seated in a theater-like room that actually rotates around a 360-degree stage. Each time the theater moves, a new scene featuring an Audio-Animatronic American family is seen. Guests follow this family through the twentieth century and explore some of the major technological advances that have occurred in the home during the early 1900s, 1920s, 1940s, and present day. The final scene depicts technology that we might be seeing in the not-too-distant future. "A whole new century is waiting for us" and "Tomorrow is just a dream away" are two of the themes of this attraction.

This is a twenty-minute show suitable for the entire family. The theater is air-conditioned, and guests get to sit down and relax as the show takes place. The waiting area is outside, but covered. Carousel of Progress operates seasonally. Consult the *Guide Map: Magic Kingdom* for details.

✔ This is a must-see attraction.

≡FAST FACT

Walt Disney himself created the Carousel of Progress, which has been seen by more people than any other show in U.S. history. As you're waiting to go into the revolving theater, you'll see a video presentation (on monitors) that features Walt Disney and provides some history behind this unique attraction.

Tomorrowland Transit Authority

Ages 2–4:	★
Ages 5–10:	★
Ages 11–15:	★★
Ages 16–Adult:	★★
Senior Citizens:	★★★

For a ten-minute, rather relaxing tour of Tomorrowland, climb aboard Tomorrowland's energy-efficient, pollution-free mass-transit system that travels about 10 miles per hour and follows a mile-long track. You'll get a sneak peek inside Space Mountain and pass by just about all of Tomorrowland's other rides and attractions.

Tomorrowland Indy Speedway

Ages 2–4:	★
Ages 5–10:	★★★
Ages 11–15:	★★★
Ages 16–Adult:	★
Senior Citizens:	★

People of all ages (who meet the 52-inch height restriction) can drive these sports cars along a 2,000-foot-long track—whether or not they have a real-life driver's license. These gasoline-powered cars have rack-and-pinion steering and disc brakes, but they're confined to a track that keeps the driver totally safe. Drivers can reach cruising speeds of about 7 miles per hour as they take a single lap around the track.

The ride lasts about five minutes and gives young people a true feeling of being in the driver's seat of a car. Drivers beware: Even in these cars, minor fender benders are common, especially if you get stuck behind a slow driver. Instead of spending time at this raceway, teens and adults looking for a real thrill should steer over to Epcot (or take the monorail) and experience Test Track.

Buzz Lightyear's Space Ranger Spin

Ages 2–4:	★
Ages 5–10:	★★★
Ages 11–15:	★★★
Ages 16–Adult:	★
Senior Citizens:	★

Designed with kids in mind, this attraction lets young guests take on the role of Space Rangers as they join their hero, Buzz Lightyear, on an adventure to save the universe's crystollic fusion cell supply (i.e., batteries). Riders climb aboard a ZP-27 space cruiser and take a lighthearted voyage through ten interactive scenes. While the vehicles move forward by themselves as the adventure unfolds, riders can make their vehicles spin, since there are things to see all around. Using a light gun (attached to the vehicle), riders can shoot at targets in order to obtain the highest possible score.

The Galaxy Palace Theater

Ages 2–4:	★★
Ages 5–10:	★★★
Ages 11–15:	★★★
Ages 16–Adult:	★
Senior Citizens:	★

Mickey Mouse and his Disney pals entertain guests with plenty of colorful costumes, singing, and dancing. Performances are held throughout the day, but show times vary based on the time of year and on weather conditions. On sunny days, make sure you apply plenty of sunblock (and wear a hat). This is an outdoor amphitheater, so you'll be exposed to the sun. Be sure to arrive about twenty minutes early to ensure that you'll get a good seat. The show offered here changes periodically. Consult the *Guide Map: Magic Kingdom* for show details and times.

📼 TRAVEL TIP

Near the entrance of The Magic Kingdom, located under the train station, you'll find locker rentals ($7 per day, plus a refundable $2 key deposit) and ATM machines.

Shop 'Til You Drop

Located throughout The Magic Kingdom are dozens of shopping opportunities, including specialty shops, general gift shops, and plenty of souvenirs to choose from. All of the shops in The Magic Kingdom offer complimentary package delivery to your WDW Resort hotel. For an additional fee, your purchases can be shipped (via FedEx) to any location worldwide. Keep in mind that even though FedEx is being used for shipping, it could take up to two weeks for your items to arrive at their destination, due to order processing delays at Disney World. Before shipping your items, ask how long it'll take for the order to be processed.

If you find something you really like but can't afford at the moment, or you don't want to lug it home, you can order any item available from any WDW shop by calling ☎(407) 363-6200 during business hours. Many of the items available at Walt Disney World are not sold at any of the Disney Stores and are not available from the Disney Catalog.

⊕ HOT SPOT

While you can buy Disney-themed hats at virtually any shop within WDW, the only place to pick up monogrammed Mickey ears (like the ones worn by the original Mouseketeers on *The Mickey Mouse Club*) is at The Chapeau, a small shop at the end of Main Street U.S.A. The hats can be monogrammed while you wait and they remain one of the best bargains at the park in terms of a memorable and personalized souvenir.

Capturing Your Memories on Film

Disposable cameras, Kodak film, a selection of Kodak digital cameras, batteries, and other camera accessories are sold at Exposition Hall within Town Square (along Main Street U.S.A.). Here, two-hour film developing is available, and video camcorders can also be rented. If you bring your own camcorder and the battery dies, the Kodak Camera Center will recharge your battery *free!* Keep in mind, however, that the prices on film and batteries aren't cheap. You can save a lot by buying your film, batteries, and camera accessories outside of WDW.

At the various gift shops throughout WDW, you'll also find a large selection of picture frames, photo albums, and even Disney-themed "Capture the Magic" scrapbooking supplies and kits.

CHAPTER 7

Kid-Oriented Areas of The Magic Kingdom

WHILE THE ENTIRE WDW RESORT WAS CREATED TO entertain and inspire people of all ages, there are certain lands within The Magic Kingdom specifically designed for young children, under the age of twelve (along with their parents). Thus, if you're traveling with young people, plan on spending extra time within these areas.

Fantasyland

This area of The Magic Kingdom offers many attractions specifically for young kids, featuring some of Disney's classic characters from movies like *Snow White and the Seven Dwarfs, Cinderella, Peter Pan, Alice in Wonderland,* and *The Little Mermaid.* Anyone traveling with young kids should plan on spending at least one full day experiencing everything that Fantasyland has to offer.

💼 TRAVEL TIP

During peak travel times (especially holidays), plan on allocating an average of forty-five minutes per ride or attraction. This includes wait times.

Cinderella's Castle

Ages 2–4:	★★★
Ages 5–10:	★★★
Ages 11–15:	★★★
Ages 16–Adult:	★★★
Senior Citizens:	★★★

This is the best-known landmark in all of The WDW Resort, and one that people from all over the world come to see. It's also the most photographed building in the park. Inside the castle is a glass tile mosaic mural that tells the story of Cinderella. This castle is 180 feet tall and is twice the height of Sleeping Beauty's Castle located at Disneyland.

Kids especially will enjoy eating breakfast, lunch, or dinner with Cinderella in the castle at Cinderella's Royal Table. Make your breakfast reservations several days early. Whether or not you decide to eat inside the castle, you'll definitely want to wander through it.

✔ This is a must-see attraction.

Cinderella's Surprise Celebration

Ages 2–4:	★★★
Ages 5–10:	★★★
Ages 11–15:	★★
Ages 16–Adult:	★
Senior Citizens:	★

Several times throughout the day (see the *Guide Map: Magic Kingdom* brochure for details), Cinderella's Surprise Celebration takes place on the castle's front stage. This is a musical show that stars Cinderella and other classic Disney characters. After the show, there's a meet-and-greet opportunity that provides an awesome chance for parents to photograph their kids in front of the castle with the various characters, or for kids to collect their autographs.

💼 TRAVEL TIP

Young kids in particular (ages four to ten) love meeting the Disney characters and getting their autographs. For about $6, you can purchase an official Disney Autograph Album (from any Disney gift shop) that your child can transform into a personalized souvenir by collecting the autographs of the characters they meet within the parks and Disney hotels.

Cinderella's Golden Carrousel

Ages 2–4:	★★
Ages 5–10:	★★★
Ages 11–15:	★★
Ages 16–Adult:	★
Senior Citizens:	★

This is one of the world's largest carrousels, and one of The Magic Kingdom's original attractions. Cinderella's Golden Carrousel holds seventy-two hand-carved horses that are truly works of art that guests of all ages can ride upon. Along with the exquisitely decorated horses, the entire carrousel features medieval decor. This ride was built in 1917 and was acquired from an amusement park in New Jersey that's no longer in existence. It has since been totally refurbished and modernized, but it still has its original beauty and charm. The ride itself lasts about two minutes.

═FAST FACT

Most families (with kids) visit the park in the morning. As the day progresses, however, kids get hungry and tired, so as evening rolls around, most families with kids tend to leave the park. Thus, late afternoons, evenings, and at night are the best times for adults and teens to experience the areas of The Magic Kingdom described within this chapter.

Dumbo the Flying Elephant

Ages 2–4:	★
Ages 5–10:	★★★
Ages 11–15:	★★
Ages 16–Adult:	★
Senior Citizens:	★

The Magic Kingdom's younger guests can fly high above Fantasyland in cars shaped like Dumbo (the elephant), who uses his oversized ears to fly. Inspired by Disney's animated movie *Dumbo*, this two-minute ride is for kids only.

If the line is very long for Dumbo the Flying Elephant, similar rides (but with different themes) are offered elsewhere. There's The Magic Carpets of Aladdin in Adventureland, and within Disney's Animal Kingdom, check out TriceraTop Spin.

It's a Small World

Ages 2–4:	★★★
Ages 5–10:	★★★
Ages 11–15:	★★★
Ages 16–Adult:	★★★
Senior Citizens:	★★★

Whether you're spending one hour or several days exploring The Magic Kingdom, this is one attraction that nobody should miss. It's been called the "happiest cruise that's ever sailed," and you'll quickly discover that this description is totally accurate.

This is a colorful, ten-minute boat ride that takes guests through several large indoor areas filled with Audio-Animatronic children from around the world, all singing "It's a Small World" in different languages. It's a Small World is absolutely delightful and is well worth waiting in line to experience. (There's almost always a shorter wait if you get into the left line queue.) During the ride, be sure to look upward as well as to the sides, because there are exciting and adorable things happening all around you. Kids love the laughing hyenas, about five minutes into the ride, while adults will find the final scene on the ride extremely heartwarming.

As they leave, many people feel inclined to toss a coin into the water and make a wish. If you're traveling with someone in a wheelchair, special boats are available (upon request) to accommodate wheelchairs.

✔ This is a must-see attraction.

══FAST FACT

It's a Small World was created by Walt Disney and his team of Imagineers for the 1964–1965 New York World's Fair, and was later added to Disneyland, and then to The Magic Kingdom at WDW, where it continues to entertain guests.

Mad Tea Party (a.k.a. The Teacups)

Ages 2–4:	N.S.
Ages 5–10:	★★★
Ages 11–15:	★★★
Ages 16–Adult:	★★
Senior Citizens:	N.S.

Inspired by Disney's *Alice in Wonderland*, this ride is virtually guaranteed to make you totally dizzy. It's the type of ride that most kids love, but that's suitable for anyone who has the stomach for it. Guests sit in oversized teacups that spin around each other. At the same time, individual guests can make their own teacup spin around its own axis. The ride lasts about two minutes and is best experienced on an empty stomach.

Peter Pan's Flight

Ages 2–4:	N.S.
Ages 5–10:	★★★
Ages 11–15:	★★★
Ages 16–Adult:	★
Senior Citizens:	★

Guests ride in pirate galleons over London on a nonstop, three-minute journey to Never Never Land, where Captain Hook and the Lost Boys will be waiting. Think of this ride as an animated, three-dimensional storybook that tells a condensed version of the Peter Pan story. This ride is definitely kid-oriented and will be of little interest to adults traveling without young kids. Don't be surprised if this ride has one of the longest lines in Fantasyland. This attraction may be too scary for very young children.

Snow White's Scary Adventures

Ages 2–4:	N.S.
Ages 5–10:	★★★
Ages 11–15:	★★★
Ages 16–Adult:	★
Senior Citizens:	★

Young guests in particular will enjoy this three-minute ride, which depicts several popular scenes from Disney's *Snow White and the Seven Dwarfs* animated classic. The Audio-Animatronic dwarfs are really cute, but kids might get a bit scared by the wicked witch's multiple appearances, so it's a good idea to prepare children by telling them what to expect. Once again, this ride should be experienced by people traveling with kids, otherwise could be skipped. This attraction may be too scary for very young children.

The Many Adventures of Winnie the Pooh

Ages 2–4:	★★★
Ages 5–10:	★★★
Ages 11–15:	★★
Ages 16–Adult:	★
Senior Citizens:	★

This colorful ride takes guests on a whirlwind visit with the classic *Winnie the Pooh* characters from the Hundred Acre Wood. As guests ride in honey pot–shaped vehicles, they bounce along with Tigger, float through a floody place with Piglet, and then enter the mysterious world of Heffalumps and Woozles. Colorful Animatronic figures and three-dimensional sets are used to convey the storyline of this adventure.

🧳 TRAVEL TIP

The Many Adventures of Winnie the Pooh is designed specifically for young children (and their parents). Since this is an extremely popular ride, be sure to take advantage of FASTPASS to avoid waiting in long lines.

Mickey's PhilharMagic

Ages 2–4:	★★
Ages 5–10:	★★★
Ages 11–15:	★★★
Ages 16–Adult:	★★★
Senior Citizens:	★★★

One of the newest attractions within The Magic Kingdom is also one of the most spectacular. This 3D movie takes place in a large, custom-designed theater that actually interacts with visitors. For example, when water shoots on screen, guests will feel droplets of water shot at them. (Don't worry, it's only a few drops. You won't get drenched.)

This movie features state-of-the-art computer animation, tons of special effects, and stars some of Disney's most beloved characters, including Donald Duck. Mickey's PhilharMagic is presented on a 150-foot by 28-foot movie screen. Special 3D glasses are provided when you enter the air-conditioned theater. The show is presented continuously throughout the day and should not be missed!

✔ This is a must-see attraction.

Mickey's Toontown Fair

People traveling with young children (ages three to twelve) will definitely want to check out The Magic Kingdom's newest land, which was designed specifically for kids. This area features many of Disney's classic characters, including Mickey Mouse, Minnie Mouse, Donald Duck, and Goofy. Mickey's Toontown Fair is a colorful, cartoon-like town that's a blast for kids, but it offers little of interest to adults. Near the entrance of this area, you'll find Pete's Garage. Here you'll find restrooms and public phones. If you want to meet Mickey Mouse and Minnie, Donald, and Goofy, the best place to do this is within Mickey's Toontown Fair.

🧳 TRAVEL TIP

Many of the gift shops throughout The WDW Resort offer Pal Mickey, a fully interactive, 12" plush Mickey Mouse toy that talks. As you explore the various theme parks, Pal Mickey shares appropriate tidbits of information, tells jokes, and interacts with your child based on where you are within the parks. Pal Mickey is priced at $60; however, you can rent it for $8 per day. It's most suitable for kids between the ages of four and ten.

Donald's Boat

Ages 2–4:	★★★
Ages 5–10:	★★★
Ages 11–15:	★
Ages 16–Adult:	N.S.
Senior Citizens:	N.S.

Kids get to explore this boat-shaped playground with a nautical theme. This boat is hardly seaworthy, however. In fact, it has so many leaks, kids who explore it are virtually guaranteed to get a bit wet. The shooting fountains offer an excellent way for kids to cool off on a hot day. On cooler days, you might want to instruct your kids to stay dry by avoiding the shooting water. (A cold and wet kid is an unhappy kid.) Otherwise, have a dry change of clothes on hand.

Mickey's Country House and Judge's Tent

Ages 2–4:	★★★
Ages 5–10:	★★★
Ages 11–15:	★★★
Ages 16–Adult:	N.S.
Senior Citizens:	N.S.

After exploring Mickey's yellow, green, and red country home and yard, young visitors get to meet Mickey in person. This is an excellent photo opportunity and a chance for your children to meet the Mouse one-on-one. While Disney characters make appearances every day throughout Walt Disney World, if you want to be guaranteed that your child will get a chance to meet Mickey (and shake hands, etc.), this is the place to visit. The wait, however, could be up to one hour. Mickey's Country House is a colorful four-room cottage where Mickey lives. Guests can explore it before meeting Mickey.

Minnie's Country House

Ages 2–4:	★★★
Ages 5–10:	★★★
Ages 11–15:	★★★
Ages 16–Adult:	N.S.
Senior Citizens:	N.S.

Young guests get to explore Minnie's pink-and-purple country home, and then explore the backyard, where Minnie herself will be waiting to greet guests in her gazebo. This is another excellent photo opportunity and a chance to interact with one of Disney's most popular characters. Be prepared to experience a wait to meet Minnie in person.

☰FAST FACT

Mickey's Toontown typically opens a little later than the rest of the park and sometimes closes earlier. Be sure to check your *Guide Map: The Magic Kingdom* brochure or the Information Board (at the end of Main Street U.S.A.) for details and plan your day accordingly.

The Barnstormer at Goofy's Wiseacre Farm

Ages 2–4:	N.S.
Ages 5–10:	★★★
Ages 11–15:	★★★
Ages 16–Adult:	N.S.
Senior Citizens:	N.S.

Young people will love Toontown's only thrill ride—a roller coaster with a "car-toon" twist that's fast enough to give young people a bit of excitement, without being too scary. Near the exit of the Barnstormer is a fun snack shop where guests can make their own strawberry shortcake. Kids must be at least 35 inches tall to experience this mild thrill ride.

Toon Park

Ages 2–4:	N.S.
Ages 5–10:	★★★
Ages 11–15:	★★
Ages 16–Adult:	N.S.
Senior Citizens:	N.S.

This playground looks like a 3D cartoon, and virtually everything within it is made out of foam, including the grass and animal statues. Toon Park is a fun and safe place for your kids to have fun while the adults sit on the sidelines.

Toontown Fair Hall of Fame

Ages 2–4:	N.S.
Ages 5–10:	★★★
Ages 11–15:	★★
Ages 16–Adult:	N.S.
Senior Citizens:	N.S.

This gallery features many of Disney's most popular characters from animated movies. Guests can also meet and greet multiple Disney characters who appear throughout the day.

Toontown Fair Railroad Station

Ages 2–4:	★★
Ages 5–10:	★★
Ages 11–15:	★★
Ages 16–Adult:	★★
Senior Citizens:	★★★

Climb aboard the WDW Railroad, which makes stops at Main Street U.S.A. and Frontierland.

⊕ HOT SPOT

Within Mickey's Toontown Fair, the main shopping opportunity can be found in County Bounty, a gift shop that sells an assortment of Disney-themed merchandise.

Meet the Characters

Located between Fantasyland and Tomorrowland, Ariel's Grotto is where you'll usually find Ariel and possibly other characters from Disney's *The Little Mermaid*, who are on hand to meet guests, take pictures, and sign autographs in an area that's designed to look like Ariel's undersea home. If you're traveling with kids, stopping by this area provides for an excellent photograph and autograph opportunity, and the line typically isn't too long.

The Fantasyland Character Festival is where you'll find a handful of Disney characters who will be on hand to meet and greet guests, sign autographs, and take pictures. While you typically won't find Mickey or Minnie here, at least a few other classic characters can typically be found here throughout the day.

Within the Fairytale Garden in Fantasyland, at several times throughout the day, young guests can hang out with Belle (from *Beauty and the Beast*) as she tells a story about her adventures within a small and intimate setting. Show times are listed in the *Guide Map: Magic Kingdom* brochure. Be sure to arrive early, since space is limited.

Other Kid-Oriented Attractions

The other lands within The Magic Kingdom also offer kid-oriented attractions. In addition, all of the parades and shows will appeal to the younger crowd. If you're traveling with kids, the following rides, shows, and attractions (highlighted in the previous chapter) should not be missed:

- Astro Orbiter (Tomorrowland)
- Buzz Lightyear's Space Ranger Spin (Tomorrowland)
- Country Bear Jamboree (Frontierland)
- The Magic Carpets of Aladdin (Adventureland)
- Swiss Family Treehouse (Adventureland)
- Tomorrowland Indy Speedway (Tomorrowland)
- Tom Sawyer Island (Frontierland)

Rides Not Suitable for Young Children

Due to the turbulent, thrill-ride nature or themes presented within some of the rides and attractions within The Magic Kingdom, some simply aren't suitable for young kids (under age six). Some of these rides and attractions include Splash Mountain, Big Thunder Mountain Railroad, the Haunted Mansion, Peter Pan's Flight, Snow White's Scary Adventures, Space Mountain, and the Mad Tea Party.

As a parent, you'll need to make a judgment call based on the information provided within this book and after seeing the ride, show, or attraction for yourself once you get to the theme park.

CHAPTER 8

Epcot Offers a Peek at Tomorrow

OUT OF ALL OF THE THEME PARKS AND THINGS TO do and see at The WDW Resort, Epcot is probably the most un-Disney. In other words, you won't be seeing flashy parades and Disney animated characters. What you will find, however, is that Epcot is a theme park designed primarily for teens and adults, offering attractions to entertain, thrill, and educate.

Park Overview

Epcot is really two totally different theme parks in one. There's Future World, which offers rides and attractions, each showcasing or demonstrating man's progress in science and technology. And then there's the World Showcase, which is designed to examine the cultural achievements, food, artistic products, and classic architecture of eleven countries from around the world.

Guests of all ages, especially adults, will find Epcot to be educational and thought provoking. This theme park takes an extremely innovative and entertaining approach to teaching people about the world we live in. Make sure that you wear comfortable shoes when you visit Epcot, because a considerable amount of walking is required.

There's an awful lot to see and do at Epcot. In order to see everything, plan on spending a minimum of two days visiting this park. Ideally, you'll want to spend one full day exploring Future World, and one day visiting the World Showcase pavilions. If you can't allocate this much time to visiting this park, choose a handful of attractions that are of interest to you from each area.

Looking at a map of Epcot, you'll discover that the park is laid out in the shape of an eight. The bottom loop comprises the attractions, shops, restaurants, and rides in Future World. The top loop comprises the World Showcase pavilions, which circle around the World Showcase Lagoon. For parents and educators, Epcot features two Discover Centers in Future World that offer educational resources and products.

Getting to Epcot

Just like The Magic Kingdom, Epcot is connected to the WDW monorail system, so you can reach this park via monorail by departing from the Ticket and Transportation Center. If you're staying at the Grand Floridian, the Contemporary, or the Polynesian (all WDW Resort hotels along a monorail route), take the monorail from the hotel to the Ticket and Transportation Center, then switch monorails and take the one that goes directly to Epcot's main entrance.

To reach Epcot's World Showcase entrance (a.k.a. The International Gateway entrance), take a short walk along a paved pathway from the Disney Yacht and Beach Club, Swan, Dolphin, and BoardWalk hotels. Instead of entering through Epcot's main entrance, which puts you in Future World (in front of Spaceship Earth), you'll enter the park from the back, in between the France and United Kingdom pavilions.

From all other WDW Resort hotels, you can take a WDW bus to Epcot's main entrance. If you're arriving at Epcot by car, there are several parking lots located near the main entrance. Follow the directions given by the parking attendants, write down the exact location where you parked your car, then hop aboard the free tram that'll take you to the park's main entrance. Parking costs $7 per day. Keep your parking ticket so that you can leave and re-enter the parking lot during a single day. Guests who are staying at any WDW Resort hotel and are already paying for parking at their hotel will receive free parking at any of Epcot's parking lots.

💼 TRAVEL TIP

To go against the crowds and thus cut down the amount of waiting time you'll experience at each attraction, consider visiting Future World in the afternoon or evening, when it is the least crowded. The best time to visit the pavilions in the World Showcase is as soon as this part of the park opens in the morning.

Admission to Epcot

Admission to Epcot requires a ticket. For details about the various ticket and pricing options for visiting Epcot and all of the theme parks within The WDW Resort, see Chapter 3.

Same-Day Re-entry

As you leave Epcot, be sure to have your hand stamped as you exit in order to be granted readmission into the park later that day or evening. In addition to the hand stamp, be sure to retain your ticket stub. The hand stamps are designed to be water-resistant, so don't worry if your hand gets wet if you choose to return to your hotel in the middle of the day to go swimming, and then want to return to Epcot later that evening. Try to refrain, however, from scrubbing your hands clean with soap until your day's visit to the park is complete.

Hours of Operation

The hours Epcot is open vary throughout the year; however, during much of the year, the park is open from 9:00 A.M. to 9:00

P.M., although there are exceptions. Future World is typically open from 9:00 A.M. to 7:00 P.M., though the popular Spaceship Earth and Innoventions attractions remain open until 9:00 P.M. The World Showcase, on the other hand, typically opens daily at 11:00 A.M. and remains open until 9:00 P.M. During the summer or during a peak holiday period, Epcot's hours are extended. To obtain the exact park operating hours for the dates of your visit, call ✆(407) 824-4321.

What to Bring

Make sure you wear comfortable shoes! Depending on the weather, you might want to take along a jacket (you can always store it in a locker). Try to avoid carrying too much stuff with you. You'll enjoy your visit more if your hands are as free as possible.

Don't forget to bring your camera, along with plenty of film and batteries. Avoid having to purchase high-priced film, batteries, or camera supplies in the park.

In case of rain, plan on getting a bit wet. Wear a raincoat or plan on purchasing an inexpensive Mickey Mouse poncho. Avoid bringing an umbrella into the park. You'll find it frustrating trying to walk around the crowded park with an open umbrella. For an up-to-the-minute weather report for the Orlando area, call ✆(407) 824-4104.

≡FAST FACT

Most of the things to see and do within Epcot are located inside. In fact, many of the attractions even allow you to wait in line indoors. You will, however, have to walk outside to go from attraction to attraction in Future World and from pavilion to pavilion in the World Showcase.

Choose a Place to Meet

As soon as you arrive at either Future World or the World Showcase at Epcot, choose a place where you'll meet up with the other people in your group if you happen to get separated. Choose to meet on the half-hour or on the hour, after being separated.

If you're traveling with children, upon arriving at Epcot, set some ground rules. Instruct your kids to stay close to you at all times. They should know that if they get lost, they should immediately contact any Disney cast member.

There are several good meeting locations in Future World, such as in front of Spaceship Earth or in front of the fountain near Epcot's main entrance. While visiting the World Showcase, you can choose a meeting location in front of a particular pavilion, such as the American Adventure, which is located exactly halfway around World Showcase Lagoon (opposite Future World).

Guest Relations

Located near Spaceship Earth is the Epcot Guest Relations building. The Disney cast members here are exceptionally helpful and will answer any and all of your questions regarding what to see and do at Epcot or anywhere at The WDW Resort. You can also make dining reservations here, or borrow a special wireless translator device that will translate the audio portion of many attractions within Epcot into Spanish, Japanese, Portuguese, German, or French.

≡FAST FACT

All of the guest services found at The Magic Kingdom, the Disney-MGM Studios, and Disney's Animal Kingdom are also available at Epcot, including ATMs, first aid, telephones, water fountains, locker rentals, and restrooms (with baby-changing stations). See Chapter 3 for details.

The Rating System

To help you choose which rides, shows, and attractions are most worth seeing while visiting Epcot's Future World and World

Showcase, this book offers star-based ratings for each ride and attraction based on the age group each will most appeal to. Each ride and attraction has earned between one and three stars.

★ = Rides and attractions that earned just one star aren't worth waiting for and could be skipped, especially if your time within the theme park is limited.

★★ = Rides and attractions that earned two stars are good, but they don't fall into the "must-see" category.

★★★ = The rides and attractions that earned three stars are definitely worth seeing and should not be missed.

N.S. = This denotes rides and attractions that are "Not Suitable" for a specific age group.

Future World

Epcot's Future World comprises multiple large buildings that house the various shows, rides, and attractions. This section provides information about everything there is to see and do in this portion of Epcot. Plan on spending between forty-five minutes and three hours at each of these attractions. As you'll see, some of the attractions contain multiple rides, shows, or things to experience. (If the park is extremely crowded, more time may be required.)

Spaceship Earth

Ages 2–4:	N.S.
Ages 5–10:	★★★
Ages 11–15:	★★★
Ages 16–Adult:	★★★
Senior Citizens:	★★★

Whether you approach Epcot via car, bus, or monorail, you can't miss seeing this 16-million-pound, 180-foot-tall, silver landmark as you approach the park. Inside this oversize golf ball–like object is an entertaining and informative attraction that explores the history of communication.

Spaceship Earth is the first major attraction you reach once you enter into Epcot's Future World from the main entrance. As a result, the line to experience Spaceship Earth's fourteen-minute-long ride is usually long. Once guests board the Omni-Mover transport inside the geosphere, they're seemingly transported back in time to discover how humans first learned to communicate. Throughout the attraction, Audio-Animatronics, lasers, and all sorts of other special effects are used to showcase communication and communication technology past, present, and future.

As the ride comes to an end, guests disembark from the Omni-Mover and find themselves in the AT&T Global Neighborhood. Guests can also enter this area through a separate entrance. This is a hands-on exhibit that showcases up-and-coming communication technology and offers a firsthand look at equipment like video telephones, and state-of-the-art ways of surfing the Internet.

The best time to experience Spaceship Earth is late afternoon or during the last ninety minutes before Epcot's Future World closes for the day.

⊕ HOT SPOT

Located in Innoventions plaza is the digital Epcot Tip Board. This information board lists the current wait times for all of the major attractions at Epcot, so you can better plan your day at the park. Show times are also available at this location.

Innoventions

Ages 2–4:	N.S.
Ages 5–10:	★★
Ages 11–15:	★★★
Ages 16–Adult:	★★★
Senior Citizens:	★★★

The purpose of Innoventions is to showcase technologically advanced products and services from many of the world's technology leaders. Innoventions is a large hands-on and visually exciting exhibit that's constantly changing. Its goal is to offer guests a preview of consumer electronics and computer technology that's new, but not necessarily currently available in American homes. What sets Innoventions apart from other attractions at Epcot is that almost everything that's on display is interactive, so you actually get to try things out, not just look at products or see someone else demonstrate them.

Whether you're a computer guru or totally computer illiterate, Innoventions gives people of all ages a chance to learn about current and future technology in a fun, but casual, setting. You're free to visit and walk through only the areas of Innoventions that are of interest to you, and spend as much or as little time as you want in each area. If you happen to see a product you're interested in, helpful people are available at each area of the pavilion to answer your questions or supply you with free informational brochures.

The Land

The overall theme of The Land is an exploration of our planet and how it produces food to support humanity and all of the other creatures living on Earth. The Land is divided up into four separate attractions: Living with The Land, Circle of Life, Food Rocks, and a Greenhouse Tour. Once you enter into this six-acre complex, plan on spending a minimum of one to three hours here.

Ages 2–4:	N.S.
Ages 5–10:	★★
Ages 11–15:	★★
Ages 16–Adult:	★★★
Senior Citizens:	★★★

Living with The Land is a fourteen-minute boat ride that takes guests through a manmade rain forest as well as The Land's massive greenhouses, where plant research is being conducted. All of the plants you see in the greenhouses are alive and real. Along the boat ride, however, to create some of the scenes you'll be seeing, artificial plants and special effects are used. This ride will appeal to people of all ages and is meant to be highly educational as well as entertaining.

Ages 2–4:	★★★
Ages 5–10:	★★★
Ages 11–15:	★★
Ages 16–Adult:	★★
Senior Citizens:	★★

The **Circle of Life** attraction located in The Land pavilion is a twenty-minute movie shown on a massive screen (23" by 60") that combines live action with animation. This movie stars characters from *The Lion King*. Designed to appeal to younger guests, the attraction focuses on the many dangers that face our environment. Environmental responsibility, demonstrated in ways that kids and adults alike will understand, is a central theme of this movie.

Ages 2–4:	★★★
Ages 5–10:	★★★
Ages 11–15:	★★
Ages 16–Adult:	★★
Senior Citizens:	★★

Food Rocks is another kid-oriented attraction within The Land pavilion, offering a fifteen-minute concert featuring upbeat and original music. The setting is a kitchen, and the performers include vegetables, a milk carton, and silverware. While guests will recognize many of the songs that are performed, all of the lyrics have been changed, giving each song a food theme. We're all taught never to play with food, but until you experience this show, you probably haven't thought too much about how entertaining food can be.

Ages 2–4:	N.S.
Ages 5–10:	N.S.
Ages 11–15:	★★
Ages 16–Adult:	★★★
Senior Citizens:	★★★

If you have a green thumb, enjoy gardening as a hobby, or just want to get a close-up look at the exotic plants growing within The **Land's Greenhouses** and see how they're maintained, one-hour guided tours are offered throughout the day.

Reservations for this tour can be made only on the day of your visit, and must be made in person by visiting the tour desk located at the **Green Thumb Emporium** (found inside The Land pavilion). There's a small fee (under $10 per person) to participate. The tour, however, will appeal mainly to adults interested in gardening and agriculture.

⊕ HOT SPOT

Space for these walking tours is extremely limited, but guests have the unique opportunity to see firsthand how plants are being grown without soil, and learn how NASA and the U.S. Department of Agriculture are working together on research being conducted at Epcot.

Soarin' over California (Opening 2005)

Ages 2–4:	N.S.
Ages 5–10:	★★
Ages 11–15:	★★★
Ages 16–Adult:	★★★
Senior Citizens:	★★★

One of the most popular attractions at Disney's California Adventure in Anaheim, California, will soon be soaring over to Orlando. It will open within Epcot's The Land pavilion sometime in 2005.

Thanks to a combination of motion simulators and Omnimax movie technology, you'll feel as if you're soaring over California as you're given a beautiful airborne tour of historic landmarks and national parks. You'll see the Golden Gate Bridge, Redwood forests, Napa Valley, Yosemite, and other landmarks in a way you've never seen them before. As you experience this realistic movie on the giant screen in front of you, you'll be suspended 45 feet in the air in what's designed to feel like a hang glider. Your movements are perfectly synchronized with the movie.

While there is a mild thrill element to this attraction, it's relatively calm and visually stunning. It's well worth experiencing this four-minute "flight" across California, which allows you to see 180 degrees around you. Unless you're prone to get motion sickness, this ride/attraction is suitable for everyone (except very young kids). The best seats are in the front row of each vehicle. The calmest ride is offered in the back seats of each vehicle. Once this ride opens, you'll definitely want to utilize FASTPASS to experience it.

✔ This is a must-see attraction.

The Living Seas

Ages 2–4:	★★★
Ages 5–10:	★★★
Ages 11–15:	★★★
Ages 16–Adult:	★★★
Senior Citizens:	★★★

Unless you've had the opportunity to ride in a real-life submarine or go scuba diving in the Caribbean, you haven't seen what life is truly like in the ocean. The Living Seas is much more than just the world's largest fish tank. Some of the world's most renowned oceanographers, researchers, and scientists, along with Disney's Imagineers, have created an attraction that allows guests to get a close-up view of life under the sea without ever having to get wet. What you'll see when you enter this pavilion is nothing short of spectacular.

The attraction begins with a walking tour through a gallery that chronicles man's journey into the oceans, using submarines and deep-sea diving equipment. Next, you'll see a short, two-and-a-half-minute movie that shows some of the deep-sea diving and ocean exploration equipment that's currently being used for research.

Your next stop is Sea Base Alpha, the world's largest aquarium, in which guests travel through glass tunnels that allow them to see ocean wildlife in its natural environment—a coral reef on the ocean floor. The reef you'll be seeing is manmade, but the fish and exotic marine life are all real. Sea Base Alpha also offers hands-on activities and interactive video screens that help to explain various oceanographic topics. Once you enter into The Living Seas, plan on spending at least thirty to sixty minutes here.

On some evenings around 7:00 P.M., if you're lucky you'll get to see Mickey Mouse in scuba gear diving into the tank and swimming with the sea life.

✔ This is a must-see attraction.

⊕ HOT SPOT

For $140 per person, guests can participate in two very special tours. The Dolphins in Depth program is three-and-a-half hours long and allows guests to interact directly with dolphins and meet the researchers who work at The Living Seas pavilion. For those who are certified scuba divers, DiveQuest allows guests to rent scuba-diving equipment and explore the 6-million-gallon tank with a guide. Advanced reservations are required to participate in either the Dolphins in Depth or DiveQuest programs. Call ✆(407) WDW-TOUR.

Universe of Energy

Ages 2–4:	★★
Ages 5–10:	★★
Ages 11–15:	★★★
Ages 16–Adult:	★★★
Senior Citizens:	★★★

The Universe of Energy was one of the original pavilions in Epcot's Future World. In 1996, however, it was totally revamped to provide guests with an entirely new and far more entertaining experience. The forty-five-minute presentation, called *Ellen's Energy Adventure,* features actress/comedian Ellen DeGeneres and scientist Bill Nye (The Science Guy). It's shown every seventeen minutes throughout the day.

As you might have gathered from the name, this attraction explores how energy is created and used around the world. Not only does this attraction explain all of the different options available for creating energy now and in the future, but it does so in a way that's entertaining and not preachy.

✔ This is a must-see attraction.

Wonders of Life

Ages 2–4:	★★
Ages 5–10:	★★
Ages 11–15:	★★
Ages 16–Adult:	★
Senior Citizens:	★

This attraction takes a look at life on the planet Earth and examines health and fitness issues facing busy humans. In addition to all sorts of high-tech hands-on displays and exercise equipment for guests to try out, the Fair Grounds area of this pavilion features three theaters.

⊕ HOT SPOT

Plan on spending between two and four hours here if you want to experience all of the shows, movies, and attractions within Wonders of Life.

An eight-minute multimedia show, called *Goofy About Health,* features the classic Disney character Goofy. This movie is shown continuously in a 100-seat theater designed so guests can come and go as they please. This movie is informative, entertaining, and is suitable for people of all ages.

Ages 2–4:	★
Ages 5–10:	★★
Ages 11–15:	★★
Ages 16–Adult:	★★
Senior Citizens:	★★

Also in this area of the pavilion is the **AnaComical Players Theater**, the home of an improvisational acting troupe that performs a comical show utilizing audience participation. Performances are held at predefined times throughout the day.

Ages 2–4:	★
Ages 5–10:	★★
Ages 11–15:	★★
Ages 16–Adult:	★★
Senior Citizens:	★★

In a third theater, *The Making of Me* movie is shown. Featuring actor/comedian Martin Short, this fourteen-minute film focuses on Martin's character, who contemplates where he came from. As part of this presentation, Martin's character travels back in time to witness his parents grow up, meet, and get married. Ultimately, he even watches his own birth. For this scene, footage of an actual birth is shown. While this entire movie discusses sexual intercourse, it does so in a nongraphic and extremely tasteful and nonoffensive way. Parents should decide for themselves if this material is suitable for their children to see.

⊕ HOT SPOT

At the Met Lifestyles Review area of the Wonders of Life pavilion, computers are available where guests can enter their age, weight, height, how much they exercise, and other information. This information is used by the computer to suggest various ways guests can reduce the stress in their lives and at the same time become more physically fit.

Ages 2–4:	★★
Ages 5–10:	★★★
Ages 11–15:	★★★
Ages 16–Adult:	★★
Senior Citizens:	★★

Another attraction in the Wonders of Life pavilion is **Cranium Command**, a seventeen-minute show that uses movie footage and Audio-Animatronics to take guests into the mind of a twelve-year-old boy. This comical and extremely creative show examines how the brain works, and features the voice talents of well-known celebrities like John Lovitz, Charles Grodin, George Wendt, Dana Carvey, and Kevin Nealon. Cranium Command is suitable for people of all ages.

Ages 2–4:	N.S.
Ages 5–10:	★★
Ages 11–15:	★★★
Ages 16–Adult:	★★★
Senior Citizens:	★★

Body Wars uses flight-simulator technology (like Star Tours at the Disney-MGM Studios) to send guests on a turbulent thrill ride inside the human body. The five-minute ride makes guests feel like they've been shrunk to a size smaller than a single cell and placed inside a ship capable of exploring the human body. This ride explains how the human immune system works and uses realistic special effects to make guests feel like they're actually traveling inside of a body. This ride is extremely turbulent, so make sure your seatbelt is securely fastened and that your belongings are all safely stowed. This ride is exciting, but not suitable for young kids (under 40 inches tall) or anyone with heart problems or back problems or who suffers from motion sickness. This is the most popular attraction in the Wonders of Life pavilion, so expect to wait between twenty minutes and one hour to experience it.

Imagination!

Ages 2–4:	★
Ages 5–10:	★★★
Ages 11–15:	★★★
Ages 16–Adult:	★★
Senior Citizens:	★★

The Epcot ride/attraction **Journey Into Your Imagination**, which opened in conjunction with this theme park, has been totally revamped yet again, creating a totally different attraction. This latest ride, Journey Into Imagination with Figment, stars the adorable purple dragon, Figment (as in figment of your imagination), and explores human imagination and our five senses in a fun, whimsical, and musical way. After experiencing the six-minute ride, guests wind up within ImageWorks and Kodak's "What If" Labs. This is a totally interactive, walk-through area that features technological exhibits and activities for people of all ages. The entire attraction, including the wait queue, is located within an air-conditioned building.

Ages 2–4:	★★
Ages 5–10:	★★★
Ages 11–15:	★★★
Ages 16–Adult:	★★★
Senior Citizens:	★★

Also located in the Journey Into Imagination pavilion is the **Honey, I Shrunk the Audience** show, which is loosely based on Disney's *Honey, I Shrunk the Kids* movie. Rick Moranis and Marcia Strassman, along with the kids from this movie series, reprise their roles for this comical fourteen-minute 3D movie. Ultimately, after the theater is invaded by 3D movie mice, and you see the on-screen characters miniaturized, the audience itself becomes the unwilling victim of Professor Wayne Szalinski's shrinking machine. This movie is exciting, extremely entertaining, and offers lots of surprises. While you'll be handed special 3D glasses as you enter into the theater, do not place them over your eyes until you're seated and instructed to do so. The 3D glasses can be placed directly over prescription eyeglasses.

✔ This is a must-see attraction.

Test Track

Ages 2–4:	N.S.
Ages 5–10:	★
Ages 11–15:	★★★
Ages 16–Adult:	★★★
Senior Citizens:	★

When you experience this attraction, you take on the role of a test driver for General Motors. Your responsibilities include testing new models of automobiles while they're still in the concept phase. This is a challenging job that takes skill, guts, and a love for speed. That's the premise behind Epcot's thrill ride Test Track.

The preshow/line queue takes place within an industrial-looking test laboratory filled with equipment and vehicle components.

There are simulated brake, wheel, suspension, airbag, seat belt, and windshield tests.

As the ride begins, get ready to buckle up and travel along bumpy terrain, through hairpin turns, into freezing cold chambers, and along 50-degree banked curves at speeds up to 65 miles per hour. Guests experience this ride in specially designed six-passenger vehicles that travel along the mile-long track.

✔ This is a must-see attraction.

💼 TRAVEL TIP

Due to its popularity, be prepared for a long wait or take advantage of FASTPASS. If you don't mind experiencing this ride without the people you're traveling with, take advantage of the singles' line. This line tends to move much quicker, but you'll wind up riding with strangers. Guests must be at least 40 inches tall to experience Test Track.

Innoventions Fountain

Ages 2–4:	★★
Ages 5–10:	★★
Ages 11–15:	★★
Ages 16–Adult:	★★
Senior Citizens:	★★

Every fifteen minutes, a computer-controlled, fully choreographed shooting water performance is presented at this fountain, located outside in Innoventions Plaza. This short show is nothing compared to IllumiNations: Reflections of Earth (presented nightly), but it offers a nice diversion as you're walking by.

Mission: SPACE

Ages 2–4:	N.S.
Ages 5–10:	N.S.
Ages 11–15:	★★★
Ages 16–Adult:	★★★
Senior Citizens:	N.S.

Epcot's newest attraction (which opened in late 2003) is also this theme park's most thrilling! Imagine what it would be like if you were an astronaut traveling deep into space. Well, the closest thing you'll probably ever get is this high-tech ride/attraction that was created in conjunction with NASA and Hewlett-Packard. Mission: SPACE has replaced the old Horizons pavilion at Epcot and was in development for more than five years.

Get ready to blast off into the future—the year 2036—and travel on a mission to Mars aboard an X2 spacecraft. You'll take on the role of your ship's pilot, navigator, engineer, or commander. During the ride, prepare to experience some of the G-forces involved in your spaceship's liftoff, sensations of weightlessness while in deep space, and the turbulence of a somewhat rough landing on Mars.

Including the preshows and the interactive area after the main ride, plan on spending about forty-five minutes experiencing Mission: SPACE. The actual ride lasts about four minutes and uses state-of-the-art centrifuge technology, sophisticated visual imaging, and incredible audio effects to create a very realistic space flight simulation experience. To experience Mission: SPACE, you must be at least 44 inches tall. It's not recommended for anyone who easily gets motion sickness.

Mission: SPACE is a high-tech thrill ride unlike anything offered at any theme park! It might not look like a roller coaster, but it offers the same type of excitement. This is definitely Epcot's most popular and exciting attraction, so be prepared for a long wait (sixty to ninety minutes during peak times). You'll definitely want to utilize FASTPASS or wait in the "singles" line.

✔ This is a must-see attraction.

═FAST FACT

Walt Disney Imagineering has seamlessly blended storytelling, engineering, imagination, and technology to create Mission: SPACE. It took a team of more than 650 Imagineers, five NASA astronauts, plus experts from NASA and the Jet Propulsion Laboratory more than 350,000 hours to develop this truly amazing space simulation adventure ride from concept to reality.

Dining in Future World

These restaurants and snack shops located in Epcot's Future World are open during park hours (but most close at 7:00 P.M.). For exact hours or to make a reservation at any of the full-service establishments, call ✆(407) WDW-DINE. The following are dining options available at Epcot's Future World:

Coral Reef—This is a full-service restaurant located in The Living Seas pavilion. The backdrop for this dining room is the attraction's 6-million-gallon aquarium. The majority of the menu items served at this restaurant are seafood dishes. Priority Seating reservations are definitely recommended. Lunch and dinner are served daily.

Garden Grill—This full-service restaurant serves breakfast, lunch, and dinner hosted by Disney characters, including Mickey Mouse and Minnie Mouse. Lunch and dinner entrees include chicken, fish, and steak dishes.

Electric Umbrella—Located near Innoventions, this is Future World's largest fast-food dining establishment. Entrees include hamburgers, cheeseburgers, hot dogs, sandwiches, salads, and a variety of snack items and beverages.

Fountain View Espresso & Bakery—Freshly baked items such as croissants and a wide range of extremely tasty desserts are offered at this dining spot located near Innoventions. Espresso, cappuccino, coffee, wine, beer, and other beverages are available.

Pure & Simple—This snack shop, located within the Wonders of Life pavilion, offers a selection of healthy snack foods, like fresh fruit, salads, frozen yogurt, muffins, juices, and oat bran waffles with fruit toppings. Breakfast, lunch, and dinner are served, and counter service is available.

Sunshine Season Food Fair—Located on the lower level of The Land pavilion in Future World, this food court offers soups and salads, as well as baked goods, bagels, fresh fruit, cinnamon rolls, Danish, and other breakfast treats. There's also a barbecue stand,

Chinese food stand, a sandwich shop, and the Potato Store. The Beverage House offers a large list of tropical (alcoholic and non-alcoholic) frozen drinks, plus beer, wine, bottled water, and soda.

═══FAST FACT

Throughout Epcot, you'll find snack carts that sell ice cream, snack foods, and beverages.

Shopping in Future World

As you probably expect, gift shops and souvenir stands are located throughout Epcot's Future World. **Gateway Gifts** and the **Camera Center** are located near the park's main entrance. Here you can pick up souvenirs or film for your camera. Video cameras can be rented at the Camera Center, and same-day film processing is available. You will, however, pay a premium if you purchase film or batteries anywhere at WDW or have your film developed at the park.

The **Centorium** is located in the midst of Innoventions and offers a large selection of Disney character merchandise, gifts, and souvenirs with the Epcot logo. This is the largest gift shop in Epcot.

For Disney fans and collectors, the **Art of Disney Epcot Gallery** is one of the most exciting shops at Epcot, because on display (and available for purchase) is Disney animation artwork, including actual production animation cells and limited edition cells. Other Disney collectibles are also displayed in a museum gallery–like setting. Whether you're looking to add to your Disney art collection, you're hoping to start a collection, or you just want to see some of the stunning artwork that's on display, be sure to stop by this gallery for a visit. It'll appeal mainly to adults.

The World Showcase

Each of the pavilions in the World Showcase represents a country and showcases its culture, architecture, food, art, music, and history.

These pavilions are staffed by natives of the featured country and offer an authentic look at what each country has to offer. To make your trip around the world more exciting, many of the pavilions offer live shows, musical performances, and some type of ride or movie attraction. Specialty shops are also featured within the pavilions, so you can pick up unique souvenirs that were handcrafted or manufactured in the featured country.

The World Showcase as a whole is designed more for adults than children, although there's always so much to see and do in this area of Epcot, people of all ages will enjoy the experience of traveling to exotic countries without ever stepping foot on an airplane. These pavilions are described in the order that you'll encounter them if you begin at the main entrance of the World Showcase (approached by coming through Future World) and proceed in a clockwise direction (traveling to the left).

⊕ HOT SPOT

The full-service, fine-dining restaurants within these pavilions offer some of the best food available anywhere in WDW. Reservations for these relatively high-priced restaurants are strongly recommended. Call ✆ (407) WDW-DINE as far in advance as possible. Same-day reservations are also available, but if you don't mind waiting, you can simply show up for a meal at one of the full-service restaurants.

Mexico

A large pyramid-like structure is the home of the Mexico pavilion, where you can experience **El Rio del Tiempo: The River of Time**. This is a six-minute boat ride that takes a look at life in Mexico past and present. Movies, animated sets, and Audio-Animatronics are used to provide the visuals along the boat trip. The lines for this attraction will probably be long in the morning, so if you wait until late in the day or evening, your wait will be less. Live entertainment is provided both inside and outside of the pavilion throughout the day.

At the **Plaza de Los Amigos** marketplace area, you can shop for piñatas, sombreros, pottery, colorful paper flowers, and other genuine Mexican souvenirs. For a higher-priced selection of merchandise, visit **Artesanias Mexicanas**. Products from northern Mexico are showcased at **El Ranchito del Norte**, while **La Familia Fashions** offers clothing and accessories for women and children, along with jewelry.

As for the Mexican dining experience offered at this pavilion, **San Angel Inn** is a second location for a famous restaurant located in Mexico City. Here you'll be able to choose from an assortment of delicious Mexican entrees, including tacos as well as fish, meat, and chicken dishes. This is a full-service restaurant and reservations are strongly recommended. Lunch and dinner are served daily.

A less expensive dining option at the Mexico pavilion is offered at **Cantina de San Angel**. Here you can snack on various types of filled soft tortillas and other fast-food items. Lunch, dinner, and snacks are served, and counter service is offered. Nearby outdoor tables are provided, or you can enjoy your food as you walk around the World Showcase Promenade.

Norway

This pavilion offers you the opportunity to learn about some of the history, culture, and folklore of Norway. The architecture of this pavilion depicts several different styles from around the country, plus from the country's past. For example, one of the main structures is a Norwegian castle that was modeled after a fourteenth-century fortress that can still be seen in Oslo's harbor.

The main attraction of the Norway pavilion is the **Maelstrom**, a ten-minute ride that uses boats modeled after those used by Vikings over 1,000 years ago. Your journey begins with a look at the country's past and at its ancient folklore. After the boat ride, your look at Norway continues in a theater, where a movie depicting life in modern Norway is presented. This is a popular attraction that's often less crowded in the evenings.

One of the buildings that make up this pavilion is a re-creation of a wooden stave church. Inside you'll discover a gallery that offers scenes and objects designed to help guests better understand this country's culture.

The Puffin's Roost is a shop that displays an assortment of Norwegian gifts, handmade items, clothing, jewelry, toys, and other souvenirs.

At the **Akershus** restaurant, located inside the castle, guests are treated to an authentic royal Norwegian (all-you-can-eat) buffet, which includes a wide array of hot and cold dishes. This is considered a fine-dining experience. Norwegian hosts and hostesses are always on hand to answer questions and add to the ambiance. Lunch and dinner are served daily. Reservations are strongly recommended.

Kringla Bakeri og Kafe offers less expensive snacks and candies as well as open-faced smoked salmon, roast beef, and turkey sandwiches. One treat that's sold here is kringles, which are candied pretzels that Norwegians eat on special occasions. Beers from Norway are served. Counter service is available, and nearby outdoor seating is provided.

💼 TRAVEL TIP

This part of Epcot requires a lot of walking. If you have physical limitations that might keep you from being able to walk around the entire World Showcase Lagoon and explore the pavilions, you should seriously consider renting a wheelchair so that you don't miss any part of this fascinating area of Epcot.

China

As you approach the China pavilion, you'll quickly notice the authentic architecture and hear the Chinese music that's played constantly near the pavilion so passersby can get a taste of China, even without dropping into the pavilion. Inside the pavilion's **Temple of Heaven**, live music is performed almost continuously, while in the nearby courtyard, you can catch a performance by a team of highly talented acrobats. This courtyard features landscaping made up of plants that are native to China.

In addition to the live performances, the China pavilion features a Circle-Vision 360 movie, *Reflections of China*, which was updated in late 2003. This presentation shows locations in China that foreigners had never seen prior to this movie's premiere at Epcot. You'll see stunning footage of Beijing's Forbidden City, the Great Wall of China, and many other beautiful locations.

As you leave the movie theater, you'll have a chance to walk through an exhibit of Chinese art. The gallery exhibit changes every six months but always includes pieces from well-known artists that are on loan from private collectors and world-renowned museums.

TRAVEL TIP

To help make the trek around the lagoon a bit easier, water taxis are available that depart from docks located near several of the pavilions. In addition, double-decker buses continuously travel around the lagoon, making stops at all of the pavilions.

Your visit to the China pavilion can also include a shopping excursion to the Yonh Feng **Shangdain Shopping Gallery**, located on the Street of Good Fortune. Here you can purchase authentic Chinese merchandise like silk robes, paper fans, and umbrellas, as well as antiques and other souvenirs.

If you're in the mood for a tasty Chinese lunch or dinner, the **Nine Dragons** restaurant offers a wonderful full-service dining experience. The food is prepared in a variety of different cooking styles, including Mandarin, Hunan, Cantonese, and Szechuan. On the menu, you'll find a wide range of entrees listed, along with Chinese teas, beers, and wines. Reservations are strongly recommended.

For lunch or dinner, **The Lotus Blossom Café** is Epcot's answer to Chinese fast food. Nearby outdoor seating is provided. The food served here is considerably less expensive than the full-service

Nine Dragons restaurant, and you'll finish eating much faster, allowing you to continue exploring the World Showcase.

Germany

The Germany pavilion is a re-creation of a small German village, although the architecture of the various buildings and structures was borrowed from many different areas of the country. On the hour, a glockenspiel located within the pavilion can be heard playing an original tune, and throughout the day, live musical entertainment is often featured.

By exploring the pavilion, you'll encounter several small shops, each featuring unique German items. At **Der Bucherwurm**, you'll find books about Germany, artwork, and souvenir items. **Volkskunst** is a small shop that sells clocks and watches, as well as other handcrafted items. If you're looking for a special gift for a child (or a collectible doll for yourself), check out what's offered at **Der Teddybar**, a lovely toy shop.

Participate in a daily wine tasting or take home a bottle of German wine by visiting **Weinkeller**, a wine shop that offers more than 250 varieties of German wine that were produced and bottled by **H. Schmitt Sohne**. Crystal jewelry and glass items are offered at **Kunstarbeit In Kristal**. You'll be able to satisfy your sweet tooth at **Sussigkeiten**, a confectionery shop that offers many German sweets.

At **Glas Und Porzellan**, you'll find glass and porcelain items made by Goebel. Collectors of Hummel figurines will find a huge assortment of these collectibles on display, plus there's often a Goebel artist on hand answering questions and demonstrating how these pieces are hand-painted. This is a wonderful shop for adults to browse through, even if you have no intention of making a purchase.

Lunch and dinner are served daily at the Germany pavilion's fine-dining restaurant, called **Biergarten**. Guests sit at large tables (often with total strangers) and can enjoy a selection of authentic German cuisine and drink Beck's beer. During dinner hours, live entertainment is offered every hour on the half-hour, so be sure to time your dining experience accordingly. Reservations are strongly recommended.

At **Sommerfest**, bratwurst sandwiches are the specialty, but you'll also find treats like soft pretzels, apple strudel, and other German snacks. Counter service is provided and nearby outdoor seating is available. Located in between the Germany and China pavilions is a snack shop that offers soda, bottled water, frozen yogurt, and ice cream.

⊕ HOT SPOT

No matter what time of year you're visiting Epcot, it's always the Christmas holiday season at Die Weihnachts Ecke, a German Christmas shop that sells ornaments, holiday decorations, and holiday-oriented gift items. Those who collect tree ornaments will be able to purchase some wonderful and unique additions for their collection here.

Italy

In addition to fine Italian food, guests get a true taste of Italy when they visit this pavilion. In the courtyard of this pavilion, not only will you see and hear live music performed, but you'll also get a chance to see the **Living Statues**. Performers stand motionless and periodically change positions. Despite the best efforts of guests to distract these performers, they remain expressionless and motionless except to change positions.

Delizie Italiane is a marketplace area that sells chocolates and other sweets, while **La Cucina Italiana** is a gourmet shop that offers Italian pastries and dessert items. Take-home gourmet food items and accessories are also sold here. For more expensive gifts, such as glassware or porcelain figurines, be sure to visit **La Bel Cristallo** ("The Beautiful Crystal"). Jewelry made from silver and gold, along with other items, is sold at **La Gemma Elegante**.

An authentic and delicious Italian dining experience is offered during lunch and dinner hours at **L'Originale Alfredo di Roma**

Ristorante. The specialty of the house is fettuccine, although you'll find a range of Italian entrees available. The kitchen of this restaurant is located behind a large glass window, so guests can see the chefs at work.

The American Adventure

Located halfway around the World Showcase Lagoon is the **American Adventure**. A large colonial-style building is the main structure of this pavilion. Inside, guests are invited to see a twenty-nine-minute attraction called the **American Adventure Show**, which features Audio-Animatronic characters that bring some of America's heroes and most famous historical figures and entertainers to life.

Live music is presented at the American Adventure pavilion, which is almost always crowded. Outside of the main pavilion, located in front of the World Showcase Lagoon, the **America Gardens Theater** offers various concerts and performances that constantly change. Show times and details about the various shows are posted in front of the theater, at Guest Relations, and at the Tip Board. The nearby **All-American Red, White & Blue** gift shop sells items that are patriotic and that represent the country. American flags, clothing, books, and other products are available, along with Coca-Cola merchandise.

⊕ HOT SPOT

Many of the pavilions in this part of Epcot offer food that is totally foreign to most young people. Stop at the Liberty Inn to find all-American food that your children will recognize and relate to.

There is no full-service restaurant in this pavilion, but the **Liberty Inn** offers all-American food like hamburgers, hot dogs, salads, soda, and cookies. Counter service is available, and nearby seating is provided. Lunch, dinner, and snack items are served.

If you're lucky enough to travel to WDW during the Christmas holiday season (late November through late December), you won't want to miss the Candlelight Processional, which is held two or three times per night at the America Gardens Theater. This magical and heartwarming holiday performance lasts about one hour, and features a 450-voice choir, a fifty-piece orchestra, and a celebrity narrator.

≡FAST FACT

Guests are invited to walk through the Hall of Flags, where forty-four flags that at some point in American history represented our country (or various parts of it) are displayed.

Japan

The Imperial Palace is the main focal point of this pavilion. Outside, you'll see and hear Japanese music performed, and you might even get to see stilt-walkers dressed like exotic birds perform. Native landscaping is seen around the pavilion. **The Bijutsu-Kan Gallery** offers an ever-changing exhibit of traditional and more modern Japanese art.

The Mitsukoshi Department Store offers a huge assortment of Japanese products, gifts, and souvenirs offered at a range of prices from extremely affordable to extremely expensive. This is definitely one of the most interesting shops to browse through at Epcot.

One of the very best restaurants in Epcot's World Showcase is **Mitsukoshi**, a Japanese steak house where your food is prepared by talented chefs right at your table. The **Tempura Kiku** area of this restaurant serves batter-dipped, deep-fried entrees made from beef, chicken, and seafood. The main dining room offers a full menu of Japanese dishes, all cooked at your table in an extremely entertaining style. At the large tables, you'll probably be seated with strangers as you enjoy this fine-dining experience. Lunch and dinner are served daily. Reservations are strongly suggested.

Yakitori House offers less expensive Japanese cuisine that can be enjoyed for lunch, dinner, or a snack. Guydon and yakitori are among the main menu selections served here.

Morocco

Inside the **Gallery of Arts and History**, guests have the opportunity to see authentic Moroccan artwork. Also on hand at the **Moroccan National Tourist Office** within this pavilion are travel experts who can help you plan your next vacation to their country. Be sure to take a few minutes to watch the slide show that's presented at this office continuously.

If you're in the market for a hard-to-find fez or another article of Moroccan clothing, drop by the **Tangier Traders** shop. **The Marketplace in the Medina** shop sells handcrafted baskets and other handmade items. If it can be made out of brass, you'll find it at a shop called the **Brass Bazaar**. Additional brass items can be purchased at **Berber Oasis**, a smaller gift shop also found in this pavilion. Kids are sure to find a toy or souvenir at **Medina Arts**, a shop that sells toys, clothing, and other items featuring characters from Disney's *Aladdin* motion picture.

As you dine at **Marrakesh**, you'll be entertained by belly dancers and live musical performances. The food served is genuine Moroccan cuisine, which includes chicken brochette, couscous, and roast lamb. The live entertainment makes this dining experience extremely memorable and enjoyable. Reservations are strongly recommended. Lunch and dinner are served daily.

≡FAST FACT

The buildings that make up this pavilion are designed to showcase the authentic architecture of Morocco, and the insides of these buildings are true works of art. Disney reports that over nine tons of handcrafted tiles were imported and laid inside this pavilion.

France

A re-creation of the Eiffel Tower is the prominent landmark at this pavilion. The main attraction here is the *Impressions de France* movie that offers a comprehensive and visually stunning look at France in eighteen minutes.

Plume et Palette is a beautiful shop that sells cosmetics, fragrances, and bath products imported from France. There's also an area that sells oil paintings and prints by well-known French artists. At **La Signature**, an assortment of gift items is available, including collectibles and tapestries. **The Galerie des Halles** also sells an assortment of affordable souvenirs from France, including musical CDs. Posters, prints, and other items imprinted with artwork from famous artists such as Monet and Renoir are available from **La Casserole**.

If you're in the mood for fine French food for lunch or dinner, make a reservation to eat at **Bistro de Paris**, a full-service restaurant that's located one flight above **Chefs de France**. Here, a traditional French bistro menu is served daily. Downstairs at Chefs de France, some of the country's finest chefs are invited to showcase their talent at this posh restaurant. This, however, is one of the most expensive restaurants at Epcot. A special children's menu is available, and lunch or dinner reservations are strongly recommended.

≡FAST FACT

France is responsible for producing over 20 percent of the wine consumed in the world. Wine collectors and connoisseurs will find a vast selection of French wines on sale at La Maison du Vin. Daily wine tastings are held here. There's a small fee to participate in a wine tasting, but you'll receive a special souvenir glass that's yours to keep.

United Kingdom

Guests who visit this pavilion get to enjoy the authentic architecture, landscaping, and shops. There's even a hedge maze that's located just outside of the pavilion's cottage. At the **Pooh Corner** shop, you'll find an incredible assortment of merchandise based on Winnie the Pooh. Meanwhile, at the **Crown & Crest**, you'll find dart boards, chess sets, and other unique gifts and items. The beautiful chess sets range in price from $250 to $900. Sweaters made of lamb's wool are available at **Pringle of Scotland**.

Lords & Ladies is the home of china products manufactured and sold by **Royal Doulton, Ltd.** Figurines and fine china are available at a wide range of prices, but even if you don't want to buy anything, this store is worth visiting just to browse. For handmade products from Wales, visit the **Magic of Wales** shop. English teas, teapots, biscuits, and fine candies are sold at the **Tea Caddy**.

When you're ready to eat lunch, dinner, or a snack, check out the menu at **Rose & Crown Pub and Dining Room**. This authentic English pub offers fish and chips and an assortment of other entrees. Seating in the pub area is available on a first-come-first-served basis; however, reservations are suggested for the dining room.

Canada

If you're traveling around Epcot's World Showcase Lagoon clockwise, then your trip around the world ends at Canada. A seventeen-minute movie, *O Canada!* is shown in Circle-Vision 360 and offers a visual tour of this country. There are no seats in this theater, so be prepared to stand while the movie is shown all around you.

At the **Northwest Mercantile**, a selection of Canadian clothing, like lumberjack shirts, as well as other items and handcrafted products can be purchased. **Le Cellier** is open only during certain times of the year but offers a selection of Canadian food in a casual environment that's not too expensive compared to the other restaurants located in the World Showcase pavilions.

Lunch, dinner, and snacks are served in a cafeteria-style setting. For a quick snack, consider stopping at the **Refreshment Port**. Canadian beer and wine are available, along with frozen yogurt, fresh fruit, and ice cream.

Outside of the Canada pavilion, you're likely to see live performances by Canadian folk dancers and the **Caledonia Bagpipe Band**.

IllumiNations: Reflections of Earth

Ages 2–4:	★★
Ages 5–10:	★★★
Ages 11–15:	★★★
Ages 16–Adult:	★★★
Senior Citizens:	★★★

Every evening (just after dark), thousands of people gather around the World Showcase Lagoon for an incredible display of fireworks, lasers, and dancing fountains, all synchronized to music. This thirteen-minute show can be seen from anywhere around the lagoon, but you'll want to stake out your viewing location up to one hour early if the park is extremely crowded. This is one of the most spectacular nighttime shows presented anywhere at WDW, so if you're visiting Epcot, plan on staying into the evening so you don't miss this magical and visually stunning show.

✔ This is a must-see attraction.

💼 TRAVEL TIP

IllumiNations changes every year, so if you're making a return visit to Epcot, the show you saw during your last visit will be different. Check with Guest Relations or the Tip Board for specific show times. You can also call ☎(407) 824-4321.

Tapestry of Dreams Parade

In addition to the nighttime IllumiNations performance, Epcot now has its own parade, which pays tribute to children from around the world, and the dreams and legacy of Walt Disney. This thirty-minute parade features colorful floats; larger-than-life puppets; and 112 cast members who sing, dance, and entertain guests who line the parade route.

Featuring original music, Tapestry of Dreams is presented twice every evening. The parade travels between the Mexico and Morocco pavilions within Epcot's World Showcase. Unlike the parades within The Magic Kingdom and Disney's Animal Kingdom, for example, this one is more adult-oriented, because there's less of an emphasis on the Disney characters. Instead, the large puppets, beautiful floats, and costumed performers are showcased. People of all ages will enjoy this parade.

Leave a Legacy

Epcot offers guests the opportunity to leave their legacy in the form of a digital photo that gets mounted on a series of sculptures located near the main entrance to the park. Guests have an opportunity to purchase "memory tiles" upon which a digital photograph (taken at the park) is etched. One or two images can be included on each tile.

══FAST FACT

From home, people can view the sculpture and the individual tiles at a specially created Web site (✑*www.disney.go.com/ millenniumlegacy*).

The cost of one image is $35. For two images on one tile, the price is $38. With every tile purchased, a verification certificate gets mailed to the purchaser that lists the exact location of the tile on the Legacy Sculpture.

Calling All Pin Collectors

Throughout the entire WDW Resort, one hobby that an ever-growing number of guests adopt during their visit is pin collecting. Disney continues to issue collectible and commemorative enamel pins relating to special events at WDW, as well as pins for each ride, attraction, show, parade, and Disney character.

There are literally thousands of pins to choose from and collect, ranging in price from a $6.50 to $8.50 (retail). Serious collectors, however, will sometimes pay hundreds of dollars for limited edition and extremely rare pins on the secondary collector's market.

You'll find **Disney Pin Traders kiosks** in every WDW theme park as well as in the Disney hotels. You can also purchase special lanyards, display cases, hats, frames, and books to showcase your pin collection. Guests are also encouraged to trade pins with Disney cast members and each other.

Visit *www.officialdisneypintrading.com* for a complete overview of Disney Pin Trading, including news about pin releases, a calendar of upcoming events, and a guide to pin trading etiquette. Different pins are offered at each Disney theme park as well as aboard Disney Cruise Lines. To obtain hard-to-find pins for your collection, also check out *www.DisneyAuctions.com*. Pin collecting is a fun, relatively inexpensive and addicting hobby for people of all ages.

≡ FAST FACT

The Walt Disney World Resort releases more than 350 new pins per year, including ten to twelve limited edition pins, ten to twelve core pins, and five to ten special event pins per month. There are more than eighty locations on WDW property that sell pins, including forty Official Pin Trading Stations.

While visiting WDW, you can participate in organized pin trading events. For example, **Mickey's Pin Trading Nights** take place from 7 P.M. to 10 P.M. on Thursday nights at Disney's All-Star Sports Resort, on Friday nights at Disney's Contemporary Resort, and on Sunday nights at Disney's BoardWalk.

CHAPTER 9

The Disney-MGM Studios

THE DISNEY-MGM STUDIOS THEME PARK OFFERS AT least one day's worth of quality entertainment with a Hollywood theme. This chapter describes all of the shows, attractions, rides, restaurants, shops, and guest services available at The Disney-MGM Studios, and will help you plan an exciting visit to this popular WDW Resort theme park.

Park Overview

The Disney-MGM Studios is the home to many highly popular attractions and shows suitable for the entire family. The theme park portion of this complex, where the rides and attractions are located, was inspired by the Golden Age of Hollywood.

The Studios opened to the public in 1989. Since then, millions of tourists, not to mention hundreds of the world's most famous celebrities, have visited this working studio facility/theme park. Even on the busiest of days, you should be able to see most of the shows and attractions, plus experience most (if not all) of the rides and tours that are of interest to you and your family, during one full day at The Disney-MGM Studios.

Getting to the Studios

If you're arriving at the studios by car, you'll want to park in the specified lot, which costs $7 per day for non-WDW Resort hotel guests. Guests of WDW Resort hotels who are already paying for parking at their hotel receive free parking at the studios. Once you pay for parking, you're allowed to exit the parking lot during the day, and re-enter later that day at no charge. Since this parking lot is huge, be sure to write down the exact location where your car is parked, and then take the free tram to the park's entrance. If you arrive midday and the parking lot is full, proceed to the nearby Dolphin or Swan hotel and take the water shuttle to the Studios.

A free water launch from several WDW Resort hotels, including the Dolphin, Swan, Yacht Club, Beach Club, and BoardWalk, goes directly to the studio's entrance. The boats go back and forth throughout the day and are the quickest way to reach the studios from the above-mentioned hotels.

Those coming from The Magic Kingdom, Epcot, and all other WDW resorts, take the specially marked WDW bus directly to the Studios. Guests traveling to this park from the Fort Wilderness Hotel, the Disney Village Marketplace, or Pleasure Island must take a WDW bus to the Transportation and Ticket Center, and then switch buses to get to the Studios.

═FAST FACT

Admission to The Disney-MGM Studios requires a ticket. For details about the various ticket and pricing options for visiting this theme park, and all of the theme parks within The WDW Resort, see Chapter 3.

Same Day Re-entry

As you leave The Disney-MGM Studios, be sure to have your hand stamped as you exit in order to be granted readmission into the park later that day or evening. In addition to the hand stamp, be sure to retain your ticket stub. The hand stamps are designed to be water-resistant, so don't worry if your hand gets wet if you choose to return to your hotel in the middle of the day to go swimming, and then want to return to the Studios later that evening. Try to refrain, however, from scrubbing your hands clean with soap until your day's visit to the studios is complete.

Hours of Operation

The Disney-MGM Studios are open seven days per week, typically from 9:00 A.M. to 7:00 P.M. During the summertime and on certain holidays and peak periods, the Studios remain open later. To determine the hours of operation on the date(s) you're planning to visit the park, call ☎(407) 824-4321.

What to Bring

Make sure you wear comfortable shoes! Depending on the weather, you might want to take along a jacket (you can always store it in a locker). Try to avoid carrying too much stuff with you. You'll enjoy your visit more if your hands are as free as possible.

Don't forget to bring your camera, along with plenty of film and batteries. The Disney-MGM Studios is a working motion picture and television studio, so you might run into some popular celebrities as well as your favorite Disney characters. Avoid having to purchase high-priced film, batteries, or camera supplies in the park.

💼 TRAVEL TIP

In case of rain, plan on getting a bit wet. Wear a raincoat or plan to purchase a Mickey Mouse poncho. Avoid bringing an umbrella into the park. You'll find it frustrating trying to walk around the crowded park with an open umbrella. For an up-to-the-minute weather report for the Orlando area, call ☎(407) 824-4104.

The Tip Board

Located at the junction of Hollywood and Sunset Boulevard is the Studios Tip Board. This information board lists the current wait times for all of the major attractions in the Disney-MGM Studios. Stationed at this board is a Disney cast member who is in constant contact with the operators of all of the park's major attractions. Accurate wait times for each ride are posted, so you can better plan your day. Show and parade times are also available at this location. The very best time to visit the park and not have to deal with huge crowds is on Sunday morning.

As a general rule, if you're planning on focusing your attention on experiencing only The Disney-MGM Studios' most popular rides and attractions, it'll take you an average of forty-five minutes per attraction. This, however, depends on how crowded the park is and which attractions and rides you're trying to experience. If you're heading to one popular ride but notice that a line is particularly short for another attraction that you were planning to check out later in the day, adjust your schedule and go where the lines are the shortest.

⊕ HOT SPOT

Oscar's Classic Car Souvenirs, near the park's main entrance, is also the place where you can rent wheelchairs, strollers, or Electronic Convenience Vehicles. Behind this service station, you'll find lockers that can be rented by the day, as well as an ATM, restrooms, a stamp machine, and public telephones.

Another good rule to follow is to always travel against the crowds. For example, many rides and attractions will have two lines. Most people automatically head to the right. You'll probably find that the lines to the left will be shorter.

Choose a Place to Meet

As soon as you arrive at the Studios, choose a place where you'll meet up with the other people in your group if you happen to get separated. Two ideal meeting places are in front of the Mann's Chinese Theater and at the Crossroads to the World (located near the park's main entrance).

🧳 TRAVEL TIP

If you're traveling with children, set some ground rules upon arriving at this park. Instruct them to stay close to you at all times. Young people should know that if they get lost, they should immediately contact any Disney cast member.

The Rating System

To help you choose which rides and attractions are most worth seeing while visiting the Disney-MGM Studios, this book offers star-based ratings for each ride and attraction, based on the age group each will most appeal to. Each ride and attraction has earned between one and three stars.

★   = Rides and attractions that earned just one star aren't worth waiting for and could be skipped, especially if your time within the theme park is limited.

★★   = Rides and attractions that earned two stars are good, but they don't fall into the "must-see" category.

★★★ = The rides and attractions that earned three stars are definitely worth seeing and should not be missed.

N.S. = This denotes rides and attractions that are "Not Suitable" for a specific age group.

The Studios' Rides and Attractions

Like all of the Disney theme parks, there's a lot to see and do at the Disney-MGM Studios. Here's a rundown of what you'll discover as you explore this fun-filled "Hollywood"-themed theme park.

Hollywood Boulevard

As soon as you enter The Disney-MGM Studios, you'll find yourself on Hollywood Boulevard, which is lined with a wide assortment of shops. To add to the overall atmosphere of Hollywood in the 1940s, you'll find an assortment of "Streetmosphere" performers who interact with guests while staying in character. Since the shops on Hollywood Boulevard are open thirty minutes after the park's official closing time, save your shopping for later in the day. The daily character parade goes down Hollywood Boulevard. For parade times, visit the Tip Board.

≡FAST FACT

As you go down Hollywood Boulevard, you can walk to the right and follow Sunset Boulevard, which leads directly to the Tower of Terror 4 and the Rock 'n' Roller Coaster Starring Aerosmith, two of the most popular thrill rides within the park. Along Sunset, you'll also find additional shops, plus the Theater of the Stars, which is the home of the *Beauty and the Beast* stage show.

The Twilight Zone: Tower of Terror 4

Ages 2–4:	N.S.
Ages 5–10:	N.S.
Ages 11–15:	★★★
Ages 16–Adult:	★★★
Senior Citizens:	N.S.

The Hollywood Tower Hotel cost the Walt Disney Company more to build than virtually all of the other WDW Resort hotels, only this one won't ever be used to accommodate living guests. This hotel looks like it's from Hollywood's Golden Age, but that it hasn't been maintained too well over the years. The Hollywood Tower Hotel is where you can experience the Twilight Zone: Tower of Terror 4, which is arguably the most thrilling of thrill rides in all of Walt Disney World.

The attraction starts with a preshow and a brief tour of the hotel. Guests then board the elevator, which is rather unique, because you get to sit down as you ride upward. When you reach one of the top floors, you'll experience some of the most incredible visual special effects you've ever seen. That is, just before you plummet down thirteen floors (157 feet) in what feels like a free fall. The drop lasts about three seconds, but it's very intense. Just when you think the thrill is over after the massive drop, the elevator starts rising upward again, only to drop guests a second time. In fact, there's now a random generator that determines when you drop and how many times the drop occurs during a ride.

To experience Tower of Terror 4, guests must be at least 40 inches tall. This ride is not recommended for anyone with heart or back problems, nor should it be experienced by pregnant women. Whatever you do, avoid eating before experiencing this ride or you'll be sorry. As you take the thirteen-floor drop, a photo will be taken of you, which can be purchased as a souvenir as you leave the hotel.

✔ This is a must-see attraction.

📷 TRAVEL TIP

Within The Disney-MGM Studios, you can utilize FASTPASS at the following rides and attractions: Indiana Jones: Epic Stunt Spectacular, Rock 'n' Roller Coaster Starring Aerosmith, Star Tours, The Twilight Zone: Tower of Terror 4, Voyage of the Little Mermaid, and Who Wants to Be a Millionaire—Play It!

The Great Movie Ride

Ages 2–4:	★★★
Ages 5–10:	★★★
Ages 11–15:	★★★
Ages 16–Adult:	★★★
Senior Citizens:	★★★

"Hooray for Hollywood" is the theme of this twenty-two-minute ride that utilizes over fifty Audio-Animatronic characters to re-create scenes from some of the most famous motion pictures of all time. This ride is located inside the Mann's Chinese Theater. As you're waiting to board the ride, once inside the theater, you'll see many authentic props and costumes from classic movies, and then when the ride begins, the movies will come to life before your eyes as you ride in a vehicle that takes you from scene to scene. The Great Movie Ride is thoroughly entertaining for people of all ages.

✔ This is a must-see attraction.

Jim Henson's Muppet Vision 3D

Ages 2–4:	★★★
Ages 5–10:	★★★
Ages 11–15:	★★★
Ages 16–Adult:	★★★
Senior Citizens:	★★★

Kermit, Miss Piggy, and all of the classic Muppet characters are featured in this attraction's twelve-minute preshow that's followed by a comical and rather bizarre twelve-minute 3D movie. Muppet fans of all ages will truly love this attraction.

✔ This is a must-see attraction.

═FAST FACT

The theater itself was designed for this show, and it looks a lot like the set from *The Muppet Show* television series. During the movie, the theater itself actually becomes part of the show.

Star Tours

Ages 2–4:	N.S.
Ages 5–10:	★★★
Ages 11–15:	★★★
Ages 16–Adult:	★★★
Senior Citizens:	★★

What happens when you combine the creative talent of Disney's Imagineers with the imagination of George Lucas? The result in this case is Star Tours, a ride that's based on the original *Star Wars* movies and features characters like R2-D2 and C3-PO. As an intergalactic tourist, you and thirty-nine other guests will board a StarSpeeder and experience a whirlwind tour of the galaxy. Using flight-simulator technology, the StarSpeeder is on hydraulics and is perfectly synchronized with the movie you'll be watching on the ship's main view screen.

The overall effect is that you'll feel like you're actually traveling at ultrafast speed through space, when, in reality, your StarSpeeder is only a few feet off the ground. Star Tours is a fast-paced and tur- bulent roller-coaster-like ride with a *Star Wars* twist. Be prepared for a long wait to ride this attraction, but while you're waiting to board the StarSpeeder, you'll be entertained by an elaborate preshow that includes Audio-Animatronic characters from the *Star Wars* movies and video monitors that feature Star Tours travel infor- mation.

This ride is suitable for people of all ages, except very young children (under the age of three) and people who suffer from back problems, heart conditions, motion sickness, et cetera. Once you board the StarSpeeder, stow all of your loose clothing, purse, camera bag, et cetera, and fasten your seatbelt. This ride is bumpy, but not scary. The best time to ride this attraction is late in the evening. If the line for this ride doesn't go outside of the building, the wait will be less than twenty minutes.

✔ This is a must-see attraction.

"Honey, I Shrunk the Kids" Movie Set Adventure

Ages 2–4:	N.S.
Ages 5–10:	★★★
Ages 11–15:	★★★
Ages 16–Adult:	N.S.
Senior Citizens:	N.S.

This outdoor playground looks like a scene from the popular live-action Disney movie, *Honey, I Shrunk the Kids*, because everything is extremely over- sized, making young guests feel incred- ibly small as they climb, crawl, jump, and slide around. This attraction offers adults a chance to sit down and relax, while the children have fun exploring this playground.

Voyage of the Little Mermaid

Ages 2–4:	★★
Ages 5–10:	★★★
Ages 11–15:	★★★
Ages 16–Adult:	★★★
Senior Citizens:	★★★

Here's an exciting opportunity to go under the sea without ever getting wet. Voyage of the Little Mermaid is an extremely innovative live show that features costumed characters and unique life-size puppets, along with special effects. Scenes from the animated Disney movie *The Little Mermaid* are re-created. This is an extremely popular attraction, especially among kids, so be prepared to wait up to one hour to experience this show. Be sure to take advantage of FASTPASS to cut your wait time. Very young children might get scared by some of the special effects used during the seventeen-minute show.

✔ This is a must-see attraction.

⊕ HOT SPOT

Located on the cement ground in front of the Mann's Chinese Theater, the home of the Great Movie Ride, are actual hand imprints, and in some cases, foot imprints, from real-life celebrities who have visited the Disney-MGM Studios since 1989. Spend a few minutes to check out which stars have left their permanent mark imprinted in the sidewalk.

Indiana Jones Epic Stunt Spectacular!

Ages 2–4:	★
Ages 5–10:	★★
Ages 11–15:	★★★
Ages 16–Adult:	★★★
Senior Citizens:	★★★

This live-action stunt show was choreographed by Glenn Randall, who was the stunt coordinator for all of the *Indiana Jones* movies. While you won't see Harrison Ford, you will see talented stuntpeople re-create scenes from this movie series. Fireworks, explosions, and other special effects are used to add extra drama to this exciting show.

The Indiana Jones Epic Stunt Spectacular is presented several times throughout the day (show times are listed in front of the theater and at the Tip Board). About 2,000 people fit into the theater, so if you arrive between fifteen and thirty minutes early, you're virtually guaranteed a seat for this high-action thirty-minute show. A few brave guests are selected at the start of each show to be "extras." Not only do audience members get to see dozens of stunts performed, they also learn how stunts are actually performed in movies so that nobody gets injured.

Stunt Show Spectacular (Opening in 2005)

Ages 2–4:	N.S.
Ages 5–10:	★★★
Ages 11–15:	★★★
Ages 16–Adult:	★★★
Senior Citizens:	★★

In 2005, Stunt Show Spectacular will make its debut at The Disney-MGM Studios. This high-action live show, inspired by a similar show now seen at Disneyland Paris, will feature specially designed cars, motorcycles, and jet skis, plus tons of special effects. The show is visually spectacular, and audience members will discover how those exciting car chases and collision scenes seen in movies and on TV are actually created and filmed. Highly skilled stunt drivers show off their skills throughout each performance. There will be some audience participation involved with this exciting show.

Beauty and the Beast

Ages 2–4:	★★
Ages 5–10:	★★★
Ages 11–15:	★★★
Ages 16–Adult:	★★★
Senior Citizens:	★★★

After Disney's *Beauty and the Beast* animated movie was released and became an instant classic, a live adaptation of this movie was created for guests of the Disney-MGM Studios. This thirty-minute live-action performance stars actors and costumed characters. The show re-creates several scenes from the movie.

This show inspired the hit Broadway musical and is presented several times throughout each day. Show times are displayed in front of the theater and at the Tip Board. While the theater holds more than 1,500 people, be sure to arrive between fifteen and thirty minutes early to get the best seats (depending on how crowded the Studios are on the day of your visit).

Starting fifteen minutes before the scheduled show time, audience members are treated to an upbeat, comical, and truly entertaining musical performance by a four-man singing group, called Four for a Dollar. The group performs a medley of popular hits, like *Love Potion Number Nine*.

Sorcery in the Sky Fireworks Spectacular

Ages 2–4:	★
Ages 5–10:	★★★
Ages 11–15:	★★★
Ages 16–Adult:	★★★
Senior Citizens:	★★★

This incredible fireworks presentation is shown at night, but only during WDW's peak seasons (during the holidays and during certain times in the summer). The fireworks are launched from above the Mann's Chinese Theater, so the best viewing location is from Hollywood Boulevard, in front of the Mann's Chinese Theater. When you're facing the theater, the clearing to the left is an excellent viewing location.

All of the fireworks are choreographed to music from *Fantasia* as well as other classic Disney films. The entire show lasts about ten exciting minutes.

✔ This is a must-see attraction.

📋 TRAVEL TIP

Check with the Tip Board for the exact show times, and be sure to stake out your viewing spot between thirty minutes and one hour early. (You want an unobstructed view looking over the Mann's Chinese Theater.)

Fantasmic!

Ages 2–4:	★★
Ages 5–10:	★★★
Ages 11–15:	★★★
Ages 16–Adult:	★★★
Senior Citizens:	★★★

Adapted from the highly popular show that was originally created for Disneyland, this nighttime spectacle combines lasers, special effects, dancing waters, fiber optic effects, classic Disney animated movie footage, Disney characters, a cast of over fifty performers, and plenty of Disney music. This is all choreographed perfectly into a twenty-five-minute performance that you'll remember forever. This is perhaps the most spectacular show at The WDW Resort. Fantasmic! should not be missed. Fantasmic! is extremely popular, but the capacity of the outdoor theater is limited. To stake out a good location and ensure you'll get a seat, plan to arrive at least one hour early for the performance.

To combine a memorable dinner with the memorable performance of Fantasmic!, consider taking advantage of the park's "Fantasmic! Dining Experience." After enjoying a full dinner at the Hollywood Brown Derby, Mama Melrose's Ristorante Italiano, or Hollywood & Vine, you'll receive a voucher that guarantees seating for that evening's Fantasmic! performance. The dinner/show combo is priced between $19.99 and $36 per adult and $9.99 for kids (ages three to eleven). Admission to the park is still required and only a limited number of dinner packages are available per day. Visit the Guest Information Board at Hollywood Junction to make your reservation as early in the day as possible.

✔ This is a must-see attraction.

Rock 'n' Roller Coaster Starring Aerosmith

Ages 2–4:	N.S.
Ages 5–10:	N.S.
Ages 11–15:	★★★
Ages 16–Adult:	★★★
Senior Citizens:	★

The latest ride added to the Disney-MGM Studios is a state-of-the-art roller coaster with a musical twist. As you experience this high-speed indoor coaster, 125 speakers will rock your world with Aerosmith music. When this coaster launches, you'll go from zero to 60 miles per hour in under two seconds, but that's just the start of the experience, which offers plenty of unexpected turns, loops, and twists.

The entire experience (including preshow) lasts about ten minutes. Having quickly become one of the most popular attractions at this park, a sixty- to ninety-minute wait for it is typical. To save time, be sure to take advantage of FASTPASS. Riders must be at least 48 inches tall.

⊕ HOT SPOT

The Radio Disney Studios are where several national radio programs originate from. Since these studios feature large glass windows and speakers outside, you can spend a few minutes watching a live radio broadcast take place. You can listen to Radio Disney in Orlando by tuning your radio to AM-990. To find the Radio Disney station in your home city, visit ✑www.RadioDisney.com.

Mickey's Sorcerer's Hat

Ages 2–4:	N.S.
Ages 5–10:	★
Ages 11–15:	★
Ages 16–Adult:	★★
Senior Citizens:	★★

In December 2001, a giant sorcerer's hat (adapted from the hat Mickey Mouse wore in *Fantasia*) was built directly in front of the Mann's Chinese Theater to commemorate Walt Disney's 100th birthday. Using interactive kiosks located behind this giant, 122-foot-tall, 156-ton hat, guests get a peek at events in Disney history. There's also a stage and courtyard area where Disney characters and musical acts appear throughout the day.

Sounds Dangerous—Starring Drew Carey

Ages 2–4:	N.S.
Ages 5–10:	★
Ages 11–15:	★★
Ages 16–Adult:	★★
Senior Citizens:	★★

This interactive show stars comedian Drew Carey and showcases how audio special effects are created for television shows and motion pictures. For this presentation, you're invited to a taping of a fictional television series pilot (that stars Drew Carey). The show lasts about twelve minutes and takes place within an indoor theater (The ABC Sound Studio). Keep in mind, a portion of this comedy show, which focuses on audio, is done in complete darkness. While this isn't meant to be scary, it might not be suitable for very young children.

Disney Stars and Motor Cars Parade

Ages 2–4:	★
Ages 5–10:	★★
Ages 11–15:	★★
Ages 16–Adult:	★★
Senior Citizens:	★★

In this twenty-five-minute daily parade, guests have a chance to see some of Disney's most famous characters as they ride down Hollywood Boulevard in a fleet of custom automobiles. The parade route begins near Star Tours and ends near the Crossroads (at the entrance of the studios). In all, sixty-three Disney characters are featured, along with a handful of Disney-MGM Studios guests who are preselected to participate in this upbeat parade. By sitting along the curb of Hollywood Boulevard, guests will have a chance to interact with some of the characters as they pass by, so have your camera ready.

Who Wants to Be a Millionaire—Play It!

Ages 2–4:	N.S.
Ages 5–10:	★
Ages 11–15:	★★★
Ages 16–Adult:	★★★
Senior Citizens:	★★★

America's attention has been captivated by a television game show that asks a simple question, "Who wants to be a millionaire?" Well, you can watch the syndicated version of the TV game show at home, or you can experience Who Wants to Be a Millionaire—Play It! and be part of the competition and excitement, whether you're sitting in the audience or in the famous "hot seat." As soon as you step into the soundstage that houses this attraction, you'll find yourself sitting in the midst of a faithful re-creation of the *Who Wants to Be a Millionaire?* TV studio set. This attraction allows you to experience what it would be like to watch a taping of the real-life game show. While you won't see TV host Meredith Vieira in-person, a stand-in host does an excellent job keeping audience members and contestants entertained. Every seat in the theater is interactive, which means you can play along. And, if you're quick (and accurate) when it comes to providing answers, you may find yourself in the "hot seat" competing for prizes. (Sorry, in this version of the game, no cash is awarded.) The show is presented multiple times throughout the day. See the *Guide Map: Disney-MGM Studios* for show times. Be sure to utilize FASTPASS to save time and avoid a long wait. For more information about the actual TV show, visit this Web site: *www.millionairetv.com.*

✔ This is a must-see attraction.

══FAST FACT

This interactive attraction lasts about thirty minutes and is extremely faithful to the format of the *Who Wants to Be a Millionaire?* TV game show, but with a few minor exceptions that allow the entire "studio audience" to be involved in the game.

Walt Disney: One Man's Dream

Ages 2–4:	N.S.
Ages 5–10:	★
Ages 11–15:	★
Ages 16–Adult:	★★★
Senior Citizens:	★★★

In conjunction with Walt Disney's 100th birthday celebration, which kicked off in December 2001, the Disney-MGM Studios created a self-paced, walk-through exhibit that showcases the life of Walt Disney and pays tribute to his many achievements. This exhibit contains extensive memorabilia from the Walt Disney archives, much of which has never been displayed to the public before.

According to Disney Imagineer Roger Holzberg, the senior show producer/director of this attraction, "When we were researching the attraction, we found that many of our guests under the age of fifteen did not know Walt Disney was a real person. They thought it was just a company name."

Walt Disney: One Man's Dream features a short film of Walt Disney's life that explores the extraordinary hardships he overcame. "He is an individual, not an icon," added Holzberg. "This tells the story of Walt the man, and we hope that guests will be moved by the scope of his imagination, what he accomplished, and what he inspired."

Anyone who truly appreciates the accomplishments of Walt Disney as a television and motion picture producer, animator, and theme park creator will enjoy this museum-like exhibit, which is not particularly kid-oriented. The entire experience lasts about twenty-five minutes and is entirely indoors.

Playhouse Disney—Live on Stage!

Ages 2–4:	★★★
Ages 5–10:	★★★
Ages 11–15:	★
Ages 16–Adult:	★
Senior Citizens:	★

Designed specifically for the under-ten crowd that watches *Playhouse Disney* on The Disney Channel, this live musical show features characters from *Jim Henson's Bear in the Big Blue House*, *Rolie Polie Olie*, *Stanley*, and stars from *The Book of Pooh*. This is a fun twenty-minute show that's colorful, upbeat, and will provide plenty of entertainment for kids (especially those familiar with the characters from the various TV shows on The Disney Channel). If you're traveling with young kids, this adorable show should not be missed!

On days when the park is crowded, be sure to arrive at the theater at least twenty to thirty minutes prior to the posted show time. To ensure that kids, in particular, get the best view of the action, all audience members sit on a carpeted floor within the air-conditioned theater.

✔ This is a must-see attraction.

═FAST FACT

Multiple shows are presented throughout the day. Check the *Guide Map: Disney-MGM Studios* for show times.

The Osborne Family Spectacle of Lights

Ages 2–4:	★★★
Ages 5–10:	★★★
Ages 11–15:	★★★
Ages 16–Adult:	★★★
Senior Citizens:	★★★

Between late November and early January each year, the Disney-MGM Studios celebrate the holiday season by transforming the "backlot" area of the working motion picture studio portion of the theme park into a holiday winter wonderland. Opening every evening after dark, this walk-through attraction is absolutely breathtaking and is suitable for the entire family.

One of the primary focal points of this extravagant light display is a 70-foot-tall Christmas tree that's adorned with over 58,000 lights. In all, however, over 350 miles of Christmas lights are used to create this attraction, which requires 800,000 watts of electricity to bring it to life. As you explore this holiday attraction, be on the lookout for the over forty hidden Mickeys that can be found within the decorative display. Even if you don't celebrate Christmas, this attraction is still worth experiencing.

✔ This is a must-see attraction.

⊕ HOT SPOT

At several times throughout each day, you can meet Mickey, Minnie, and other popular Disney characters in front of Mickey's Sorcerer's Hat (at the end of Hollywood Blvd.). Throughout the day, you can also often spot Mickey Mouse along Mickey Avenue, Lilo & Stitch near the Magic of Disney Animation pavilion, and characters from Toy Story in front of Al's Toy Barn. Check the *Guide Map: Disney-MGM Studios* booklet for exact character appearance times.

The Disney-MGM Studios Backlot Tour

One of the things that makes a trip to the Disney-MGM Studios so special is that you actually have the opportunity to visit a motion picture, television, and animation studio, where movies and television programs are being produced. The actual studios can be seen by taking either of the two main tours that are available throughout the day.

The Magic of Disney Animation

Ages 2–4:	N.S.
Ages 5–10:	★
Ages 11–15:	★★★
Ages 16–Adult:	★★★
Senior Citizens:	★★★

While not an attraction per se, this thirty-five-minute movie/tour combination offers guests a walking tour of the working Disney Animation Studios facility in Orlando. Not only will you learn how animated movies and television shows are created, but you'll also see animation artwork and have a chance to see actual animators at work. The best time to experience this tour is on a weekday, during business hours (because that's when the animators will be working).

Disney's *Mulan* and *Lilo & Stitch* are the only full-length animated features so far to be produced entirely at the Orlando animation facility, although the animators here contributed to *The Lion*

King, Aladdin, Pocahontas, Beauty and the Beast, and *The Hunchback of Notre Dame,* along with other, more recent, films. Chances are you'll get a chance to see many of the animators who worked on these movies, plus get a sneak peak at future animation projects that Walt Disney Animation is working on.

✔ This is a must-see attraction.

The Studio Backlot Tour

Ages 2–4:	★
Ages 5–10:	★★
Ages 11–15:	★★★
Ages 16–Adult:	★★★
Senior Citizens:	★★★

When guests participate in this tour, they'll ride in trams that take them on a thirty-five-minute tour of the Disney-MGM Studios production facilities (a.k.a. the Backlot). Although the Disney-MGM Studios are rarely still used to film live-action TV shows and movies, you'll see movie sets, outdoor "facades," as well as soundstages where movies and TV shows are filmed. You'll also see the studio's wardrobe/costume facility, plus get a chance to see costumes from classic movies. Along the tram tour, you can expect a few surprises as well, like the Special Effects Water Tank show. In 2004, this tour is being revamped slightly as the backlot area gets expanded to include new cityscapes, including Chicago and San Francisco.

═FAST FACT

This is a working television studio. Some of the shows that have been produced here include *The New Mickey Mouse Club, Sheena, Full House, Wheel of Fortune, World Championship Wrestling, ESPN College Football Awards, Talk Soup, Step by Step, Barbara Walters Special,* and *Live! With Regis & Kathie Lee.*

For anyone interested in a behind-the-scenes look at how movies are made, this tour offers this and more. Tours are given throughout the day. Check with the Tip Board for departure times.

Dining at the Disney-MGM Studios

The following are the dining locations at the Disney-MGM Studios. For full-service restaurants, especially during peak lunch and dinner hours, be sure to make a reservation in advance. To make a restaurant reservation up to sixty days in advance for any full-service restaurant in The Walt Disney World Resort, call ☎(407) WDW-DINE.

For same-day reservations, visit the restaurant of your choice, or stop at the Tip Board. While several of these restaurants offer somewhat fancy atmospheres and are considered fine-dining experiences, casual attire is acceptable. (After all, you're on vacation at a theme park. Throw on your favorite T-shirt and shorts, but don't forget your wallet.)

The Hollywood Brown Derby

This full-service restaurant is a re-creation of the Brown Derby in Hollywood, where some of Hollywood's biggest and most famous stars used to dine. This is one of the very best restaurants located anywhere in The WDW Resort. While it's rather expensive, it's a wonderful place to enjoy lunch or dinner. Reservations are strongly recommended, and a children's menu is available.

The original Brown Derby is where owner Bob Cobb created the now-popular Cobb Salad in the 1930s. Comprising salad greens, bacon, turkey, tomato, egg, avocado, and blue cheese, this is one of the restaurant's most popular dishes. While the lunch and dinner entrees are incredible, just wait until you see what's offered for dessert. The Hollywood Brown Derby is located in the heart of the Disney-MGM Studios, along Hollywood Boulevard, and like the original restaurant, it is a popular dining location for visiting celebrities and dignitaries.

Mama Melrose's Ristorante Italiano

Open for lunch (and dinner during WDW's busy seasons), this Italian restaurant serves pizzas baked in a wood-burning oven.

Seafood, steak, and chicken dishes (grilled on a hardwood charbroiler) are also popular entrees. Although this is one of the Studios' more expensive restaurants, the food is delicious. Reservations are strongly recommended.

50's Prime Time Café

This 1950s-style diner features television monitors located throughout the restaurant (and on the tables) that show black-and-white clips from popular 1950s sitcoms. Instead of serving food on traditional plates, the meals, while cooked fresh, are presented like old-fashioned TV dinners. Hamburgers, turkey burgers, roast beef sandwiches, salads, and other staple diner items can be found on the menu of this theme restaurant, which will appeal to the entire family.

≡FAST FACT

The food here isn't cheap, because you're paying for the atmosphere. A special children's menu is available. In addition to serving lunch and dinner, this is a great place to stop for a snack. Reservations are strongly recommended, or you'll find yourself waiting for a table.

Sci-Fi Dine-In Theater

This full-service theme restaurant simulates a 1950s drive-in movie theater. The tables are in the shapes of popular cars, and fiber-optic special effects are used to simulate stars on the ceiling as guests dine and watch a movie screen that shows continuous science fiction movie trailers and cartoons from the 1950s. Lunch and dinner are served daily, and popcorn is always served as an appetizer. Reservations are strongly recommended.

Fast Food

If you're not looking for a full-service restaurant, the following options are available for lunch, dinner, and snacks throughout the day. These dining locations are considerably less expensive than the above-listed restaurants.

Backlot Express—A fast and inexpensive dining choice at the Studios is the Backlot Express, which also offers counter service and a Hollywood studio theme. Hamburgers, hot dogs, salads, dessert items, fresh fruit, and soda are among the most popular menu selections. Beer and wine are also available.

Commissary—All of the major Hollywood studios offer a commissary, where actors, actresses, and motion picture or television crews can grab a quick bite to eat on the studio lot. What you will find is fast food. Hamburgers, hot dogs, chicken sandwiches, salads, sodas, bottled water, and ice cream are among the menu options.

Dinosaur Gertie's—This snack shop looks like a giant dinosaur located along Echo Lake. What you'll find here is frozen slush in a variety of flavors—the perfect way for your kids to cool down and get a sugar rush on a hot day.

Hollywood & Vine Buffeteria—Serving breakfast, lunch, and dinner, this cafeteria offers a wide selection of inexpensive menu items. As for the décor, you'll find a huge mural depicting Hollywood landmarks such as several major studios.

Min & Bill's Dockside Diner—Soft-serve ice cream and sandwiches are available at this lakeside diner.

Soundstage Restaurant—This is one of the few places in the Disney-MGM Studios where you're virtually guaranteed to see Disney characters and have a chance to meet them, get autographs, and take pictures. You'll have the opportunity to dine at the all-you-can-eat buffet. Chicken, beef, salads, and seafood dishes are usually among the offerings.

Starring Rolls Bakery—This is the perfect place to stop for breakfast if you're on the go and don't want to waste a minute sitting around eating when you could be experiencing a show, ride, or attraction at the Studios. For lunch, a variety of sandwiches (served on freshly baked croissants) are available.

Studio Catering Co.—Snacks and desserts are the specialty of this eating establishment, which you'll come across at the end of the Studio Backlot Tour tram ride. Beer is available here.

Sunset Ranch Market—This area comprises several food stands along Sunset Boulevard (located on the way to the Tower of Terror). Hot dogs; frozen yogurt; popcorn; assorted fresh fruit; and all sorts of soda, juice, and bottled water are available.

Toy Story Pizza Planet—This themed restaurant will remind guests of Disney's *The Toy Story* movie. Individual pizzas are the featured items, although salads, Italian ices, and other snacks are also available.

Shopping at the Studios

While visiting the Studios, chances are you'll want to pick up some souvenirs. Whether you're looking for Disney-themed clothing, collectible Disney animation cells, one-of-a-kind autographed Hollywood memorabilia, or some other gift or souvenir item, chances are you'll find it at one of the shops located within this park. If you're looking for something in particular, but don't know where to find it, call the Disney Merchandise Hotline at ✆(407) 824-5566. A few of the unique gift shops at The Disney-MGM Studios that are worth checking out include:

Animation Gallery—Limited-edition Disney animation cells, original Disney artwork, and other collectibles are available here. This gallery is located in the Animation building. While most of the artwork and collectibles are rather expensive, you can also purchase books and posters. Even if you're not in the buying mood, if you're interested in Disney animation, you'll want to drop into this air-conditioned gallery and enjoy what's on display. A Disney animator/artist is usually on hand to answer questions and to demonstrate how animation cells are created. This gallery will appeal more to adults, Disneyana collectors, and Disney animation fans.

The Darkroom—In addition to being able to rent video camcorders from this shop, you can also purchase Kodak film, batteries, disposable cameras, and just about any photographic accessory you need. Two-hour photo processing is also available from here, as well as from several other shops within the Studios that have a sign to this effect in the window or on the counter.

Mickey's of Hollywood—Logo-imprinted Mickey Mouse, Walt Disney Studios, and Disney-MGM Studios merchandise and clothing are the main thrust of what's offered at this shop.

Planet Hollywood Super Store—Theme dining Hollywood-style is possible only at Planet Hollywood restaurants. The world's largest Planet Hollywood restaurant can be found at Disney's West Side. For souvenirs from Planet Hollywood, however, drop into this popular shop.

Sid Cahuenga's One-of-a-Kind—Out of all the shops within this park, with the exception of the Animation Gallery, only this one offers extremely interesting and unique non-Disney merchandise. What you'll find here are one-of-a-kind autographed photos, posters, and books, plus items once owned by celebrities.

The Writer's Shop—This small shop is a bookstore where the Disney-MGM Studios often hosts well-known authors for special book-signing events. There's also a gourmet coffee kiosk within the shop.

CHAPTER 10

Disney's Animal Kingdom

BY COMBINING THE TALENTS OF ZOOKEEPERS, wildlife experts, and Disney Imagineers from around the world, Disney's Animal Kingdom has become a unique collection of innovative rides, shows, parades, and attractions that combine the thrill of a Disney theme park with the unpredictable excitement of seeing exotic wild animals up close in re-creations of their natural habitats.

Park Overview

Several years ago, the Walt Disney Company set aside 500 acres of The Walt Disney World Resort to create a totally new type of theme park—one that features a lively cast of animals, but that would be unlike any zoo or wildlife sanctuary. Construction of this theme park began in August 1995. Disney's Animal Kingdom is now larger than The Magic Kingdom, Epcot, and the Disney-MGM Studios, and offers what the company calls "a new species of theme park entertainment."

So, what's Disney's Animal Kingdom all about? It's about seeing the animals that live on our planet in a whole new light and learning about them. It's also about fun, exploration, and excitement.

On April 22, 1998, the hard work and dreams of thousands of Disney Imagineers and cast members came to fruition as Disney's Animal Kingdom opened to the public. Here, guests come face-to-face with more than 1,500 animals (representing more than 250 species) in a theme park that only Disney's Imagineers could conceive. Since its grand opening, this park has continued to expand, with new rides, shows, and attractions that you'll learn about in this chapter.

While guests will see Mickey and his pals in the park, Disney's Animal Kingdom is designed to educate as well as entertain, in an environment that is less commercial than The Magic Kingdom. Messages and lessons about wildlife preservation and conservation are intertwined into virtually every experience that guests have while visiting this exciting theme park.

Area Divisions

Located in the center of this theme park is Safari Village, which contains the Tree of Life (a 145-foot masterpiece with 325 animals carved into its trunk). Just like The Magic Kingdom, Disney's Animal Kingdom is divided into areas, which include Discovery Island, Camp Minnie-Mickey, Africa, the Oasis, Rafiki's Planet Watch, Asia, and DinoLand U.S.A. Each of these areas has a totally different theme, yet all involve interaction with animals that are alive, from the past, or from the imagination of Disney's Imagineers.

Throughout this park, you'll find many rides, shows, and attractions suitable for young kids (under age twelve); however, Camp Minnie-Mickey and, more recently, DinoLand U.S.A. have become the kid-oriented areas of this theme park. So, if you're traveling with kids, be sure to allocate extra time for these two areas.

≡FAST FACT

Disney's Animal Kingdom offers beautiful landscaping that includes 600 species of trees, 350 species of grasses, along with 1,800 species of shrubs, vines, ferns, mosses, epiphytes, and perennials. More than 100,000 trees and more than 4 million individual plants, trees, grasses, and shrubs have been planted on the park's 500 acres.

Animal Care

To ensure that the animals living in this theme park are always given the very best care, the Walt Disney Company has hired hundreds of the most prominent animal specialists, curators, animal keepers, veterinarians, and animal behavioral specialists from over 200 leading zoos, educational institutions, and wild animal parks from around the world.

Depending on when you visit Disney's Animal Kingdom and how crowded the park is, you'll easily be able to spend between one and one-and-a-half days experiencing everything this theme park has to offer.

Animal Viewing

As you plan your time at Disney's Animal Kingdom, pace yourself—lots of walking is required. Since some of the park's most popular attractions involve seeing live animals, keep in mind that many of the animals tend to be more active and visible to the public in the mornings and late afternoons when the temperature is cooler. The majority of the animals are allowed to roam freely in their habitats, so at times they may not be visible to guests, simply because they're napping in the shade. Thus, try to experience the live animal attractions early or late in the day.

The very best time to see the animals, especially the ones in the Kilimanjaro Safaris, is when it's cool, overcast, or raining. Obviously, this isn't ideal for vacationers, but the animals tend to come out and be far more visible and lively.

Virtually all of the live animals you'll be seeing at Disney's Animal Kingdom are wild. They have not been trained or domesticated. They are kept in habitats designed to simulate their natural environments as closely as possible. All of the animals are kept on strict diets in order to keep them healthy. Thus, while as a guest at Disney's Animal Kingdom you can purchase all sorts of food and snacks for yourself, it's critical that you do not share your food or beverages with any of the animals, no matter how tempting it might be to toss a few pieces of popcorn, for example, to one of the animals you encounter.

≡FAST FACT

Admission to Disney's Animal Kingdom requires a ticket. For details about the various ticket and pricing options for visiting Disney's Animal Kingdom and all of the theme parks within The WDW Resort, see Chapter 3.

Same Day Re-entry

As you leave Disney's Animal Kingdom, be sure to have your hand stamped as you exit in order to be granted readmission into the park later that day or evening. In addition to the hand stamp, be sure to retain your ticket stub. The hand stamps are designed to be water-resistant, so don't worry if your hand gets wet if you choose to return to your hotel in the middle of the day to go swimming, and then want to return to Disney's Animal Kingdom later that evening. Try to refrain, however, from scrubbing your hands clean with soap until your day's visit to Disney's Animal Kingdom is complete.

What to Bring

Make sure you wear comfortable shoes, because you'll be doing a tremendous amount of walking! Much of your time will be spent outdoors while visiting this theme park, so depending on the weather, you might also want to take along a jacket (you can always store it in a locker). Sunglasses, a cap (with a visor), and sunblock are also important items to have with you, especially if the weather is sunny.

Try to avoid carrying too much stuff with you. You'll enjoy your visit more if your hands are as free as possible. Don't forget to bring your camera, along with plenty of film and batteries. Avoid having to purchase high-priced film, batteries, or camera supplies in the park.

In case of rain, plan on getting a bit wet. Wear a raincoat or purchase a Mickey Mouse poncho. Avoid bringing an umbrella into the park. You'll find it frustrating trying to walk around the crowded park with an open umbrella. During a rainstorm, crowds will be smaller; however, some outdoor shows and attractions will be closed or cancelled.

The Information Board

Located next to the Creature Comforts shop inside the park is one of the park's Attraction Information Boards. A second board is located outside the Disney Outfitters store, across from the Island Mercantile. These boards list the current wait times for all of the major attractions in Disney's Animal Kingdom, and also list the show times for the various parades and stage performances.

Stationed at each board is a Disney cast member who is in constant contact with the operators of all of the park's major attractions. Accurate wait times for each ride and attraction are posted, so you can better plan your day at Disney's Animal Kingdom. If you have any questions about planning your day at the park, the cast members overseeing the Attraction Information Board will be able to provide answers. Other Disney cast members who are always in the know are those roaming the park carrying walkie-talkies.

The Disney cast members manning the Information Board will be able to assist you in determining how early you should arrive to the shows and how long you'll have to wait for the various attractions, based on how crowded the park is on the day of your visit.

≡FAST FACT

While it's critical that guests refrain from feeding any of the animals that live within Disney's Animal Kingdom (because each animal has a very specialized diet), the team of animal experts that care for the animals feed them over three tons of food per day.

Transportation

Located just outside the main entrance of Disney's Animal Kingdom is a 6,000-car parking lot. There is a daily parking fee if you're not a guest of a WDW Resort hotel. Guests can also be dropped off and picked up right near the park's main entrance when they use the WDW buses. When using the complimentary bus service, plan on spending thirty to sixty minutes each way getting to and from the park from any location within The WDW Resort complex.

Where you'll wait for the bus (outside of the park's main entrance) to take you back to your hotel or to another Disney theme park, there are no nearby benches, telephones, or restrooms, so take advantage of these facilities before leaving the park. You could wind up waiting between twenty and thirty minutes for the right bus to take you where you want to go. The bus stop is, however, covered, so you'll remain pretty sheltered during bad weather.

A faster, but more expensive, mode of transportation for getting to and from Disney's Animal Kingdom is taking a taxi. Guests will, however, ultimately save a tremendous amount of commuting time by renting a car for the duration of their vacation at The WDW Resort. (Renting a car at the Orlando International Airport is cheaper than taking taxis within The WDW Resort and much faster and less frustrating than dealing with the WDW bus.)

Tours

For an additional fee, private and small group tours are available that will give you a special behind-the-scenes look at Disney's Animal Kingdom. These tours are given by people who are extremely knowledgeable about the animals, and are designed for teens and adults. For more information about the tours that are available, call ✆(407) WDW-TOUR. Since the tours are limited to small groups, make your reservations as early as possible.

Mickey's Jammin' Jungle Parade

All of the Disney theme parks are known for their daytime, character-oriented parades. Disney's Animal Kingdom is now the home to Mickey's Jammin' Jungle Parade, a fifteen-minute extravaganza featuring Mickey, Minnie, Rafiki, thirteen other Disney characters, and a cast of over sixty dancers and performers. Complete with an African jungle theme, this parade features original music and a format that encourages guest participation along the parade route. Mickey's Jammin' Jungle Parade is definitely suitable for the entire family.

The parade route begins at the Tusker House Gate at Harambe Village, then winds through Disney's Animal Kingdom (around Discovery Island) and returns to the Tusker House Gate. During the parade, it becomes extremely difficult for guests to leave the theme park (because the parade route blocks the entrance/exit), so plan your exit accordingly. Also, be prepared for large groups of people to leave the park immediately after this parade.

📖 TRAVEL TIP

For parade times, see the *Guide Map: Disney's Animal Kingdom*. If the parade is being held around sunset, be sure the spot you choose to watch the parade is away from the setting sun. You don't want to be watching the oncoming parade and staring directly into the sun. If you're taking pictures during the parade, remember that Mickey makes an appearance on the last float.

The Disney Wildlife Conservation Fund

While many people believe that some of Disney's theme parks and attractions are overly commercial, the underlying theme of the rides, shows, and attractions at Disney's Animal Kingdom is to promote the conservation of animal habitats around the world. The Disney Wildlife Conservation Fund promotes global wildlife conservation by working directly with scientists, educators, and organizations that are committed to preserving Earth's biodiversity.

The Disney Wildlife Conservation Fund provides financial support and resources to over 200 programs in over twenty-four different countries. To help raise money and awareness for this fund, each of the gift shops located in Disney's Animal Kingdom encourages guests to make a $1 donation to the fund when they make a purchase. All of the contributions are combined with the funds of the Walt Disney Company Foundation and are distributed to the wildlife conservation programs that the Disney Wildlife Conservation Fund supports. To obtain a list of these organizations, write to: The Disney Wildlife Conservation Fund c/o Conservation Initiatives, Walt Disney World Co., P.O. Box 10,000, Lake Buena Vista, Florida 32830.

🧳 TRAVEL TIP

To save money when dining at Disney's Animal Kingdom, consider purchasing the "Meal Plus Certificate." Priced at $11.99 (adults) and $5.99 (kids), this certificate can be redeemed at several of the park's dining establishments for one entrée and beverage. You'll also receive coupons that can be redeemed later in the day anywhere in the park for one popcorn or ice cream, plus one bottled soda or water. (When purchased separately, the price of an ice cream is $2.50, a box of popcorn is $2.75, and a bottled soda or water is $2.50.)

The Rating System

To help you choose which rides and attractions are most worth seeing while visiting Disney's Animal Kingdom, this book offers star-based ratings for each ride and attraction based on the age group each will most appeal to. Each ride and attraction has earned between one and three stars.

★   = Rides and attractions that earned just one star aren't worth waiting for and could be skipped, especially if your time within the theme park is limited.

★★   = Rides and attractions that earned two stars are good, but they don't fall into the "must-see" category.

★★★ = The rides and attractions that earned three stars are definitely worth seeing and should not be missed.

N.S.   = This denotes rides and attractions that are "Not Suitable" for a specific age group.

≡FAST FACT

Walt Disney's love for animals began when he was four years old. His family moved from Chicago to a 45-acre farm in Marceline, Missouri. Growing up, Walt helped to care for the animals on the farm and learned how to draw them.

The Oasis

The Oasis is a park area that separates Entrance Plaza from the rest of the Animal Kingdom. As you walk through this area, you'll see exotic plants as well as colorful birds in the trees. It's about a three-minute walk from the main entrance to Discovery Island.

Discovery Island

This island is the hub from which you'll depart on your animal-based adventures. The centerpiece of this island is the Tree of Life, which is the home of It's Tough to Be a Bug! On this island, you'll experience live entertainment, see exotic birds and wildlife, and get a preview of what this park is all about.

The Tree of Life

Not only is the Tree of Life the centerpiece of Disney's Animal Kingdom, it's also a stunning work of art. A picture of the people you're traveling with standing in front of this tree will make the perfect addition to your vacation photo album.

Here's the scoop on this manmade masterpiece:

Animal Carvings: 325 animals

Chief Sculptor: Zsolt Hormay and a team of three Native American artists, plus artists from France, Ireland, Indianapolis, and Central Florida. It took eighteen months to create the carvings on the Tree of Life.

Height: 145 feet (14 stories tall)

Number of Branches: 8,000

Number of Leaves: 103,000

Trunk Width: 50 feet

Width at Root Base: 170 feet

The Tree of Life Garden

Pathways have been created throughout Safari Village so guests can wander around and enjoy the landscaping and wildlife.

It's Tough to Be a Bug!

Ages 2–4:	★
Ages 5–10:	★★★
Ages 11–15:	★★★
Ages 16–Adult:	★★★
Senior Citizens:	★★★

When you enter the theater (located in the trunk of the Tree of Life), you become an honorary bug and begin to see the world from a bug's point of view. Not only is this a 3D movie with incredibly lifelike special effects, but the entire theater becomes part of the adventure, so expect to see, hear, and feel what's happening. Remember, the best seats are in the sixth or seventh row close to the center. As you enter the theater, you'll be given a pair of 3D glasses. Don't put the glasses over your eyes until you're seated and the Audio-

Animatronic character who hosts the show (a bug, of course) tells you to put on the glasses.

The theater holds 430 guests and shows are presented continuously throughout the day. This is, however, one of the most popular attractions in the park, so be prepared to wait in line. It's Tough to Be a Bug! appeals to people of all ages, whether they like real-life bugs or not. Like all of the attractions at Disney's Animal Kingdom, this one has a positive message. Let's just say you'll think twice before zapping a bug with a can of bug spray or a fly swatter when you get home. Because this 3D movie takes place within a custom-built theater that's interactive, young children (under the age of eight) may get frightened by some of the special effects.

✔ This is a must-see attraction.

⊕ HOT SPOT

Throughout the day, bands and other forms of live entertainment perform at various locations around Safari Village. Kick back, relax, and enjoy the show!

Africa

Just in case you haven't yet traveled to Africa and experienced a real-life safari, Disney has brought Africa to Orlando. Everyone from the performers to the cast members will be dressed in African fashions, while the architecture and atmosphere in this area of the park are all authentically African.

Harambe

This area is designed to replicate a port in East Africa. The restaurants, shops, and entertainment all help guests feel like they've traveled across the world.

Kilimanjaro Safaris

Ages 2–4:	★★
Ages 5–10:	★★★
Ages 11–15:	★★★
Ages 16–Adult:	★★★
Senior Citizens:	★★★

You came to Disney's Animal Kingdom to see animals, and that's exactly what you'll see when you experience this safari ride. You'll ride on a thirty-two-passenger camouflage safari truck with a tour guide as this true-life adventure unfolds on more than 100 acres of savanna, rivers, and rocky hills. Antelope, giraffes, zebras, baboons, rhinos, elephants, crocodiles, lions, hippos, and other animals roam freely. As a result, what you see and where and when you see it will be different every time you experience this tour.

Some of the animals will come within a few feet of your vehicle. The best time to experience Kilimanjaro Safaris is in the morning or late afternoon, because that's when the animals are most active. During the hottest times of the day, many of the animals take naps in the shade. As you see the animals, the tour guide talks about animal poachers and how some species of animals are becoming extinct. Throughout this ride, keep your camera ready. There's no telling when a perfect photo opportunity will happen.

Throughout the safari, you'll see many different animals, so don't use up all of your film early on. Kilimanjaro Safaris will appeal to people of all ages and is one of this park's very best and most popular attractions. It shouldn't be missed! Each time you visit this safari, your experience will be different, because you'll see different animals and sites. Thus, if you have time to experience the Kilimanjaro Safaris twice during your visit, it's well worth it.

✔ This is a must-see attraction.

💼 TRAVEL TIP

To save time waiting in line for Kilimanjaro Safaris, be sure to take advantage of FASTPASS.

Pangani Forest Exploration Trail

Ages 2–4:	★★
Ages 5–10:	★★★
Ages 11–15:	★★★
Ages 16–Adult:	★★★
Senior Citizens:	★★★

Take a walking tour through a parklike environment and see a troop of gorillas, colorful African birds, and even a few hippos. You can walk through this area at your own pace, so the lines are usually minimal. On hand near each of the exhibits are experts who will answer questions about the animals. About halfway through this exhibit is a small building that contains computers that guests can use to learn more about naked mole rats (also on exhibit within this building). As you make your way through the Pangani Forest Exploration Trail, be sure to look up into the trees to see about thirty-five different species of exotic birds.

Wildlife Express to Conservation Station

Ages 2–4:	★
Ages 5–10:	★★
Ages 11–15:	★★★
Ages 16–Adult:	★★★
Senior Citizens:	★★

A short train ride takes you partway through the 100-acre savanna, where you'll catch glimpses of some of the same animals you'll see on the Kilimanjaro Safaris. You'll also see some of the buildings where the animals are kept at night. Your destination is Disney's Conservation Station, where animals are cared for. As you ride the train, keep your camera handy. There are some excellent photo opportunities along the way.

There may be a wait to board and ride the train to and from Conservation Station, but once you're there, you can roam freely and see things at your own pace. Thus, the waits to see the various attractions and exhibits at Conservation Station are kept to a minimum. The round-trip train ride to and from Conservation Station is 1.2 miles long.

⊕ HOT SPOT

Disney "Streetmosphere" performers take on the roles of Harambe citizens who are very pleased to have you as a guest in their African village. Guests are invited to interact with the citizens of Harambe while enjoying the live musical performances from an African contemporary band.

DinoLand U.S.A.

This area of Disney's Animal Kingdom is somewhat kid-oriented; however, it's here that you'll find the most exciting thrill ride in the park, which is far more suitable for teens and adults than it is for young kids. In this area, you'll also see life-size replicas of dinosaur skeletons and discover how fossils are found and prepared for display.

Anyone who is fascinated by dinosaurs will want to explore DinoLand U.S.A., which is sponsored by McDonald's. In this case, you'll see some innovative, educational, and highly entertaining attractions, shows, exhibits, and rides. The best time to check out this area is in the morning when the park opens.

DINOSAUR!

Ages 2–4:	N.S.
Ages 5–10:	★★
Ages 11–15:	★★★
Ages 16–Adult:	★★★
Senior Citizens:	★

This is a highly turbulent ride that takes you back in time to see a group of life-size, very realistic, Audio-Animatronic dinos. After watching a preshow movie, you'll climb aboard a twelve-person vehicle that'll transport you back to prehistoric times. Much of the ride itself takes place in dark surroundings as the vehicles follow an extremely bumpy track and travel at high speeds. Thus, young children may find it scary and senior citizens may find it too turbulent. As for everyone else, this is an awesome ride with spectacular special effects.

For the most thrilling ride, as you climb aboard your vehicle, try to grab a seat that's in the back row and on the left side of the vehicle. Be sure to safely stow loose items like hats, purses, and cameras in the seat pockets in front of you before the ride begins.

✔ This is a must-see attraction.

The Boneyard

Ages 2–4:	★★★
Ages 5–10:	★★★
Ages 11–15:	★★
Ages 16–Adult:	N.S.
Senior Citizens:	N.S.

Designed for young people, the Boneyard offers a preview of what it's like to be an archeologist or paleontologist. Best described as a huge sandbox, in this attraction, young guests get to dig for dino bones.

Cretaceous Trail

Guests of all ages can take a walking tour (at their own pace) and explore an outdoor exhibit of plants and animals that have survived on this planet since the days of the dinosaurs.

Tarzan Rocks!

Ages 2–4:	★★★
Ages 5–10:	★★★
Ages 11–15:	★★
Ages 16–Adult:	★
Senior Citizens:	★

One of Disney's recent animated films comes to life on stage during this fun-filled musical. Swing your way right into a rockin' show that's definitely on the wild side and of particular interest to kids. The show is filled with all kinds of extreme stunts and live music from the film's soundtrack. Tarzan Rocks! takes place several times throughout the day within the 1,500-seat Theatre in the Wild (found near DinoLand U.S.A.). For the best seats, arrive between fifteen and thirty minutes prior to show time. This is an excellent family-oriented show.

TriceraTop Spin

Ages 2–4:	★★
Ages 5–10:	★★★
Ages 11–15:	★★★
Ages 16–Adult:	★
Senior Citizens:	★

Up to four guests ride in triceratops-shaped vehicles that rise and tilt as they spin around a giant top while cartoon comets whiz past and playful dinosaurs pop up. This ride is very much like Dumbo the Flying Elephant (a popular kids' ride found within The Magic Kingdom's Fantasyland); however, instead of being shaped like an elephant, the vehicles resemble dinosaurs.

Primeval Whirl

Ages 2–4:	N.S.
Ages 5–10:	★★★
Ages 11–15:	★★★
Ages 16–Adult:	★★
Senior Citizens:	★

This kid-oriented roller coaster features free-spinning cars that travel along a twisting track of tight loops and short drops. It's designed to offer a mild thrill-ride experience for children and adults alike. Riders must be at least 48 inches tall. Due to the ride's excessive spinning, it's a wise idea to experience this attraction before lunch. To save time, take advantage of FASTPASS to experience this popular ride.

✔ This is a must-see attraction.

Fossil Fun Games

The Fossil Fun Games area contains TriceraTop Spin and Primeval Whirl!, in addition to a handful of classic carnival games (all of which have a dinosaur twist). Young players can win prizes for playing the carnival games, but there is an additional charge to participate.

Camp Minnie-Mickey

Disney's Animal Kingdom is the largest Disney theme park at The WDW Resort in Orlando, yet it's only in this area of the park where you'll get to meet some of the popular Disney characters, like Mickey and Minnie (dressed in safari attire). This area of the park is also where you'll see several different live shows.

Character Meet-and-Greet Areas

Located across from where *Festival of the Lion King* is presented are several trails that lead to secluded character meeting areas. Get your camera ready, because throughout the day, this is where you and your kids will get to meet Mickey Mouse and his pals up close and in person. Make sure your kids have their autograph books with them, since young people enjoy collecting the signatures of the Disney characters. (Official Disney autograph books are sold at many of the gift shops for about $5.)

Festival of the Lion King

Ages 2–4:	★★★
Ages 5–10:	★★★
Ages 11–15:	★★★
Ages 16–Adult:	★★★
Senior Citizens:	★★★

Out of all the shows and parades featured at Disney's Animal Kingdom and the other Disney theme parks, this one is the best! This live show is presented several times throughout the day, and is one of the most popular attractions at the park for people of all ages (although kids in particular will love this thirty-minute musical show).

The theater in which this show is presented is a covered "fresh-air" amphitheater that holds about 1,000 guests. The seating is on benches that are divided into four sections. All sections offer an equally good view, although if you're traveling with kids, you'll want to sit as close to the front (near the stage) as possible, since as part of the show's finale, kids are invited onto the stage to join the show.

"Festival of the Lion King" features human actors along with costumed characters and Audio-Animatronic characters, and includes nonstop singing and dancing. Several of the popular songs from Disney's *The Lion King* are performed live; however, new music has also been incorporated into this show, which is very different from the animated movie, the Legend of the Lion King

Audio-Animatronic puppet show presented at The Magic Kingdom, and *The Lion King: The Broadway Show* (at the New Amsterdam Theatre on Broadway in New York City).

✔ This is a must-see attraction.

⊕ HOT SPOT

Moving scenery, 136 colorful costumes, and acrobatic circus acts make this a fun-filled show. Since the theater is covered, you'll be out of the Florida sun and have an opportunity to sit down and relax while you're entertained.

Pocahontas and Her Forest Friends

Ages 2–4:	★★★
Ages 5–10:	★★★
Ages 11–15:	★★
Ages 16–Adult:	★
Senior Citizens:	★

Unlike Festival of the Lion King, which features a large cast of characters, this show stars a human actress who portrays Pocahontas; a life-size Audio-Animatronic tree (Grandmother Willow); and several real-life animals. The show, designed primarily for young guests, talks about the importance of preserving the planet's forests and runs about twelve minutes. It is presented throughout the day in an outdoor theater that holds 350 guests. Be sure to arrive at the theater between thirty and forty-five minutes prior to the posted show time in order to ensure yourself a seat for the performance of your choice. No food or beverages are allowed in the theater.

Rafiki's Planet Watch

Especially for young people (age fifteen and under) this area of Disney's Animal Kingdom will encourage education and exploration. The focus is on conservation and protecting our planet and its wildlife. People of all ages, however, will find much of what this area offers to be interesting.

The Conservation Station

This facility combines hands-on displays, live animal displays, and a chance to see some of the park's veterinary facilities, animal nurseries, and even where some of the food for the animals in the park gets prepared. Upon arriving at Conservation Station, guests can roam freely and see everything at their own pace. Plenty of animal experts are on hand to answer questions and conduct various types of demonstrations.

≡FAST FACT

This is one of the most educational areas of Disney's Animal Kingdom. Some of the live animals you'll see include aardvarks, chinchillas, a miniature donkey, great horned owls, porcupines, guinea pigs, and a rock hyrax. Young guests can also pet some of the animals; however, feeding them is strictly prohibited.

Affection Section

Ages 2–4:	★★
Ages 5–10:	★★★
Ages 11–15:	★★
Ages 16–Adult:	★
Senior Citizens:	★

Designed for young children, Affection Section is a petting zoo where guests can get up close to animals, pet them, and have pictures taken with them. Guests are welcome to spend as much time as they'd like in this area and proceed at their own pace. Kids who will be interacting with the animals are encouraged to wash their hands both prior to and after touching the animals. For parents, this area offers wonderful photo opportunities.

Look Backstage!

Ages 2–4:	★
Ages 5–10:	★★
Ages 11–15:	★★
Ages 16–Adult:	★★
Senior Citizens:	★★

Inside the Hall of Animal Care, guests get to see many animal experts, including vets, researchers, and keepers, work with live animals. This is an educational area where the animals are the stars. Animal experts are always on hand to answer questions. One of the favorite parts of this exhibit is the baby mammal nurseries.

⊕ HOT SPOT

There are interactive exhibits that allow guests of all ages to use touch-screen computers to learn more about animals and their habitats.

Asia

This exciting area of Disney's Animal Kingdom features one of the most popular thrill rides in the park—Kali River Rapids: A Whitewater Adventure. In 2006, Expedition EVEREST will also open in this area of the park.

Flights of Wonder at Caravan Stage

Ages 2–4:	★
Ages 5–10:	★★★
Ages 11–15:	★★★
Ages 16–Adult:	★★
Senior Citizens:	★★

Presented several times throughout the day, this live show features human bird handlers and a cast of over twenty species of trained exotic birds from around the world, some of which fly out into the audience. The Caravan Stage is an outdoor theater that holds about 1,250 guests. No food or beverages are allowed in the theater. Be sure to arrive between twenty and thirty minutes prior to a posted show time to guarantee yourself a seat for the performance of your choice.

This show presents a story about a character named Luke who is in search of lost treasures. Kids especially will enjoy this show, although it is entertaining for people of all ages. The show itself lasts about twenty-five minutes.

Kali River Rapids: A Whitewater Adventure

Ages 2–4:	N.S.
Ages 5–10:	★★★
Ages 11–15:	★★★
Ages 16–Adult:	★★★
Senior Citizens:	★

In addition to DINOSAUR!, Kali River Rapids is another thrill ride that's designed for teens and adults. Guests ride in six-passenger rubber rafts and slide down a raging and winding river through rapids and waterfalls. This is definitely one of the most popular attractions at Disney's Animal Kingdom, so be prepared to wait in line to experience it. Also, be prepared to get soaked! (If you're carrying items that aren't waterproof, be sure to store them in lockers, leave them with someone not riding this attraction, or use the watertight storage compartment on the raft.) Guests must be at least 40 inches tall to experience this rather turbulent ride.

✔ This is a must-see attraction.

💼 TRAVEL TIP

To save time waiting in line for Kali River Rapids, be sure to take advantage of FASTPASS. If you have one of the Disney ponchos, be sure to wear it on this ride to help you stay dry. As a bystander, it's possible to shoot water at guests experiencing the ride.

Maharajah Jungle Trek

Here's an opportunity to wander down jungle paths, explore temple ruins, and see some of the world's most exotic and powerful animals—Bengal tigers, Komodo monitor dragons, gibbons, and an assortment of other wild animals that are native to Asia. There are some excellent photo opportunities along this trail.

Expedition EVEREST (Opening 2006)

Ages 2–4:	N.S.
Ages 5–10:	N.S.
Ages 11–15:	★★★
Ages 16–Adult:	★★★
Senior Citizens:	★

If you visit Disney's Animal Kingdom between now and 2006, you'll see a massive construction effort under way behind the Asia area of the park. It's here that Expedition EVEREST is being built.

This will be a high-speed train adventure that combines coaster-like thrills with several surprises. Guests will board an old mountain railway destined for Mount Everest. The train will roll through thick bamboo forests, past thundering waterfalls, and along shimmering glacier fields as it climbs higher and higher through snow-capped peaks.

During the voyage, the thrills will intensify as the train races both forward and backward through mountain caverns and icy canyons as guests head for an inevitable face-to-face encounter with the mysterious yeti—known to some as the abominable snowman.

This 200-foot, high-speed thrill-ride attraction is scheduled to open sometime in 2006 and will no doubt quickly become one of the park's most popular attractions. When it opens, be sure to utilize FASTPASS to save time.

✔ This will be a must-see attraction.

Shopping at the Animal Kingdom

Like all of the Disney theme parks, you'll find many gift shops and souvenir kiosks scattered throughout Disney's Animal Kingdom. Sure, you'll find a wide assortment of Disney's Animal Kingdom logo merchandise, along with plenty of T-shirts, plush toys, and other items featuring Mickey dressed in a safari outfit, but you'll also find a great assortment of non-Disney-based items that make excellent souvenirs or great gifts.

All of the gift shops accept cash, credit cards, checks, traveler's checks, and Disney Dollars, along with your hotel room charge card (your room key, if you're staying at a Disney Resort hotel). The souvenir kiosks and carts accept cash, checks, and traveler's checks only.

Keep in mind that much of the merchandise sold at these shops is available only within this park and can't be purchased at the shops in Downtown Disney, from the Disney Stores, or through the Disney Catalog. You can, however, purchase most items sold exclusively at the park by telephone by calling ✆(407) 363-6200 during business hours. You must, however, know exactly what item(s) you want to purchase and be willing to pay by credit card.

When you make a purchase, you can take your merchandise with you (and carry it around the park), arrange to have it delivered to the park's exit so that you can pick up your purchases on your way out, arrange to have the purchase delivered to your WDW Resort hotel, or, for an additional fee, you can have your purchases shipped anywhere in the world. If you arrange to have your packages delivered to the park's exit, keep in mind that on busy days, it could take up to ninety minutes for your packages to arrive, so plan accordingly. Likewise, if you're having packages shipped, even if you pay FedEx charges, it might take up to several weeks for your purchases to actually get shipped.

Dining at the Animal Kingdom

Like all of the Disney theme parks, Disney's Animal Kingdom offers a selection of fast-food and full-service dining establishments that serve everything from snack foods to full multicourse meals. No matter where you eat within the park, it's not going to be cheap, but if you're hungry, you'll find many different food and drink choices available. Chocolate-covered frozen bananas, one of Disneyland's most popular treats (previously unavailable at the

WDW theme parks), are now available from many of the ice-cream carts throughout Disney's Animal Kingdom.

⊕ HOT SPOT

If you're looking for an animal-themed dining experience where you're surrounded by waterfalls, tropical plants, and an exciting atmosphere for lunch or dinner, you'll want to experience the Rainforest Café, located in Entrance Plaza. A second Rainforest Café is located within Downtown Disney.

CHAPTER 11

Disney's Water Parks

FOR PEOPLE WHO ENJOY THE WATER, THE WDW
Resort offers two full-size water parks that contain various kid- and
family-oriented activities that are water based. So, if visiting one or
more of these water parks is on your vacation itinerary, plan on
packing bathing suits, plenty of sunblock, and beach shoes.

Water Park Information

If you're staying at one of the Disney resorts, you're entitled to take
advantage of the swimming pools and beaches at any of Disney's
resorts. Many of the resorts offer multiple pools, whirlpools, water
slides, and kid-oriented areas. The WDW Resort also offers two
exciting water parks—Blizzard Beach and Typhoon Lagoon—that
have become favorite attractions of families traveling with kids.

Families can easily spend at least one full day at Blizzard Beach
or Typhoon Lagoon. These parks are always busiest in the mornings, so if you have a multiday Park Hopper Plus Pass, plan on
arriving around lunchtime to avoid the heavy morning crowds.
Spend the morning at The Magic Kingdom, Epcot, the Disney-MGM
Studios, or Disney's Animal Kingdom, then cool off at one of the
refreshingly wet and wildly exciting water parks.

For female guests, wearing a one-piece bathing suit is highly
recommended, due to the "rough water" and "waves" you'll be

encountering. These water parks offer family-oriented entertainment with kids and teens in mind.

═FAST FACT

Being able to swim is a prerequisite for some, but not all, of these water-based attractions. Keep in mind, Disney's water parks are either open seasonally or have limited hours during off-peak times of the year.

Hours of Operation

All of these water parks are somewhat seasonal and are open during nice weather only. Typically, the hours of operation are between 10:00 A.M. and 5:00 P.M. (with extended hours during the peak summer months). Be sure to call ✆(407) 824-4321 to ensure that the water parks will be open during your visit and to confirm exact operating hours. All of the water parks can be reached using the WDW Transportation Bus system.

💼 TRAVEL TIP

Disney's Winter Summerland Miniature Golf is located near Blizzard Beach. Families can experience this eighteen-hole miniature golf course with a winter theme for $9.76 per adult and $7.78 per child. If you play a second round of golf on the same day, the second round is half off. You can also purchase money-saving combo tickets for Blizzard Beach and Disney's Winter Summerland Miniature Golf.

Guest Services

At all of the water parks, showers and restrooms are available. Lockers may be rented on a daily basis. Life jackets are available for free, but a $25 refundable deposit is required. Towels can be rented at the various water parks for $1 each, or you can bring your own from your hotel room (but you must also return them to your hotel room at the end of the day).

Admission to the Water Parks

Admission to the three Disney water parks is included in the price of the multiday Park Hopper Plus tickets. You can, however, also purchase one-day admission tickets or annual passes for each of the water parks separately. See Chapter 3 for details. As you'll soon discover, each of the water parks has a totally different theme and a different set of activities and attractions.

Blizzard Beach

Blizzard Beach opened in 1995 and has a winter, ski-slope theme. If a 66-acre ski slope existed in the middle of Orlando, what would happen if all of a sudden the weather went from below freezing to the mid-80s and all of the snow on the mountain started to melt? That's the premise for many of the attractions at Blizzard Beach, which features some of the world's fastest water slides. The attractions include:

Chair Lift—Soar over the face of Mount Gushmore.

Cross Country Creek—If high-speed, turbulent tube rides aren't your thing, you can relax and enjoy a one-mile lazy tube ride around the entire Blizzard Beach park.

Downhill Double Dipper—Ride along a twin tube run and race against others as you travel at speeds of up to 25 miles per hour.

Melt-Away Bay—Take a dip in a one-acre wave pool.

Run-Off Rapids—Ride a tube along flume runs filled with wet and wild surprises.

Ski Patrol Training Camp—This area of Blizzard Beach is designed specifically for preteens.

Slush Gusher—This is a fast-paced and exciting slide experience that sends guests down through a snow-banked gully.

Snow Stormers—A toboggan flume ride.

Summit Plummet—Take a plunge down the world's tallest free-fall speed slide. This is a 120-foot, nearly vertical drop that allows guests to reach speeds of up to 50 miles per hour.

Teamboat Springs—This is the longest and most exciting manmade family white-water raft ride in the world. Groups of people travel down 1,200 feet of twisting rapids while riding in six-passenger tube rafts.

Tike's Peak—This kid-oriented area of Blizzard Beach offers thrill rides that younger kids will enjoy.

Toboggan Racer—Ride on foam toboggan-like sleds along an eight-lane run that goes down a water-slick mountain.

Typhoon Lagoon

When visiting Typhoon Lagoon, guests are asked to imagine a small resort village that just got hit by a typhoon. While if this happened in real life it would be a disaster, when it's done Disney style, the result is a 56-acre water park that offers a splashing good time.

The main Typhoon Lagoon swimming area is a massive wave pool that contains almost 3 million gallons of water. Along the coast of this pool is a sandy white beach. Meanwhile, Castaway Creek is a 2,100-foot-long river that allows guests to enjoy a fun-filled tubing ride that takes them through a series of themed areas.

▐ TRAVEL TIP

Since you'll be outside in direct sunlight, be sure to apply plenty of waterproof sunblock, even in overcast weather conditions. Plan on spending between three hours and an entire day at any of Disney's water parks.

Gangplank Falls, Keelhaul Falls, and Mayday Falls are the thrill rides offered at Typhoon Lagoon. Guests ride on various types of tubes as they plummet down waterfalls and other white-water terrain.

Water slides at Typhoon Lagoon provide for extremely wet and fast-paced experiences that nobody who rides them will soon forget. Humunga Kowabunga is a 214-foot slide that includes a 51-foot drop, allowing guests to travel upward of 30 miles per hour. The Storm Slides are a bit tamer, but not much. These fiberglass slides are 300 feet long and allow guests to slide down at 20 miles per hour.

For some snorkeling fun, check out Shark Reef (snorkeling equipment is provided) and explore a man-made coral reef where you'll come face-to-face with friendly leopard, nurse, and bonnet-head sharks, plus schools of exotic and colorful fish.

Ketchakiddee Creek is a water park unto itself, but it's designed only for people under four feet tall.

⊕ HOT SPOT

Surfers (or wanna-be surfers) can obtain top-notch instruction and then experience two and a half hours of surfing at Typhoon Lagoon before the park opens to the general public. The fee (which includes the instruction) is $125 per person. Reservations are required for this Surfer's Secret package. Call ✆(407) WDW-PLAY.

Other Area Water Parks

In addition to the Disney water parks, if you have access to a rental car, there are several independently owned water parks in the Orlando area that are worth checking out, especially for the young people in your group. There's **Wet 'n Wild** (6200 International Drive, Orlando, ✆407-351-1800, ✇*www.wetnwild.com*) as well as **Water Mania** (6073 West Irlo Bronson Highway, Kissimmee, ✆407-396-2626, ✇*www.watermania-florida.com*).

For people who enjoy scuba diving and would love a chance to swim with dolphins, SeaWorld's Discovery Cove offers a once-in-a-lifetime experience. See Chapter 18 for details.

CHAPTER 12

Disney Nightlife

SO, WHAT'S THERE TO DO AFTER DARK AT THE WDW Resort? Well, for adults, there is an abundance of activities, clubs, shops, and restaurants within the Downtown Disney, Pleasure Island, and Disney's West Side areas. There's also Disney's BoardWalk area, which offers an exciting nightlife for adult vacationers.

Nighttime Entertainment Overview

Downtown Disney has three unique areas: Pleasure Island, the Marketplace, and Disney's West Side. Starting at around 7:00 P.M. and going until 1:00 A.M. (or 2:00 A.M., depending on the season) every night, there's plenty to experience.

While both Downtown Disney and Disney's BoardWalk offer some family-oriented activities, several of the nightclubs are restricted to those over twenty-one years of age, since alcoholic beverages are served. After spending an exciting day at the park with the family, you might consider leaving your young kids with a babysitter and experiencing Disney's nightlife. (See Chapter 3 for child care options.)

Everyone in the family will enjoy exploring the Downtown Disney area in the late afternoon and evening, but after dark, Pleasure Island especially becomes a place designed with adults in mind. If you're visiting The WDW Resort for multiple nights, plan on spending at least one night at Pleasure Island (which has an admission fee) and at least one additional evening/night exploring everything that the Marketplace and Disney's West Side have to offer.

Getting to Downtown Disney

Plenty of free parking is available in front of Disney's West Side, Pleasure Island, and the Marketplace. Valet parking (daily between 5:30 P.M. and 2:00 A.M.) is also available for $7 (free to guests with physical disabilities). Free valet parking is also provided to WDW Resort hotel guests. From anywhere in The WDW Resort, follow the signs to Downtown Disney/Pleasure Island.

Buses run constantly to and from Disney's resort hotels and theme parks to Pleasure Island, the Marketplace, and Disney's West Side areas.

If you're staying at Disney's Dixie Landings, Disney's Old Key West Resort, Disney's Port Orleans, or Disney's Saratoga Springs Resort & Spa, complimentary boat launches are available that drop off and pick up passengers from the docks located at the Marketplace.

For a fee, taxi service is available to take you back to your hotel or anywhere in the Orlando area. Taxis can be hailed at any of the exits of the Downtown Disney area. This, however, is a costly option.

Admission Information and Prices

While there is no charge to shop and explore the Marketplace or Disney's West Side, there is an admission charge to enter Pleasure Island after 7:00 P.M. This admission fee gives you unlimited access (for the night) to all of the area's nightclubs, including:

- Adventurers Club
- BET SoundStage Club
- Comedy Warehouse
- 8Trax

- Mannequins Dance Palace
- Motion
- Pleasure Island Jazz Company
- Rock 'n' Roll Beach Club

You'll also get to see the live entertainment presented outside at the West End Stage, which includes a nightly New Year's Eve cele- bration at midnight that features fireworks. Drinks and food are not included in the admission price. Adult admission to Pleasure Island after 7:00 P.M. is $19.95 per night. An annual pass to Pleasure Island costs $54.95. Admission to Pleasure Island is included with a mul- tiday Park Hopper Plus pass and the WDW Premium Annual Pass.

People under the age of eighteen will not be permitted into Pleasure Island after 7:00 P.M. unless accompanied by a parent or guardian. No alcoholic beverages will be served to anyone under the age of twenty-one. People under the age of twenty-one will not be admitted into Mannequins Dance Palace (and some of the other clubs) under any circumstances. Be prepared to show a valid pass- port, U.S. (or foreign) driver's license with a photo, or a U.S. mili- tary ID to be served alcohol or be admitted into the adults-only clubs.

🧳 TRAVEL TIP

If you're spending three or more days (and nights) at The WDW Resort and plan on returning to Pleasure Island during each of those nights, consider purchasing an annual pass in order to save yourself some cash. A special promotion is also sometimes offered where guests can upgrade their one-night admission ticket to a six-consecutive-night admission ticket for $5 more than the one-day admission price.

Guest Services

A Guest Services office is available at the Marketplace and also inside the AMC 24 Theater building. At various locations within the Downtown Disney area you'll find ATM machines, restrooms (con- taining baby-changing facilities), and public telephones. If any type of first aid is required, contact any Disney cast member for assis- tance. For additional information about the Pleasure Island, Disney's West Side and the Downtown Disney area, call ☎(407) 934-7781.

Dining Reservations

Reservations are recommended for many of the full-service restaurants located in Pleasure Island, the Marketplace, and Disney's West Side. Check with the restaurant of your choice directly, or call ☎(407) WDW-DINE. Without a reservation, be prepared to wait up to two hours to be seated. Most of the full-service restaurants will give you a beeper, allowing you to walk around the area and shop until your table is ready. Reservations for the Rainforest Café at Downtown Disney must be made in person.

≡FAST FACT

Pleasure Island, the Marketplace, and Downtown Disney West Side are all vacation areas, so you're not expected to dress up in formal attire to dine or go dancing; however, some type of shirt and shoes must be worn at all times.

Disney's West Side

There is no charge to visit Disney's West Side. However, there is an admission fee to several of the shows, movies, and attractions. The shops in this area open at 11:00 A.M. daily and remain open until 11:00 P.M. Many of the restaurants serve until midnight.

AMC Theaters

Currently the largest movie theater complex in the Southeast, the AMC 24 Theaters offers twenty-four screens, all showing the hottest new movies in theaters with state-of-the-art sound systems.

Bongos Cuban Café

Gloria Estefan and husband, Emilio, are the owners of this 550-seat family restaurant, which serves authentic Cuban cuisine in a two-story building that's decorated with colorful hand-painted mosaic murals that depict Old World Cuba in the 1940s and 1950s. Seating is available both inside and outside, and live entertainment is presented throughout the night. The main performer each night is Desi Arnaz (well, he's an incredibly talented impersonator who looks and sounds just like the real Desi).

Like all of the full-service restaurants located at The WDW Resort, this one isn't cheap, but the food is delicious! In a typical night, Bongos Cuban Café serves up to 3,000 people. If you're planning to drop in to enjoy the restaurant's three fully stocked bars, plan on paying a $15 cover charge, which includes one drink and plenty of live entertainment and dancing.

Bongos Cuban Café is open daily from 11:00 A.M. to 2:00 A.M. "We specifically created Bongos Cuban Café for the entire family so they may enjoy the festive Cuba that once was—and will be again," said Emilio Estefan.

⊕ HOT SPOT

Designer sunglasses and prescription eyewear are available at Celebrity Eyeworks Studio. Included in this shop's inventory are replicas of sunglasses worn in recent hit films.

Cirque du Soleil: La Nouba

Within the 70,000-square-foot, custom-designed, state-of-the-art theater that's located at the end of Disney's West Side is the permanent U.S. home of Cirque du Soleil. This theater holds 1,650 guests per performance and was designed to actually be part of the show itself.

Cirque du Soleil is a nontraditional French-Canadian circus that includes specialty acts the likes of which you've probably never seen before (even if you've seen a touring Cirque du Soleil show or one of the shows in Las Vegas). Circus acts are mixed with special effects, colorful and unusual costumes, and wonderful music. This is a wonderful, memorable, and breathtaking show for people of all ages.

Two performances are held Tuesday through Saturday evenings at 6:00 P.M. and 9:00 P.M. (There are no performances on Sunday or Monday nights.) The show lasts about ninety minutes and contains no intermission. Ticket prices are $82 or $72 (adults) and $49 or $44 (children, ages three to nine). Tickets can be purchased at the box office located within the theater itself, or by calling ✆(407) 939-7600. This is a popular show, so once you know your travel schedule, reserve your tickets as far in advance as possible, especially during peak travel times. For more information about this highly unique show, visit the Cirque du Soleil Web site at ✐*www. cirquedusoleil.com.*

DisneyQuest

This interactive, high-tech attraction provides fun and exciting entertainment and dining opportunities for the whole family. When guests step into this flashy-looking 100,000-square-foot pavilion, they're taken on a virtual journey to places that could be only dreamed of.

Combining video games, virtual reality, motion simulator rides, and other high-tech forms of entertainment, DisneyQuest is an indoor theme park unto itself that will appeal mainly to teenage guys and younger kids.

Admission to DisneyQuest is included with a multiday Park Hopper Plus ticket or the WDW Premium Annual Pass. Otherwise, there's a per-day entrance fee of $31 (adults) and $25 (children). An annual pass for DisneyQuest can be purchased for $79 (adults) or $63 (children).

Disney's Candy Cauldron

If you're in the mood to sample a wide range of candy and other treats that are guaranteed to satisfy your sweet tooth, drop in to this shop for the perfect snack or after-lunch/dinner dessert.

⊕ HOT SPOT

Cappuccino, espresso, smoothies, juice, and an assortment of other drinks and yummy desserts are available at Forty Thirst Street between 7:00 A.M. and 2:00 A.M. daily.

Guitar Gallery

This is a music shop for serious guitarists and amateur musicians alike. Guitar Gallery offers a wide selection of guitars and accessories from all major manufacturers. You'll also find very rare instruments of interest to serious collectors.

House of Blues

As you've probably guessed, the Downtown Disney complex has become a mecca of themed restaurants. House of Blues serves lunch and dinner daily, between 11:00 A.M. and 2:00 A.M. in the dining room. The BB Blues Bar offers live entertainment and a fully stocked bar that's open every evening.

There's also an official House of Blues merchandise shop attached to the restaurant. In the dining room, authentic Mississippi Delta cooking is served as live blues, R&B, jazz, country, and gospel music are performed nightly. Specialties of the house include jambalaya, etouffee, gumbo, and bread pudding.

The restaurant's concert hall features regular performances by big-name recording artists, so be sure to check the schedule to see who's performing during your stay at The WDW Resort. For concert information, call ✆(407) 934-2222 or on the Internet, visit the House of Blues Web site at ✍*www.hob.com.*

Hoypoloi

This gallery/gift shop offers a large assortment of highly unusual non-Disney gift items, jewelry, and art. Tabletop fountains, wind chimes, mini Zen gardens, and other tastefully displayed items make this an extremely interesting store to browse through, especially for adults.

Magic Masters

Want to amaze and astound your friends and family members? Learn how to perform magic tricks just like a professional magician. This store is staffed by highly skilled magicians who offer demonstrations and perform short magic shows. Even if you don't plan on shopping here, it's a great place to visit for a few minutes if you want to enjoy watching magic tricks and illusions performed right before your eyes.

Magnetron

Magnets, magnets, and more magnets, of every shape, size, and color, are what you'll find at this small shop. Whether you're a collector or someone looking for a new magnet for your refrigerator, you'll find what you're looking for. Even the salespeople have magnetic personalities.

⊕ HOT SPOT

Mickey's Groove is a Disney-owned shop offering an assortment of Disney-themed merchandise, including apparel.

Planet Hollywood

As you approach Disney's West Side, you can't miss seeing Planet Hollywood, the giant globe-shaped restaurant that's jam-packed with Hollywood memorabilia, movie props, posters, photos, costumes, and giant monitors that constantly show music videos and movie clips.

Menu entrees range in price from about $10 to $25 each, and include salads, pizzas, burgers, steaks, pastas, and a wide assortment of desserts. Planet Hollywood also offers a fully stocked bar and nonstop entertainment. The Crunch Chicken appetizer is awesome! This is a great place to go for lunch, dinner, or a late-night dessert.

Dining at Planet Hollywood is an interactive and highly entertaining experience, so be sure to bring your camera. Also, don't be surprised if you run into a popular celebrity or pop star dining right along with you.

Planet Hollywood on Location

In addition to being the home of the world's largest Planet Hollywood restaurant, Disney's West Side also features two Planet Hollywood merchandise shops. This is where you can pick up official Planet Hollywood Orlando and Planet Hollywood America apparel, toys, and other logoed merchandise. You'll discover that some of the limited-edition clothing is endorsed by big-name recording artists and pop groups. To see a preview of the merchandise, visit ✎*www.PlanetHollywood.com.*

⊕ HOT SPOT

Hand-rolled fresh cigars and other smoking accessories are available at Sosa Family Cigars. You'll find a knowledgeable staff on hand to answer your questions and make recommendations.

Starabilias

This unusual antique and collectibles showroom and store allows you to take home valuable pieces of authentic pop culture and history. Whether or not you consider yourself a collector, Starabilias is a fun place for adults and teens to explore.

Here, you'll find genuine items such as an antique Coca-Cola vending machine (which can be yours for $8,995), a 1930s Texaco gas pump (suggested retail price $10,000), and a Ty Cobb–autographed baseball bat (which you can own for $10,000). A wide range of autographed memorabilia from politicians, recording artists, Hollywood's superstars, and historical figures is available.

The inventory of this store changes regularly. In addition to high-priced collectibles, you'll also find a selection of inexpensive toys and collectibles. For a preview of the items you'll find at Starabilias, or to place an order online, you can visit the company's Web site at ✎*www.Starabilias.com.*

Virgin Megastore

Three massive floors in this store offer thousands upon thousands of music CDs, cassettes, videos, laser discs, DVD movies, computer games, video games, magazines, music accessories, and books. There's even a Virgin Megastore café located on the top floor. Throughout this store, you'll find CD-listening stations, computers to try out the hottest new games, and over twenty video/laser stations for previewing movies. Live musical performances, author appearances, and other special events are held regularly at this store.

Wolfgang Puck Café

Spago's is a premier restaurant in Hollywood where the biggest stars go for dinner and to be seen. Owner/chef Wolfgang Puck has also created the California Pizza Kitchen (CPK) restaurants (now located throughout the country), as well as the Wolfgang Puck Cafés. This chain can best be described as an overpriced, albeit extremely trendy, CPK restaurant. Pizzas and California cuisine are what's offered on the menu. A basic four-cheese ten-inch pizza (which will feed one or two people max) is priced at $9.95. Reservations are strongly recommended, so call ☎(407) 939-3463.

Pleasure Island

Most people think of Pleasure Island as a Magic Kingdom for adults who enjoy dancing, drinking, and having fun. Whether you like disco dancing or dancing to the latest hits, there's a dance club at Pleasure Island that'll appeal to you.

There are also clubs that allow you to enjoy comedy shows, live jazz performances, and rhythm and blues music. One flat nightly admission fee gives you unlimited access to all of the clubs within Pleasure Island. (All food and drinks are extra.) In addition to the various nightclubs, Pleasure Island offers carnival-like games and several unique shops, not to mention a nonstop street-party atmosphere that doesn't end until 1:00 A.M. or 2:00 A.M. (depending on the season). Pleasure Island offers "the largest nightly street party on the planet."

═FAST FACT

Every night at 11:45 P.M., live dancers appear on the West End Stage, inviting guests to participate in an outdoor New Year's Eve celebration that's complete with a short fireworks show at exactly midnight. Throughout the night, live music is performed on the West End Stage, while elsewhere (outside) you'll hear a live DJ playing all of the hottest dance music.

8Trax

Disco is back and at 8Trax, you can boogie down to the hottest hits from the 1970s. Disco lights surround the dance floor and fully stocked bar. There are also video monitors located throughout the club that continuously show classic music videos from the disco era. There's always a party atmosphere here as you're taken back in time.

Adventurers Club

Modeled after an adventurers club from the 1930s, this club features live stage shows and actors who roam around (in character) and mingle with the crowds. The humor is a bit dry and rather sophisticated, and the décor of this club is rather unusual. Full bar service is available. This club tends to attract an older (thirty-plus) crowd.

The Comedy Warehouse

One of the funniest thirty to forty minutes you'll spend at The WDW Resort will be at the Comedy Warehouse, where a troupe of five improvisational comedians and a piano/keyboards player perform five off-the-wall shows per night. Since this is improvisational comedy, the show is totally based around comments and suggestions from the audience. The more creative the audience's input is, the funnier the show itself will be.

The Comedy Warehouse holds a large audience, but seating is on a first-come basis, so arrive at least thirty minutes prior to show time to ensure you'll get a seat. (If Pleasure Island is extremely crowded, arrive forty-five minutes to one hour early.) All seating is on bar stools, except for a few small tables in front near the stage. Shows earlier in the evening tend to be less crowded than the ones presented between 11:00 P.M. and 1:00 A.M.

DTV

Character-based Disney merchandise, clothing, and souvenirs are sold here. If you happen to need an aspirin, you can purchase personal care items from any checkout counter/cashier within this store.

⊕ HOT SPOT

One of the newest additions to Pleasure Island is the BET SoundStage Club, a rhythm-and-blues club that offers live DJs playing dance music, as well as live entertainment.

Hub Video Stage

Located opposite the DJ tower is this small stage, featuring a large video wall, where music videos are played in conjunction with the music that's heard throughout the outdoor area of Pleasure Island. Live performances are also presented here.

Island Depot

Stroller and wheelchair rentals, along with the Pleasure Island lost and found, are located near the Rock 'n' Roll Beach Club building. You can also purchase a selection of official Pleasure Island merchandise at the shop in this building. An ATM is nearby.

Mannequins Dance Palace

This is Pleasure Island's premier dance club. It features a rotating dance floor, a state-of-the-art lighting and sound system, live DJs, and plenty of nonstop popular dance music. The club was recently renovated to maintain its cutting-edge atmosphere. You must be twenty-one years or older to enter into Mannequins, which offers a fully stocked bar and small cocktail tables. Throughout the night, Pleasure Island's Explosion Dancers perform.

Pleasure Island Jazz Company

Live jazz music is performed throughout the night in this club, which also sells cigars and offers a full bar service. The crowd here tends to be a bit older and more sophisticated compared to the people you'll find at the other clubs. Plenty of small tables and chairs are available, so plan on relaxing, having a few drinks, and enjoying some extremely good classic jazz.

Motion

Pleasure Island's newest club offers nonstop Top-40 music. This club features a casual party atmosphere and live DJs. Local Orlando residents, off-duty Disney cast members, and tourists alike gather here for great nighttime entertainment. While Mannequins Dance Palace appeals to a slightly older crowd (twenty-one-plus), those over eighteen will find that this club offers a great atmosphere for socializing and dancing.

Portobello Yacht Club

For a fine-dining experience, Portobello Yacht Club is one of the few nontrendy, nonthemed restaurants located in the Downtown Disney area. While the food is a bit pricey (between $21 and $35 per person), what you'll find here is award-winning Northern Italian cuisine that includes seafood, pasta, and chicken dishes, along with wood-burning-oven pizzas and some incredible desserts. Lunch is served starting at 11:30 A.M., and dinner is served until midnight daily.

⊕ HOT SPOT

A variety of carnival-like games are offered at Pleasure Island near Motion. Large plush toys are awarded as prizes. There's an additional fee to try your luck or show off your skills on games.

Reel Finds

Genuine celebrity autographs and photos are sold in this shop. If you're looking for an autographed picture of a cast member from *Star Trek: The Next Generation, Start Trek Voyager,* or *Star Trek: Deep Space Nine,* you'll find it here for $180 and up, depending on the individual cast member you're looking for. A photo of the entire *Diff'rent Strokes* cast, for example, sells for $220. Dozens of other photos and movie scripts are also available, so if you're a movie buff, you'll enjoy checking this place out.

Rock 'n' Roll Beach Club

Nonstop rock-and-roll music from the past and present is played continuously throughout the evening and late into the night. This club has a beach-party theme and features a mix of live performances and talented DJs who keep cranking out the music. Snacks and full bar service are available.

Superstar Studios

If you've ever had dreams of becoming a recording artist, here's your chance to star in your own music video. Take the videocassette of your performance home with you as a souvenir (for a fee, of course) and show it to your friends and family—it'll be good for a laugh.

≡FAST FACT

Disney animation cells, collectible figurines, and Disney poster artwork is sold at the Suspended Animation gallery. Some of the stuff sold here is rather expensive, but it's fun to browse, especially if you enjoy Disney's classic animated movies. A limited number of autographed animation cells are also available.

The Marketplace

This entire shopping area is dedicated to everything Disney, but there are also plenty of shops that offer unique non-Disney merchandise. It's easy to spend an evening here browsing, shopping, and enjoying the festive atmosphere, whether or not you plan on making purchases.

In addition to the shops, restaurants, and activities available at the Marketplace, there are also dozens of kiosks that sell unique handcrafted souvenirs and snacks. The Marketplace is open daily from 9:30 A.M. to 11:00 P.M. Most of the full-service restaurants open at 10:30 A.M. and serve until 11:00 P.M.

Art of Disney

This is an upscale gallery that sells high-priced Disney animation and artwork. Some of the pieces on display here are absolutely stunning. Less expensive Disney posters and figurines issued by the Walt Disney Collector's Society are also available.

Boating at Cap'N Jack's Marina

During the day, a selection of boats can be rented here by the half hour or by the hour. Guests must be twelve years of age or older to rent a boat. Water sprites, canopy boats, and pontoon boats are available. For more information, call ✆(407) 828-2204.

Cap'N Jack's Oyster Bar Restaurant

Located along the coast of Buena Vista Lagoon, this restaurant features seafood dishes, including shrimp, clam chowder, and oysters, served daily between 11:30 A.M. and 10:30 P.M. Several nonseafood dishes are also available, although if you're not looking for seafood, there are plenty of other dining options available to you elsewhere.

Disney at Home

Here's your opportunity to take some of the magic of Walt Disney World home with you. Disney-themed furniture, kitchen accessories, bathroom fixtures, and household accessories (even bed sheets and pillowcases) are sold here.

⊕ HOT SPOT

Three hundred and sixty-five days a year, it's always the Christmas holiday season in Disney's Days of Christmas, a lovely shop that sells Christmas tree ornaments and other Disney-themed holiday merchandise like animated Disney character statues.

Eurospain

Lovely handmade glass and crystal merchandise is sold here, and not all of it has a Disney theme. This is a beautiful shop to browse through, but keep a close eye on your kids. The items on display here are extremely fragile. Many of the gift items can be engraved while you wait. In the center of this shop is an area where a glassblower demonstrates how some of the products in this shop are made.

Fulton's Crab House

Lunch and dinner are served daily. This is the place to eat if you're looking for an upscale environment and fresh seafood from around the world. The food here is rather expensive, but delicious. You and your children can also join popular Disney characters at Fulton's Crab House for breakfast every morning between 8:00 A.M. and 10:00 A.M. Lunch is served from noon to 5:00 P.M. Dinner is served from 5:00 P.M. until midnight.

Ghirardelli Soda Fountain & Chocolate Shop

This ice-cream parlor serves a tasty selection of shakes, ice-cream sundaes, and chocolates. It's the perfect place to drop in for a midday (or midnight) snack, especially if you're in the mood for something sweet. Indoor and nearby outdoor tables are available.

Gourmet Pantry

You'll find all sorts of kitchen goodies here, most with a Disney theme. Cookbooks, aprons, Mickey Mouse cutting boards, coffee mugs, dinner plates, pot holders, and even Mickey Mouse–shaped ice trays can be purchased here. If you want to make Mickey Mouse–shaped sandwiches (like grilled cheese) at home, the Mickey & Minnie Sandwich Maker costs $59.95. This shop also offers a full deli and bakery where you can grab a snack and eat on the go as you shop.

LEGO Imagination Center

This colorful LEGO superstore and activity center is like a magnet for young people. Throughout the store (and outside) are giant statues made from LEGO. In the courtyard that's just outside this shop, kids can walk up to the various kiosks and build their own LEGO creations. The LEGO playground is a great place for young people to hang out and have a blast (as long as they're supervised by a parent or guardian). This is one of the coolest shops/activities for kids in the Downtown Disney area. Here you can purchase virtually every LEGO play set currently available, plus LEGO-themed clothing and souvenirs.

FAST FACT

A Guest Services desk is located at Dock Stage. You can get your questions answered, make dinner reservations, or learn about special events taking place at Downtown Disney during your visit.

McDonald's

It took the McDonald's Corporation over twenty-five years, but it finally succeeded in opening a McDonald's restaurant on Disney property. This inexpensive fast-food establishment offers a large play area for kids, plus a full menu of McDonald's favorites, like Big Macs, Chicken McNuggets, French fries, and Happy Meals. The Golden Arches are located in the heart of the Marketplace. There's virtually always a crowd here, so expect a slight wait to order your food.

The Rainforest Café

Why travel to a tropical rain forest when you can enjoy a wild meal in a rain forest setting, complete with live wildlife and Audio-Animatronic creatures! Inside the restaurant you'll find huge salt-water fish tanks. Lunch and dinner are served daily (between 10:30 A.M. and 11:00 P.M.).

This is an extremely popular restaurant at the Marketplace, so be prepared to add your name to the waiting list and then have plenty of time to shop before your table becomes available. The prices here are reasonable, and a wide assortment of American cuisine and seafood is offered. This is a wonderful family-oriented restaurant that's unique and offers a very different dining experience than the many themed restaurants located nearby.

Sand Street Station

This is an outdoor playground area for young people. While this is an area in which kids can climb, run around, and have fun, they should never be left unsupervised, here or anywhere else within The WDW Resort.

Studio M

In case you were wondering what the "M" stands for, simply step foot into this shop and there will be no doubt in your mind. Studio M is divided up into small areas, each offering something unique, like Disney-themed airbrushed T-shirts created while you wait by robots (priced between $23 and $42).

You can also pick up a Mickey Mouse mug with your name on it, or meet and greet Mickey Mouse in person and have your photo taken with him. The cost of the Mickey photo session is $29.95 and includes one 8" x 10", two 4" x 5", and four wallet-size color photos of you (or your kids) and Disney's main mouse.

Team Mickey's Athletic Club

All sorts of Disney-themed sports-related apparel and sporting equipment is for sale at this shop. Mickey Mouse tennis balls, Disney-character golf balls, and Disney-themed golf bags from Belding Sports (ranging in price from $210 to $285) are among the most popular items.

⊕ HOT SPOT

Pooh Corner offers all sorts of Winnie the Pooh merchandise, from clothing to storybooks. This charming shop isn't just for kids.

Wolfgang Puck Express

This is fast food, Wolfgang Puck style. The prices here are lower than at the Wolfgang Puck Café located at Disney's West Side. Lunch and dinner are served daily. Outdoor, but covered, seating is available. Gourmet pizzas are the specialty here, although salads, sandwiches, and baked goods are also available. While this is fast food, the prices aren't too cheap. McDonald's might not be as tasty, but it's a far less expensive fast-food alternative.

World of Disney

You're about to experience the world's largest Disney Store, featuring all sorts of Disney clothing, toys, gifts, souvenirs, plush toys, collectibles, kitchen items, and other Disney-character-based products. This store is divided into twelve different (and very large) rooms. In the center of the store there's an information booth manned by Disney cast members who can help you locate any type of Disney merchandise available anywhere at The WDW Resort, The Disney Stores, and the Disney Catalog.

Once upon a Toy

This is an interactive toy shop featuring Walt Disney World attraction toys and Hasbro games that have a Disney twist.

Disney's Wonderful World of Memories

Here you'll find a large selection of picture frames, photo albums, and scrapbooking supplies, all with a Disney theme. Also available are Disney books, stationery, pens, and postcards, plus several stations where guests can create scrapbook pages and post-cards.

Earl of Sandwich

This gourmet sandwich shop is located in the heart of Downtown Disney. It's a great place to stop for lunch or dinner.

Disney's BoardWalk

Located a short walk from Epcot (and several of The WDW Resort hotels), Disney's BoardWalk offers another alternative for adult-oriented evening and nighttime entertainment. There is no admission charge to enter the BoardWalk area, although several of the clubs have a small cover charge.

This half-mile stretch of nightclubs, restaurants, shops, and activities is located along Crescent Lake and is modeled after the boardwalks of the 1920s and 1930s. While the shops and restaurants in this area are open during the day, Disney's BoardWalk is most enjoyable after dark, so you can experience the lights and festive atmosphere. If you happen to be a guest at Disney's BoardWalk Villas hotel, then the excitement of Disney's BoardWalk will happen all around you.

An ATM is located in the main courtyard area of the BoardWalk, behind the hotel (near Wyland Galleries). For additional information about Disney's BoardWalk, call ✆(407) 939-5100. Don't forget to bring your passport, U.S. (or foreign) driver's license with photo, or U.S. military ID in order to show proof of age, required for entry into some of the clubs. The hours of operation for each of the restaurants and clubs listed are subject to change based on the season.

⊕ HOT SPOT

Listen to a ten-piece swing band perform hits from the 1940s to today, and strut your stuff on the ballroom dance floor of the Atlantic Dance Club. You must be twenty-one years old or older to get into this club. There is an admission charge, and special events are held here on holidays.

Big River Grille & Brewing Works

Lunch and dinner entrees (ranging in price from $12.95 to $15.95), along with sandwiches, appetizers, salads, and desserts, are available, but the main draw of this dining establishment is the assortment of specialty beers that are served. Operating hours are from 10:00 A.M. to 2:00 A.M. daily.

BoardWalk Bakery

An assortment of freshly baked goodies is available here, along with cappuccino and espresso. All items are served to go, but if you choose, you can hang out and watch the bakers at work in the kitchen.

Disney Vacation Club Information Center

In case you're interested in learning about the Disney Vacation Club timesharing facilities offered at The WDW Resort, you can drop into this information office to schedule an appointment or obtain literature. Timeshare vacation opportunities are extremely popular in the Orlando area, so be prepared to hear a sales pitch.

The ESPN Club

Sports fans will feel like they're in heaven when they step foot into this giant sports bar, which offers dozens of sporting events shown on monitors throughout the club. Live ESPN radio and television broadcasts originate from here, so guests often get to meet their favorite ESPN personalities and sportscasters. A full and pretty inexpensive menu and bar service are available. Food entrees range in price from $7.95 to under $15, and include burgers, hot dogs, tuna salad, and Caesar salad.

There's no admission charge to hang out at the ESPN club. Operating hours are from 11:00 A.M. to 2:00 A.M. If there's a big sporting event taking place, like the Super Bowl or World Series, this club will be packed with sports fans. This club is, however, packed pretty much every evening and night.

After hanging out at the ESPN Club, you can purchase official ESPN merchandise at the nearby shop. Glasses, sports clothing, and caps with the ESPN logo are among the offerings.

⊕ HOT SPOT

Open daily for dinner only, the Flying Fish Café serves fine American cuisine including seafood and steak entrees. This is the most classy and expensive restaurant in the BoardWalk area. Reservations are recommended. Call ☏ (407) WDW-DINE.

Jellyrolls

If you're in the mood for some lighthearted musical entertainment, often with a comedy twist, drop into Jellyrolls. This is a dueling piano bar, where two extremely talented singers/musicians entertain guests simultaneously in a casual and cozy bar atmosphere. The performers change every hour or so, and each pair has its own repertoire of music. Of course, audience participation is expected, so be prepared to sing and clap along, plus request your favorite songs.

To ensure that the performers will honor your song request, write it down on a cocktail napkin and take it up onto the small stage, accompanied by a tip. Even if you don't drink, you'll easily be able to spend a very enjoyable hour or two watching the performances. There's a small admission fee ($4 or less) to enter Jellyrolls, and the drink prices are reasonable.

You must be twenty-one years old or older to be admitted into this piano bar. If you do nothing else during your visit to the BoardWalk, drop into Jellyrolls to experience the live entertainment. Of course, Jellyrolls T-shirts and other souvenirs are available near the exit.

Leaping Horse Libations

Open from 11:00 A.M. until dusk, this poolside bar offers a small menu of inexpensive food items. Relax by the pool and enjoy your favorite alcoholic or nonalcoholic beverage, along with a burger, hot dog, french fries, or ice cream. This area is mainly for guests of the BoardWalk Inn hotel, but it's open to everyone.

Seashore Sweets

Styled after an old-fashioned sweet shop, you'll find a delicious assortment of cookies, candies, taffy, hand-dipped gelato, and flavored coffees served here between 11:00 A.M. and 2:00 A.M. A limited number of small tables are available.

Souvenir Kiosks

Along with the shops, throughout the BoardWalk area you'll encounter many souvenir kiosks that offer a variety of unique products and services, such as face painting (a favorite among kids). There's also a hair wrap kiosk (also popular among young girls). At the Design Your Own Cap kiosk, you can have a baseball cap embroidered with a name or design, while you wait. Another interesting souvenir is your hand in wax, which is created by dipping your hand in hot wax. There's usually a small crowd around this kiosk because watching the hand-dipping process is somewhat interesting. A box for your wax creation is provided for easy transport home.

Wyland Galleries

Wyland is a world-renowned artist who specializes in painting and drawing dolphins, whales, and other sea life. You can see (and purchase) his work at this stunning gallery located in the heart of Disney's BoardWalk. The art on display is beautiful, so be sure to drop in to browse. Another Wyland Gallery is located in Celebration, Florida (the city that Disney built). If you can't afford the actual artwork, postcards, posters, books, and other merchandise featuring Wyland's work are also on sale.

⊕ HOT SPOT

Men's and women's fashions, resort apparel, and swimwear are sold at Thimbles and Threads, and not all of the clothing has a Disney character imprinted on it.

CHAPTER 13

A High Seas Adventure

THE MAGIC AND WONDER OF A WALT DISNEY WORLD vacation no longer has to end in Orlando. Disney's Imagineers have dreamed up a way for people of all ages, traveling with or without children, to enjoy a cruise to the Bahamas that's unlike what any other cruise ship line has to offer.

Disney Cruise Lines

Disney Cruise Lines features two state-of-the-art ships, offering three-, four-, seven-, and ten-night cruises from Cape Canaveral (located near Orlando) to destinations like Key West, St. Maarten, St. Lucia, Antigua, St. Thomas, San Juan, Grand Cayman, Cozumel, Nassau, Grand Bahama Island, and Disney's own private island, called Castaway Cay. While these may sound like fun-filled and exotic destinations (which they are), getting there is more than half the fun. The Disney Cruise Line ships offer all kinds of activities and world-class service that will make your cruise a vacation you'll remember for a lifetime. In most cases, you can combine your Disney cruise with a several-day visit to The WDW Resort, thus creating the ultimate all-inclusive Disney vacation package.

The vacations available through Disney Cruise Lines are offered at a variety of prices (with special package deals always being made available through travel agents, online travel services, and directly through Disney Cruise Lines). Since this is a family-oriented cruise ship, accommodations and itineraries are available that cater to guests of all ages.

When you board either the *Disney Magic* or the *Disney Wonder,* you will find in your cabin a daily itinerary for what's happening aboard the ship. Each evening, the next day's itinerary will be delivered to your cabin.

≡FAST FACT

If you're leaving from The WDW Resort to the cruise ship, your baggage will be picked up at your hotel early in the morning on your day of departure and be delivered directly to your stateroom aboard the ship. The bus ride from The WDW Resort to Cape Canaveral is about one hour and fifteen minutes. During the bus ride, an entertaining video will introduce you to shipboard activities and prepare you for your high seas journey.

Meet Disney Characters

What would a Disney vacation be without seeing Mickey, Minnie, and the other Disney characters? Well, while sailing aboard either of Disney's cruise ships, you'll meet up with your favorite Disney characters many times. Plenty of photo opportunities are available. The majority of character appearances are preplanned and listed with your itinerary.

Extra Charges

While the majority of activities and the dining are all included within your cruise package, alcoholic beverages, bottled water, and soft drinks cost extra. (Soda and water are served free of charge within the dining rooms, however.) There's also a charge to play Bingo onboard (because cash prizes are awarded), and separate charges apply for land-based excursions and tours when the ship stops at the various ports of call. All charges can be billed to your room (just like at The WDW Resort), so unless you leave the ship, there's no need to carry cash.

Castaway Cay

One of the highlights of a Disney Cruise Line vacation is the stop the ship makes at Disney's Castaway Cay, a 1,000-acre private island in the Abacos. During the one-day stop at this private tropical island paradise, guests enjoy an authentic island experience that features the Bahamas' best attributes, such as a half-mile-long beach area and a wide range of water sports and activities for families. There's also a secluded mile-long pristine beach that provides the ideal place to relax and unwind, plus an adults-only beach, where older people can go to enjoy quiet time. Snorkeling, sailboat and kayak rentals, bike riding, massages on the beach, and live entertainment are among the ways guests spend their time on the island.

💼 TRAVEL TIP

Kids and teens in particular will enjoy having their hair braided with beads while on the island (for an additional fee). If you want to have this done, don't wait until the end of the day. The line gets long in the afternoon, and the braiders stop taking new people about one hour before the ship's scheduled departure.

The *Magic* and the *Wonder*

If you and your family have already experienced a Disney World vacation and you're looking for something new, different, but equally exciting, set sail aboard the *Disney Magic* or *Disney Wonder* cruise ships.

Disney Cruise Line's first ship, *Disney Magic*, began service in mid-1998, with its cruises leaving from the $27 million glass-towered Disney terminal in Port Canaveral, Florida. On August 15, 1999,

Disney Wonder made its maiden voyage. Both ships are similar and hold between 1,760 and 2,400 guests per voyage.

Both *Disney Magic* and *Disney Wonder* are 85,000-ton ships that were built at the Fincantieri Shipyards in Ancona and Marghera, Italy. Each ship was designed to cater to the vacation demands of four distinct audiences: kids, teens, families, and adults. Instead of relying on ship designers from Fincantieri Shipyards to design and then build the two ships, Disney tapped the talent of its own Imagineers, giving them the task of creating a totally unique cruise ship design that would result in guests' experiencing a cruise vacation that only Disney could offer. The result is that *Disney Magic* and *Disney Wonder* are among the most technologically advanced ships afloat.

The ships offer 875 staterooms (73 percent of which offer outside views) featuring more space and attention to detail than most other cruise ships in existence. Even the smallest of the ship's staterooms will easily accommodate three guests, with many staterooms designed for families of up to six people (using bunk beds). The staterooms aboard both the *Magic* and the *Wonder* are 25 percent larger than the current industry average and have been designed to offer more storage and usable space than any other cruise ship accommodations. Many of the staterooms also feature a bathroom-and-a-half, featuring separate bath facilities. About 44 percent of the staterooms feature private verandas.

⊕ HOT SPOT

If you're interested in experiencing the many different treatments and massages available within the onboard day spa, be sure to make your appointment within several hours of first boarding the ship. Appointments for massages, facials, and other treatments fill up immediately. These services cost extra—however, the facilities are equivalent to what you'd find at a world-class day spa on land.

Pricing Your Vacation

The pricing structure for the various cruise packages is divided up much like that of The Walt Disney World Resort hotels. For example, *Disney Magic* offers twelve different stateroom categories to make it easy to choose the perfect accommodations for your family or the people you're traveling with.

Disney Cruise Line's vacation packages include airfare from major U.S. cities. Based on the package you choose, the package might also include three or four days' worth of hotel accommodations, plus unlimited admission to The WDW Resort's theme parks and other land-based recreational activities, such as ninety-nine holes of golf (on six courses).

▣ TRAVEL TIP

Some of the land-based excursions have limited space available and fill up quickly (in some cases, before the ship ever sets sail). You can book your shore excursions up to sixty days prior to sailing by calling ✆(877) 566-0968. A listing of available excursions is provided when you make your cruise reservation or online at ✑*www.DisneyCruise.com*. These excursions cost extra, but add a lot to the overall vacation experience.

Prices for the seven-night theme park/cruise vacation packages range from $829 per person (based on double occupancy) to as high as $2,499 per person (for a veranda stateroom), depending on the level of hotel and stateroom accommodations guests desire (these are 2004 prices). Three-night cruise-only vacation packages start at $439 per person (based on double occupancy) and go as high as $1,399 per person (for a veranda stateroom). The four-night cruise-only packages average between $100 and $200 higher per person than the three-night packages. When traveling with at least one adult, kids and teens receive highly discounted rates (starting at $199 per child).

Using an online service, such as *Travelocity.com* or *Hotwire.com*, discounted rates for non-peak travel periods can be found for Disney Cruise Lines.

For additional information about Disney Cruise Lines, to request a free vacation-planning brochure, or to make a reservation, call ✆(888) DCL-2500, visit any travel agent, or check out the Disney Cruise Line's Web site at ✑*www.disneycruise.com*. Be sure to inquire about early-booking discounts that could save you hundreds of dollars per stateroom for some of the cruises scheduled to take place during non-holiday periods. Special honeymoon packages are also available.

Children's Space

In order to cater to the unique needs of young guests, 15,000 square feet of the ship have been set aside as dedicated children's space. The kid- and teen-oriented areas of the ship are staffed by more than forty professional counselors, who personalize each guest's experience. Kids and teens are encouraged to participate in a wide range of organized camp-like activities.

Adult Activities

While the children are enjoying the personalized attention and the dozens of activities designed specifically for them, parents and adults traveling without children will be able to enjoy the ship's adults-only areas, including a nighttime entertainment complex that offers three themed nightclubs and shopping. There's a rock-and-roll club, a comedy club, and a piano/cappuccino club. A special adults-only alternative restaurant, a separate adults-only swimming pool, and a fully equipped day spa facility (offering the most modern exercise equipment and spa treatments, as well as educational and enrichment programs) are offered.

When parents want to leave their children and experience the nightlife aboard the ship, private babysitting service is available (for an additional fee). No matter what time it is, day or night, unlimited room service is available (and all food is included in the cruise package).

≡FAST FACT

Every night, a different Broadway-style show is presented that's suitable for the entire family. For the eighteen-and-over crowd, however, the nightlife aboard the ship includes dance clubs and an improv comedy club (where every show is totally different). In 2003, *The Golden Mickeys* show made its debut aboard both of Disney Cruise Lines' ships. This is a salute to Walt Disney and his legacy of animation magic that includes theatrical song and dance, animated film, video, and special effects.

Family Time

During times when parents and children want to spend time together, many family-oriented activities are also available on Disney Cruise Line's ships. Each ship offers three family-oriented restaurants, snack bars, a buffet, and multiple bars. Each night, guests experience a different restaurant with a different theme, but the entire staff remains the same, so your waiter will quickly get to know your personal preferences and accommodate your every need.

Of course, since The Walt Disney Company specializes in family-oriented entertainment, there is no shortage of Disney-style entertainment aboard the cruise ship. There's a 1,040-seat theater that features one of the most sophisticated show settings in the world. This theater is the home of three different Broadway-style shows. Each evening, the cruise line offers a uniquely themed production, including Disney classics and newly created shows that combine storytelling and music.

Throughout each day, the Buena Vista Theater (a 270-seat full-screen cinema with state-of-the-art Dolby Sound) shows a variety of Disney's animated classics and first-run movie releases. For less formal entertainment, the ships offer multiple lounges and the ESPN Sports Club. In this sports club, multiple screens continuously broadcast all of the latest sports news and events from around the world.

⎯⎯FAST FACT

Throughout the year, Disney Cruise Lines hosts special theme cruises, with celebrity guests making appearances, performing concerts, conducting workshops, and interacting with guests.

Dining Experiences

Out of all the dining experiences on the ships, the Animator's Palate offers the most unique dining experience. When guests first enter this dining room, everything is in black and white. As guests dine on California cuisine, the entire room begins to change—colors begin to appear on the walls, on the ceiling, and at each table. As the meal proceeds, the entire restaurant undergoes a complete transformation that's synchronized with light and sound. At the end of the meal, diners are treated to an appearance from a few surprise guests who participate in a musical finale.

The Palo restaurant (which requires separate reservations) definitely offers the most spectacular view aboard the ship, not to mention incredible food, mouthwatering desserts, and an impressive wine list. If you're celebrating a special occasion, want to enjoy a romantic dinner, or just want to relax and experience an awesome dining experience, make plans to dine at least one evening at this onboard restaurant. As a guest aboard Disney Cruise Lines, you'll automatically be invited to dine at the ships' regular restaurants. A reservation for Palo must be requested.

Guest Services

As if having the facilities and built-in entertainment venues and offering countless activities isn't enough, each ship is operated by a crew of almost 1,000 people (representing over fifty countries) who are totally dedicated to providing superior Disney-style service to all guests.

Other services aboard the ships include complete photographic services, complete laundry and dry-cleaning services, satellite telephone service, modern medical facilities, a twenty-four-hour front desk service, fax and secretarial service, and conference facilities for groups of up to 120 people.

▐█▌ TRAVEL TIP

Once you book your cruise, pay attention to the two-suitcase (plus one carry-on) baggage limitation per person and pack accordingly. Leave space for your souvenirs! Be sure to keep any medications, tickets, your passport, a change of clothes, and toiletries with you in a carry-on.

When traveling on Disney Cruise Lines, satellite telephones are available in every stateroom; however, the price per minute for making calls is extremely high. Public phones are available in Nassau; however, making an international call to the United States, even if you're using a calling card, is both expensive and time consuming. So, plan on sending postcards rather than calling your friends and family back home.

A somewhat less expensive alternative is to visit the onboard Internet Café and send e-mail home to friends, coworkers, and relatives. There's a seventy-five-cent-per-minute charge to surf the Web while aboard the ship; however, for a flat fee of $39.99 (for a three-

or four-night cruise) or $89.99 (for a seven-night cruise), unlimited Internet access is available.

Disney Cruise Lines truly offers something for everyone. Whether you're looking to schedule activities every minute of the day or night, or you just want to kick back, relax, and enjoy the sunshine, the options are plentiful. With various activities, babysitting services, and supervised camp-like activities for kids and teens, parents can easily find romantic "alone time" together, in between experiencing quality "family time" aboard the ship.

CHAPTER 14

The Universal Orlando Resort

FOLLOWING IN THE FOOTSTEPS OF THE WDW RESORT, The Universal Orlando Resort has become a vacation destination unto itself, complete with resort hotels, theme parks, and a unique restaurant/shopping area.

Overview of the Resort

Once you arrive at the Universal Orlando Resort, plan on spending at least one full day at each of the theme parks, plus your evenings/nights at CityWalk. While both theme parks are family oriented, each offers a totally different overall theme and atmosphere.

═══FAST FACT

The Universal Orlando Resort has multiple on-site ATMs. At Universal Studios Florida, there's a full-service bank on the property. The First Union National Bank offers traveler's check cashing, cash advances from credit cards, and currency exchanges.

The Theme Parks

Universal Studios Florida (like its counterpart in Hollywood, California) offers rides, shows and attractions based on blockbuster movies like *Twister, E.T.: The Extraterrestrial, The Blues Brothers, Jaws, Shrek, Men in Black, Back to the Future,* and *Terminator 2.* The majority of these aren't traditional thrill rides, yet they offer an interactive and often exciting way to experience the story behind each of these movies in a whole new way. Hence, the overall theme of this park (as well as its advertising slogan) is "Ride the Movies!"

Universal Studios Florida is divided into various themed lands. Woody Woodpecker's KidZone, for example, is a kid-oriented area. Another favorite among the younger crowd is Nickelodeon Studios. This is where some of the most popular shows from the Nickelodeon television network are actually filmed. For families and adults, Production Central, New York, San Francisco/Amity, The World Expo, and Hollywood are the other themed areas of Universal Studios Florida, each of which offers its own rides, shows, attractions, shops, and dining options (all described in the next chapter).

The second theme park within the Universal Orlando Resort is Islands of Adventure. Also divided into a series of themed areas, this park offers more traditional roller coasters and thrill rides, each with its own storyline. Here, Seuss Landing and Toon Lagoon offer an assortment of kid-oriented rides, shows, and attractions (plus shops and dining options), while the Lost Continent, Jurassic Park, and Marvel Super Hero Island will appeal more to teens and adults. Everything that Islands of Adventure has to offer is described within Chapter 16.

CityWalk

Located between these two exciting theme parks is CityWalk, a unique dining and shopping area that by day is family-oriented, but by night offers exciting nightlife activities for adults, featuring dance clubs, bars, live entertainment, and an overall party atmosphere. In addition to a state-of-the-art movie theater, CityWalk offers a handful of themed restaurants, plus several fine-dining restaurants, mixed with unique shops. Somewhat similar in concept to Disney's Pleasure Island (and Downtown Disney area), you can learn all about CityWalk in Chapter 17.

≡FAST FACT

Universal Studios offers a variety of discounts for members of AARP, HIA, and the Orlando MagiCard. Florida-resident discount offers are also available. For more information, contact the park's Guest Services office at ✆(407) 363-8000.

Driving Directions

Once you're in the Orlando area, you'll find this theme park located near the intersection of Interstate 4 (I-4) and the Florida Turnpike. Depending on where you're coming from, follow these driving directions:

From the Orlando International Airport take 528 West (the Beeline Expressway) toward Tampa. Watch for signs to Interstate 4 East (to Orlando). From Interstate 4 East, take Exit #29B (Universal Boulevard). Take a left onto Universal Boulevard and follow the signs to the Universal Orlando Resort.

Traveling East on I-4 (from the Tampa area): Exit I-4 at Exit #30A (Universal Boulevard). Take a left onto Universal Boulevard and follow the signs to the Universal Orlando Resort.

Traveling North on the Florida Turnpike (from the Miami/ Ft. Lauderdale area): Take Exit #259 (the second of the Orlando exits) and follow the signs to the I-4 Tampa exit. Exit I-4 at Exit #29B. Take a right onto Hollywood Way and follow the signs to the Universal Orlando Resort.

Traveling South on the Florida Turnpike (from the Wildwood/ Ocala area): Take Exit #259 and follow the signs to the I-4 Tampa exit. Exit I-4 at Exit #29B. Take a right onto Hollywood Way and follow the signs to the Universal Orlando Resort.

Traveling West on I-4 (from the Daytona/Jacksonville area): Exit I-4 at Exit #29B. Take a right onto Hollywood Way and follow the signs to the Universal Orlando Resort.

When driving from The Walt Disney World Resort: Take I-4 to Exit #30A (Universal Boulevard). Take a left onto Universal Boulevard and follow the signs to the Universal Orlando Resort. Driving time is about twenty minutes from most areas within The WDW Resort.

≡FAST FACT

Shuttle buses are available from many non-Disney hotels in the Orlando area, especially those along International Drive and surrounding areas. If you're staying at The WDW Resort, however, the cheapest and fastest way to get to the Universal Orlando Resort is by renting a car, although taxi and shuttle bus service is available. If you need shuttle bus service, contact Mears Transportation at ✆(407) 839-1570. The Yellow Cab Co. can be reached at ✆(407) 699-9999.

Parking at the Universal Orlando Resort

Most people arrive at Universal Orlando Resort (Universal Studios Florida, Islands of Adventure, and CityWalk) traveling by car. The theme park offers an enclosed parking garage that is equipped with a 200-camera security system, moving sidewalks, escalators and elevators, on-site wheelchair rental, and an on-site kennel. Daily parking for cars, vans, and motorcycles is $8 per vehicle. Daily parking for RVs and trailers is $10 per vehicle.

Vehicles can leave the garage and return the same day by stopping at the toll plaza upon re-entry and presenting their original parking ticket. Valet parking for cars and vans is available for an additional charge.

Taxis, buses, limousines, and shuttles to hotels and other area destinations are available outside the main entrance at the Transportation Center of the parking structure. For schedule information, contact the Guest Services office.

The distance between the Universal Orlando Resort parking complex and the theme parks is considerable. While moving walkways and escalators are used to make the trip to and from your car easier, the commute takes about twenty minutes on foot and involves walking. Much of this commute is outdoors, so if it's raining, you're going to get wet.

💼 TRAVEL TIP

Show your AAA membership card when purchasing tickets or making a purchase at gift shops or restaurants within the Universal Orlando Resort and receive up to a 10 percent discount.

Admission to Universal Studios Theme Parks

As you'll see, depending on your length of stay and which park(s) you plan on visiting, there are a variety of different ticket options available. If you'll be in the Orlando area for multiple days (and you plan to visit Universal Studios Florida and Islands of Adventure), you can save money by purchasing a multiday/multipark pass.

After purchasing your admission ticket, if you decide you want to stay longer or upgrade your admission for additional days, special discounts are offered at the Customer Service counter near the entrance of the park. You must upgrade your ticket the day it's purchased, however.

Universal Orlando Resort Theme Park Admission Prices

The following are the admission prices for Universal Studios Florida, Islands of Adventure, and CityWalk.

Type of Ticket	Adult Pass	Child Pass (ages 3 to 9)
1 Day/1 Park	$51.95	$42.95
4-Park FlexTicket	$175.95	$142.95
5-Park FlexTicket	$214.95	$179.95
2-Park Preferred Annual Pass	$169.95	$169.95
2-Park Annual Power Pass	$109.95	$109.95
Universal Orlando Bonus Pass	$94.95	$94.95
CityWalk Party Pass	$9.95	N/A
CityWalk Party Pass + Movie	$13.00	N/A

The 2-Park Preferred Annual Pass and Annual Power Pass

The 2-Park Preferred Annual Pass gives you unlimited admission to both Universal Studios Florida and Islands of Adventure for one full year. There are no blackout dates and self-parking is free. The 2-Park Annual Power Pass also offers admission to both theme parks for a full year; however, there are blackout dates during peak periods and you still pay for parking.

Along with theme park admission, being an annual passholder offers a handful of privileges, such as a 10, 15, or 20 percent discount off food and merchandise throughout the theme parks and CityWalk.

The Universal Orlando Bonus Pass

This type of admission ticket offers five consecutive days at Universal Studios Florida, Islands of Adventure, and CityWalk. You're allowed unlimited parkhopping. This type of ticket is only available online from ✐*www.usf.com*.

4-Park Orlando FlexTicket

The Orlando FlexTicket offers a way to see multiple Orlando-based attractions and theme parks and save money. If you're planning to visit Universal Studios Florida, Islands of Adventure, CityWalk, SeaWorld, and Wet 'n Wild, you'll save a fortune with this type of multiday, multipark pass. It's valid for fourteen consecutive days and offers unlimited admission to each of the parks mentioned. A 4-Park Orlando FlexTicket is priced at $175.95 per adult and $142.95 per child.

5-Park Orlando FlexTicket

The 5-Park Orlando FlexTicket is priced at $214.95 per adult and $179.95 per child (ages three to nine) and provides unlimited admission for fourteen consecutive days to all of the following theme parks:

- Busch Gardens (Tampa Bay, Florida—ticket includes free bus transportation)
- SeaWorld Orlando
- Universal Studios Florida
- Universal Studios Islands of Adventure
- Wet 'N Wild
- CityWalk

≡FAST FACT

While the Orlando FlexTicket does not include admission to any of the Disney-owned theme parks, it offers great savings to other popular Orlando area attractions. If you're planning to visit the Universal theme parks, SeaWorld, and Busch Gardens, this type of ticket is worthwhile.

CityWalk Party Pass

Enjoy unlimited admission for one night to the various clubs located within CityWalk. For a few dollars more, you can also see a movie at the twenty-screen Universal Cineplex. For movie listings, call ✆(407) 354-5998.

Same Day Theme Park Re-entry

As you leave either of the Universal Orlando Resort theme parks, be sure to have your hand stamped as you exit in order to be granted readmission into that park later in the day or evening. In addition to the hand stamp, be sure to retain your ticket stub. The hand stamps are designed to be water-resistant, so don't worry if your hands get wet if you choose to return to your hotel in the middle of the day to go swimming, and then want to return to Universal Studios Florida later that evening. Try to refrain, however, from scrubbing your hands clean with soap until your day's visit to the theme park is complete.

Universal Studios Florida VIP Tours

If you're pressed for time and want to ensure that you see and do the best of what Universal Studios Florida has to offer, consider participating in a VIP Tour. This walking tour of the park lasts about five hours, departs at either 10:00 A.M. or noon (daily), and ensures that participants get to experience many of the park's most popular shows and attractions—without waiting in lines.

Advanced reservations are required. Call ✆(407) 363-8295 during normal business hours. The cost of the VIP Tour is $125 per person.

══FAST FACT

Reservations for all tours should be made in advance by calling ✆(888) U-ESCAPE or ✆(407) 363-8295. Reservations are accepted between 9:00 A.M. and 6:00 P.M. (EST), Monday through Friday only.

Exclusive VIP Tours

This eight-hour walking tour is private and can accommodate up to fifteen people. These tours are scheduled at your convenience and will ensure that you and your group have the opportunity to see and do exactly what you want within the Universal Studios Florida park—without waiting in lines. Priority seating is provided at select restaurants and shows. The cost of this exclusive private tour is $1,700 for the entire group.

▮ TRAVEL TIP

If you plan to stay at one of the on-property Universal Orlando Resort hotels or resorts, special package deals including hotel accommodations and admission to the theme parks are available. For more information, call Universal Studios Vacations at ✆(800) 711-0080 or ✆(407) 224-7000. You can also visit ⬧*www.usf.com.*

Ultimate Escape Tours

This two-day private tour offers a true insider's perspective of Universal Studios Florida and also brings to life the stories behind Islands of Adventure. This two-day tour gives you unlimited park-to-park priority entrance to rides, shows, and attractions, plus preferred seating for the attractions of your choice. The cost is $2,600 for the entire group (up to fifteen people).

Islands of Adventure VIP Tours

VIP Tours are available (for an additional fee) that ensure you get to experience all of the thrill rides Islands of Adventure has to offer—with little or no waiting.

The VIP Tour departs daily at 10:00 A.M. and noon. The price of this tour is $100 per person. It includes a five-hour walking tour (nonprivate) of the Islands of Adventure theme park. Participants receive priority entrance and preferred seating for approximately eight popular attractions.

Guest Services

Located just inside the main entrance of each of the theme parks is the Guest Services office. Here you can take advantage of special services for guests with disabilities. Printed disability tour guides, TDD, assisted listening devices, and wheelchairs are available. Tour maps are also available in French, German, Japanese, Portuguese, and Spanish. Each park's lost and found, stroller rental desk, wheelchair rental counter, foreign money exchange, ATM, pay lockers, and mail drop-off are all located at or near Guest Services.

Getting the Most out of Your Day

Just as when you're visiting one of the Disney theme parks, it's always a good idea to save the most popular attractions for lunchtime or dinnertime, when many guests take a break to eat. At these times (between 11:30 A.M. and 1:00 P.M., and 5:00 P.M. to 6:00 P.M.), the lines are somewhat shorter. The lines for the popular attractions also tend to be shorter late in the day, since many guests try to experience the hottest rides and attractions as soon as they arrive.

📑 TRAVEL TIP

To find out the television and motion picture production schedule at Universal Studios during the time you'll be visiting, drop by the Studio Audience Center located to the right of the main entrance turnstiles to Universal Studios Florida. You can also call the Studio Audience Center at ☎(407) 224-4233 Option #5.

If the weather is bad and it's raining, you can count on shorter-than-average lines, no matter when you visit this theme park. You'll want to wear lightweight rain gear (such as a rain poncho, which can be purchased at the various Universal Studios shops) and refrain from carrying an umbrella. Navigating through the park in crowds when you're carrying an open umbrella is difficult, and if it's windy, you won't stay dry. Also, when you enter into a ride or attraction, there's often nowhere to stow your wet umbrella.

During periods of rain, you have two options. You can choose to get wet and see the rides and attractions that require you to wait outside, or you can follow the crowds and head for the indoor rides and attractions. During periods of rain, outdoor shows and attractions will be cancelled or postponed.

CHAPTER 15

The Universal Studios Florida Theme Park

WHAT STARTED OUT AS A WORKING TELEVISION AND motion picture studio in Orlando has developed into an extremely popular tourist destination. Universal Studios Florida offers guests a chance to see what happens behind the scenes in television and movie production, as well as a chance to "Ride the Movies."

Park Information

Designed to provide at least one full day's worth of entertainment for the entire family, the majority of things to see and do at this park are suitable for people of all ages. Universal Studios Florida opens every day at 9 A.M. Closing times vary, based on the season. For the exact hours of operation during your planned visit, call ✆(407) 363-8000.

Useful Phone Numbers

General Information: ✆(407) 363-8000

Hard Rock Hotel: ✆(407) 503-ROCK

Hearing Impaired TDD: ✆(407) 224-4414

Islands of Adventure Guest Services: ✆(407) 224-4233

> **Merchandise Sales & Information:** ☎(407) 363-8320
> **Portofino Bay Hotel:** ☎(407) 503-1000
> **Royal Pacific Resort:** ☎(407) 503-3000
> **Special Event Hotline:** ☎(407) 224-5500
> **Universal Cineplex Movie Schedule:** ☎(407) 354-5998
> **Universal Studios Florida Guest Services:** ☎(407) 224-4233
> **Universal Studios Florida Lost & Found:** ☎(407) 224-4244
> **Vacation Package Information:** ☎(800) 711-0080 or
> ☎(407) 224-7000

Universal Express Passes

Just like The WDW Resort's popular FASTPASS, Universal Orlando Resort offers the Universal Express pass for the majority of its popular theme park attractions. Instead of waiting in regular lines to see an attraction, you request a Universal Express pass, which will display the time you should return to the attraction in order to get right in. (You won't wait longer than fifteen minutes for any attraction using a Universal Express pass.) You can only obtain one pass at a time (for a single attraction). Universal Express passes are free of charge and if used properly, can help you save a lot of time, particularly when the park is crowded and you want to see the most popular attractions with minimal waiting.

The Rating System

Not all of the rides, shows, and attractions at Universal Studios Florida are suitable or designed for everyone. To help you choose which rides and attractions are most worth seeing while visiting Universal Studios Florida, this book offers star-based ratings for each ride and attraction, based on the age group each will most appeal to. Each ride and attraction has earned between one and three stars.

★ = Rides and attractions that earned just one star aren't worth waiting for and could be skipped, especially if your time within the theme park is limited.

★★ = Rides and attractions that earned two stars are good, but they don't fall into the "must-see" category.

★★★ = The rides and attractions that earned three stars are definitely worth seeing and should not be missed.

N.S. = This denotes rides and attractions that are "Not Suitable" for a specific age group.

Choose a Place to Meet

As soon as you arrive at Universal Studios Florida, choose a place where you'll meet up with the other people in your group if you happen to get separated. Two ideal meeting places are in front of Guest Services (near the entrance) and in front of Back to the Future . . . The Ride. Arrange to meet on the half-hour if you become separated.

⎓FAST FACT

Award-winning producer and director Steven Spielberg is one of this theme park's creative consultants. He's worked hands-on in the development of several of the park's most popular rides, shows, and attractions.

The Rides

The slogan for this theme park is "Ride the Movies," and that's exactly what you'll do when you experience the various rides at Universal Studios Florida. All of the rides and attractions are based on popular motion pictures and television shows produced by Universal Studios. Many of these rides are cutting-edge and can't be experienced anywhere else (except in some cases at Universal Studios Hollywood in California).

Back to the Future . . . The Ride

Ages 2–4:	N.S.
Ages 5–10:	★★★
Ages 11–15:	★★★
Ages 16–Adult:	★★★
Senior Citizens:	★★

This ride is absolutely awesome, so expect to wait for up to an hour (or longer) to experience it. About 90 percent of your waiting time will be under a covered awning or inside.

Once inside the ride's building, you'll see the preshow on video monitors. This preshow stars several actors from the *Back to the Future* movie trilogy, including "Doc Brown" and "Biff," although you won't see Michael J. Fox's character. Just before boarding the ride, you'll see a second four-minute preshow, which is shown to you in a small room.

As you climb aboard the actual ride, you'll step into a time-traveling vehicle, which is Doc Brown's latest invention (just like the one in the movie), except this model holds eight passengers. As the ride itself begins, prepare yourself for four minutes of turbulent excitement as you race through time.

Using state-of-the-art flight simulator, audio, and Omnimax movie technology, your vehicle will move and bounce around in a way that's perfectly synchronized with the Omnimax movie shown on a massive 80-foot-tall projection screen in front of you. You'll hear (and feel) the realistic sound effects through the 300 speakers that surround you.

To make the experience even more realistic, smoke and other special effects are used. Back to the Future . . . The Ride was two years in the making and cost over $16 million to create. This ride is as turbulent as a roller coaster, although there are no real drops (but it feels like there are).

✔ This is a must-see attraction.

E.T. Adventure

Ages 2–4:	★
Ages 5–10:	★★★
Ages 11–15:	★★★
Ages 16–Adult:	★★★
Senior Citizens:	★★

Only Steven Spielberg himself (in conjunction with Universal Studios' attraction designers) could have created this ride, which is absolutely charming. Guests sit on moving bicycle-shaped vehicles that roll and eventually fly while being piloted by E.T. himself. The visuals throughout this ride experience are stunning and realistic. As a passenger, guests have the opportunity to visit E.T.'s home planet. At the very end, E.T. even says "goodbye" to each passenger by saying his or her name (something kids absolutely love). E.T. Adventure is loosely based on the movie *E.T.: The Extra-Terrestrial.*

This is one of the most popular attractions within this park, so be prepared for a wait. Virtually all of the waiting, however, is inside, as guests wind around a maze and have a chance to see lifelike Animatronic re-creations of E.T.'s friends and relatives. Sure, E.T. Adventure is somewhat kid-oriented, but just like the movie itself, it'll appeal to everyone and shouldn't be missed.

✔ This is a must-see attraction.

═══FAST FACT

John Williams, the composer who created the original soundtrack for the *E.T.* motion picture, also created an original score for this ride. Steven Spielberg created several new characters that appear during the ride.

Earthquake—The Big One

Ages 2–4:	N.S.
Ages 5–10:	★★
Ages 11–15:	★★★
Ages 16–Adult:	★★★
Senior Citizens:	★★

Using highly realistic sets and special effects, guests feel like they're trapped within San Francisco's Embarcadero subway station during an earthquake that measures 8.3 on the Richter scale. In other words, there's a whole lot of shaking going on. Don't worry, this ride is perfectly safe, although you will bounce around a bit in the vehicle you're traveling in, while 65,000 gallons of water rush past you (you'll stay dry, however).

The Hollywood-style special effects used in this ride are impressive. This attraction is based on the 1974 movie *Earthquake,* which starred Charlton Heston and Ava Gardner. Young children might get frightened by this ride, so you might want to have them sit this one out. The ride itself lasts about six minutes.

≡FAST FACT

If the earthquake visitors experience in this attraction were real, it would register 8.3 on the Richter scale. To make this attraction more realistic, over 65,000 gallons of water are released and recycled every six minutes.

JAWS

Ages 2–4:	N.S.
Ages 5–10:	★★
Ages 11–15:	★★★
Ages 16–Adult:	★★★
Senior Citizens:	★★

Located in the area of Universal Studios Florida that re-creates the small town of Amity in which the movie *JAWS* took place, there's an exciting and somewhat scary ride/attraction starring Jaws himself. While guests remain dry (for the most part), everyone winds up face-to-face with a very lifelike Animatronic shark. The 32-foot-long creature weighs three tons and is made of steel and fiberglass, but even up close, he looks very real and very hungry. The shark travels at a rate of 20 feet per second around the attraction's manmade 5-million-gallon, 7-acre lagoon. This ride is so realistic, young children may get frightened.

Men in Black: Alien Attack

Ages 2–4:	N.S.
Ages 5–10:	N.S.
Ages 11–15:	★★★
Ages 16–Adult:	★★★
Senior Citizens:	★★

Guests team up to save Earth from alien terrorists. While riding in special vehicles through a simulated New York City, riders directly affect the environment around them as they try to shoot and capture aliens roaming freely. Each rider is equipped with a "Series IV Alienator" device with which to shoot aliens (who will also be shooting at the vehicles guests are traveling in). This exciting ride offers twelve different endings, from a hero's welcome to an embarrassing defeat. It's based on the popular *Men in Black* motion picture.

✔ This is a must-see attraction.

Curious George Goes to Town

Ages 2–4:	N.S.
Ages 5–10:	★★★
Ages 11–15:	★
Ages 16–Adult:	N.S.
Senior Citizens:	N.S.

This attraction takes the popular children's books and brings them to life in an area that kids can interact within. Kids can climb, explore, play, and even get a little wet (if they choose to). This area is not suitable for children under age three. Parents should maintain constant supervision over their kids while they play in this innovative playground area.

Woody Woodpecker's Nuthouse Coaster

Ages 2–4:	N.S.
Ages 5–10:	★★★
Ages 11–15:	★★
Ages 16–Adult:	★
Senior Citizens:	N.S.

This kid-oriented roller coaster offers an 800-foot-long track that travels through a factory filled with gears and gadgets. The coaster is a mild thrill ride that lasts for about ninety seconds. It's for young people, so don't expect any big drops, sharp turns, loops, or other surprises. The highest point on the ride is 28 feet off the ground. Guests must be at least three years old and able to sit upright to ride this coaster. Kids under 48 inches tall must be accompanied by an adult.

✔ This is a must-see attraction.

A Day in the Park with Barney

Ages 2–4:	★★★
Ages 5–10:	★★★
Ages 11–15:	★
Ages 16–Adult:	★
Senior Citizens:	★

If you're traveling with kids ages ten and under, one of the stops you'll definitely want to make while visiting this park is to see Barney, who performs in live shows throughout the day. After each show, kids get to meet their favorite purple dinosaur.

The preshow stars one of Barney's human friends, Mr. Peekaboo, but once you enter into the main theater, the main show stars Barney, Baby Bop, and BJ from the PBS television series *Barney and Friends*. Kids are invited to sing and clap along as Barney performs popular songs that kids know and love. This show is presented in a specially built indoor theater that contains a 360-degree stage (that resembles a park) and offers benches for kids (and their parents) to sit on. All of the seats in the theater offer an excellent view.

The theater itself holds 350 people. During the actual performance, no flash photography is permitted; however, during the meet-and-greet session after each performance, you're welcome to take photographs of Barney shaking hands with or hugging your child. While many adults find Barney annoying, this show is actually rather charming. Young kids will absolutely love it, and most parents will find it tolerable.

✔ This is a must-see attraction.

⊕ HOT SPOT

After the show, guests exit the theater into an adjoining gift shop that sells all sorts of Barney merchandise, so be prepared to either spend money or have to explain to your child why he or she can't have whatever Barney toy catches his or her attention. Also near the exit to the theater is a Barney-themed playground that kids will love exploring.

Animal Planet Live!

Ages 2–4:	★★
Ages 5–10:	★★★
Ages 11–15:	★★★
Ages 16–Adult:	★★
Senior Citizens:	★★

Based on programming from the Animal Planet television cable network, as the name suggests, this is a totally live, twenty-minute stage show featuring live animal trainers and a cast of animals you've seen on popular television shows and in movies. Exotic birds, trained monkeys, snakes, and famous dogs are among the animals that perform in a show that can best be described as extremely cute and enjoyable.

This is a highly entertaining and rather humorous show that is suitable for and appealing to people of all ages. The theater in which this show is presented is large, so there's seldom a wait, assuming you arrive about fifteen minutes before a scheduled show time. Show times are posted in front of the theater, on the information board locations throughout the park, and in the printed park schedule available from the ticket booths. The theater itself is covered, so you'll be sheltered from direct sunlight or rain.

After each performance, some of the animals and their trainers remain onstage to meet and greet young audience members. This provides for an excellent photo opportunity.

✔ This is a must-see attraction.

Fievel's Playland

Ages 2–4:	★★★
Ages 5–10:	★★★
Ages 11–15:	N.S.
Ages 16–Adult:	N.S.
Senior Citizens:	N.S.

This fun-filled playground is for children only. It's based on the animated movie *An American Tail* and features all sorts of activities for young kids to experience, like slides, a water flume, and a massive jungle gym. There's also a shooting fountain that allows kids to get wet and cool off on a hot day. As you make your way to or from A Day in the Park with Barney and/or E.T. Adventure, you might want to drop by this playground with your kids.

✔ This is a must-see attraction.

📋 TRAVEL TIP

For parents, there are nearby benches where you can relax while your kids play. While sitting on a nearby bench, however, keep a constant eye on the young people you're with.

Universal Studios Florida . . . Take 3!

In addition to the awesome rides, you won't want to miss these highly entertaining shows, many of which feature talented live performers (who don't lip-synch). For the majority of these shows, the wait is minimal, especially if you time your arrival to the appropriate theater correctly. On the days when the park isn't totally jammed, arrive at the appropriate theater about fifteen minutes before the posted show time. Arrive thirty minutes prior to a show if the park is crowded and you want to be assured a good seat.

When you arrive at Universal Studios Florida and purchase your ticket, you'll be given a full-color guide booklet that lists all show times and show locations. While some shows are continuous, others are presented only a few times each day, at specific times.

Some of the shows/attractions listed here, like Terminator 2: 3D and Twister, are extremely popular, so you might want to see these shows between 11:30 A.M. and 1:00 P.M., or around 5:00 P.M., when many guests take a lunch or dinner break. Another ideal time to catch these two popular attractions is during the Dynamite Nights Stuntacular show that's held every evening.

Beetlejuice's Graveyard Revue

Ages 2–4:	★
Ages 5–10:	★★★
Ages 11–15:	★★★
Ages 16–Adult:	★★
Senior Citizens:	★★

Several times throughout the day, a group of Universal Studios' official monsters get together for a fun-filled concert, featuring adaptations of popular rock-and-roll songs. This twenty-five-minute show is suitable for the entire family, and features a cast of talented performers who perform all of the songs live. Join Dracula, the Phantom of the Opera, the Wolfman, the Bride of Frankenstein, and Frankenstein himself in a lighthearted musical extravaganza.

Dynamite Nights Stuntacular

Ages 2–4:	N.S.
Ages 5–10:	★★
Ages 11–15:	★★
Ages 16–Adult:	★★
Senior Citizens:	★★

In the center of Universal Studios Florida is an eight-acre, manmade lagoon that holds 13,850,000 gallons of water. Every evening, this lagoon is the stage of an awesome show featuring high-speed powerboats, jet skis, and other aquatic vehicles performing a stunt show that's accompanied by a flashy pyrotechnics demonstration (lots of explosions).

This show will appeal to guests of all ages and offers some pretty incredible and rather dangerous stunts. Dynamite Nights Stuntacular is presented once each evening (around 6:00 P.M.) during good weather conditions only.

💼 TRAVEL TIP

If you don't want to see this show, while it's going on is an excellent time to experience the other popular attractions. If you choose to see this show, there are excellent viewing locations around the perimeter of the lagoon. Some of the best spots to watch this show from are along the Embarcadero, in the Central Park area, or along Exposition Boulevard.

Lucy—A Tribute

Ages 2–4:	N.S.
Ages 5–10:	N.S.
Ages 11–15:	★
Ages 16–Adult:	★★
Senior Citizens:	★★

This museum-like exhibit offers a salute to Lucy. It will appeal to fans of the *I Love Lucy* sitcom. This self-paced, walk-through exhibit features a handful of interactive displays, TV show clips, props from *I Love Lucy,* and other memorabilia.

Horror Make-Up Show

Ages 2–4:	N.S.
Ages 5–10:	N.S.
Ages 11–15:	★★
Ages 16–Adult:	★★
Senior Citizens:	★★

Do you like scary movies? Watch a live demonstration of how an actor is transformed into a monster using makeup and special effects. A scene from *An American Werewolf in London* is used in this demonstration.

Also, discover how decapitations, severed limbs, bullet holes, stab wounds, and other special effects are incorporated into TV shows and movies. This show is both entertaining and educational (especially if you're a horror movie buff).

The show takes place in an air-conditioned theater and utilizes special fog effects. The Horror Make-Up Show is not suitable for kids under the age of thirteen.

⊕ HOT SPOT

Stage 54 is a soundstage that houses actual props, sets, and memorabilia from a popular (current) motion picture. The interactive exhibit changes every few months, but it offers an up-close and behind-the-scenes look at how a movie is made. This is a self-paced walking tour of a soundstage (a large building where movies are actually filmed).

Terminator 2: 3D

Ages 2–4:	N.S.
Ages 5–10:	★★
Ages 11–15:	★★★
Ages 16–Adult:	★★★
Senior Citizens:	★★★

You can experience every single ride, show, and attraction at The Magic Kingdom, Epcot, The Disney-MGM Studios, Universal Studios Florida, and at every other theme park and tourist attraction in the Orlando area, but you won't see anything like Terminator 2: 3D . . . it's that good! This 3D movie/attraction cost over $60 million to produce, and reunited Arnold Schwarzenegger, Linda Hamilton, Edward Furlong, and director James Cameron in a truly spectacular twelve-minute-and-forty-one-second film that's presented in 3D.

This attraction is much more than simply a 3D movie. The theater was custom built just for this presentation, and the entire theater becomes part of the show. Three 23-foot-high by 50-foot-wide movie screens are used to project the 3D movie, while lasers, smoke, robots, special effects, and moving seats in the theater itself all add to the overall experience. Live actors (stunt doubles) literally go from the stage and leap into the movie screens using effects never used before in a theme park attraction. The story itself takes audience members from the present to the year 2029.

Whatever you do, don't leave Universal Studios Florida without experiencing Terminator 2: 3D, no matter how long the wait is. Young children might find this movie a bit scary. This show/3D movie is equivalent to a rated PG-13 movie that you'd see in a regular theater in terms of suitability for kids.

✔ This is a must-see attraction.

Revenge of the Mummy—The Ride

Ages 2–4:	N.S.
Ages 5–10:	N.S.
Ages 11–15:	★★★
Ages 16–Adult:	★★★
Senior Citizens:	N.S.

In May 2004, Universal Studios transformed the motion pictures *The Mummy* and *The Mummy Returns* into one ground-breaking new thrill ride that was ten years in the making. This fast-paced and turbulent ride combines animitronics, projected CGI computer graphic effects, original motion picture footage (starring Brendan Fraser), and motion simulator technology to create a totally new type of theme park experience. Designed for teens and adults, Revenge of the Mummy is designed to take you on a trip inside an ancient tomb, where you'll experience firsthand many of the horrors seen in the movie. Not only is this ride scary due to its fast and turbulent element (like a high-tech rollercoaster), it also creates the feeling that you're inside a horror film, complete with mummies, scarab beetles, and fireballs. This ride was "directed" by Stephen Summers, who also directed the two popular motion pictures. Just as the movies were rated PG-13, this ride should carry a similar rating.

Twister . . . Ride It Out

Ages 2–4:	N.S.
Ages 5–10:	★★
Ages 11–15:	★★★
Ages 16–Adult:	★★★
Senior Citizens:	★★★

The blockbuster movie *Twister* has been developed into another stunning special-effects-intensive attraction at Universal Studios Florida that's almost as awesome as Back to the Future . . . The Ride and Terminator 2: 3D. You'll actually experience a real-life twister from only 20 feet away and see firsthand how incredibly treacherous a tornado can be. In this case, a five-story-tall tornado is created inside this 25,000-square-foot attraction.

While a real tornado is actually created, guests remain totally safe as they watch this awe-inspiring spectacle. You'll see the tornado consume everything in its path, shatter windows, lift up and hurl life-size trucks, crush enormous signs, and ultimately burst into a massive funnel of fire. Like Earthquake and JAWS, this attraction is highly realistic and might be too scary for young people (under the age of six). For teens and adults, however, it shouldn't be missed and is well worth the wait! This attraction will blow your mind, and might get you a little wet (but not drenched). The preshow features actors from the movie *Twister* but is a bit dull.

✔ This is a must-see attraction.

≡FAST FACT

This attraction blasts wind in your face and sends cows flying through the air, and to add to the realism, 150,000 gallons of recycled water are used as part of this attraction each day.

Shrek 4-D

Ages 2–4:	★★★
Ages 5–10:	★★★
Ages 11–15:	★★★
Ages 16–Adult:	★★
Senior Citizens:	★★

Shrek and Donkey are back in a totally original 3D movie with a twist. In this adventure, you'll join Princess Fiona, Shrek, and Donkey as they take you along every step of an all-new honeymoon adventure. Along with the 3D visual effects are dozens of other visual and audio effects that add excitement and realism to this unique movie experience. Through the miracle of "OgreVision," you will see, hear, and actually *feel* the action right from your seat.

✔ This is a must-see attraction.

Jimmy Neutron's Nicktoon Blast

Ages 2–4:	★★★
Ages 5–10:	★★★
Ages 11–15:	★★
Ages 16–Adult:	★★
Senior Citizens:	★★

Replacing the attraction called The FUNtastic World of Hanna-Barbera, this all-new and state-of-the-art attraction allows you to blast off on an adventure with Nickelodeon's Jimmy Neutron. The evil Ooblar (from the planet Yokian) has stolen Jimmy's newest rocket creation, the

Mark IV. You'll blast off on a neutronic trip as you board your rocket and follow Jimmy, his best friend Carl, and Jimmy's faithful robotic dog Goddard on a wild chase through your favorite NickToons. Along the way, you'll meet up with familiar faces from *SpongeBob SquarePants*, *The Fairly Odd Parents*, *Hey Arnold!*, and *Rugrats*. It's a colorful, fun, and lighthearted adventure no child will want to miss!

Universal Studios Florida . . . Take 4!

Along with the rides and shows, there are also plenty of interactive entertainment opportunities available throughout this theme park. There's an additional charge to participate in some of these activities. These attractions aren't anywhere near as entertaining or exciting as the rides and shows, but if you have some free time, they're worth checking out.

Amity Pitch & Skill Games—Play an assortment of carnival-like games that require both skill and luck. These games can be found near the entrance of the Jaws ride. The cost to participate is $1 per try. Prizes are awarded to winners.

AT&T at the Movies—Learn about the history and future of moviemaking from this interactive attraction.

Caricature Artist—Located at kiosks throughout the theme park are artists who will create caricatures of guests while they wait. There is a charge to take home this personalized souvenir.

Sega's Coney Island Arcade—Check out some of the hottest new arcade games here. Just as in any arcade, be prepared to pay for each game you want to play.

Sega's Space Station Arcade—This is a second arcade located in the Universal Studios Florida park.

Nickelodeon Studios Florida

The most popular cable network for kids, Nickelodeon, has a full production facility located in the heart of Universal Studios

Florida. Special forty-five-minute, kid-oriented guided tours of this studio complex are given throughout the day. Kids get a chance to see some of their favorite Nickelodeon shows in production.

At the entrance to this studio area is a 17-foot green slime geyser (instead of a fountain). The Nickelodeon Studios Tour is included in the general admission price to Universal Studios Florida. In addition to seeing the sets of popular Nickelodeon shows (and maybe even having the opportunity to see actors and actresses from those shows), free tickets for kids to be in the audience during show tapings are often available.

Kids of all ages will enjoy this fun-filled and informative tour of Nickelodeon Studios, which includes a stop at the gack kitchen, where guests learn how green slime is created. Special Nickelodeon merchandise is sold near the exit of the Nickelodeon Studios. If you're traveling with kids, plan on spending at least two hours exploring the Nickelodeon Studios, experiencing the Game Lab, and taking the guided tour.

Meet the Characters

At Universal Studios Florida, kids have the chance to meet some of their favorite animated idols, who roam around the park continuously and participate in special meet-and-greet sessions held at specific times and locations in the park throughout the day.

Some of the characters you're apt to meet at Universal Studios Florida include Boo Boo Bear, Yogi Bear, Scooby Doo, Fred Flintstone, Frankenstein, Harry Henderson, George Jetson, Fievel Mousekewitz, Rocky and Bullwinkle, Barney Rubble, Winnie Woodpecker, and Woody Woodpecker. Oh, and kids also get a chance to meet and greet that lovable purple dinosaur . . . Barney! As you explore Universal Studios, you'll also meet celebrity look-alikes ranging from Beetlejuice and Charlie Chaplin to Groucho Marx and Marilyn Monroe.

If you're traveling with kids, be sure to take photos of them meeting these characters and celebrity look-alikes. They'll make a perfect addition to your family photo album. You'll also want to bring along an autograph book so that your children can collect the autographs of the "celebrities" they meet. Autograph books are an inexpensive souvenir that kids really appreciate and look forward to taking home to show their friends.

Dining Opportunities

Whether you're looking for a quick bite or a full sit-down lunch or dinner, there are many dining opportunities available in the main Universal Studios Florida theme park area, plus plenty of other restaurants in the CityWalk area. Reservations are accepted at some of the Studios' full-service restaurants. Here is a list of some of your dining options:

Animal Crackers—Hot dogs, chicken fingers, and smoked sausage hoagies are among the fast-food and snack options served here.

Beverly Hills Boulangerie—Sandwiches, pastries, and cappuccino are among the popular menu selections. Counter service and nearby tables are offered.

Boardwalk Funnel Cake Co.—Funnel cakes and soft drinks make up the menu here.

Brody's Ice Cream Shop—Ice cream, sundaes, and floats are the dessert and snack items you can purchase here and enjoy on a hot day.

Café LaBamba—Rotisserie chicken, burgers, sandwiches, and BBQ ribs are the popular entrees served here. Counter service and nearby seating are offered.

Captain Quint's Seafood and Chowder House Restaurant—Enjoy a fresh selection of coastal seafood and chowder.

Chez Alcatraz—Hot dogs, shrimp cocktail, clam chowder, and sandwiches are served here. Counter service and nearby seating are offered.

Finnegan's Bar & Grill—This is a full-service restaurant that serves traditional Irish-American food and beverages. Live entertainment and a fully equipped bar are provided for your pleasure. During mealtimes, be prepared to wait for a table.

The Fudge Shop—The name says it all. Homemade fudge is created here daily.

International Food Bazaar—Everything from pizza to fried chicken, tacos, burgers, sweet-and-sour chicken, and a wide range of desserts is offered here. Counter service with nearby seating is offered.

Lombard's Landing—At this full-service restaurant, you'll find seafood dishes like fresh lobster, as well as steak, pasta, and sandwiches. During lunch and dinner periods, expect to wait for a table.

Louie's Italian Restaurant—Pizza, pasta, Italian desserts, and a full espresso bar are offered here. Counter service and nearby tables are provided.

Mel's Drive-In—This 1950s diner offers burgers, fries, shakes, and other popular diner entrees. Limited indoor table service is offered. While you eat, you'll be entertained by a disc jockey who plays popular 1950s and 1960s music. Outside seating is more readily available. This is one of the better mid-priced eating places within the park.

Midway Grill—Sausage hoagies, Philly cheese steaks, and beer are served here.

Schwab's Pharmacy—In addition to ice cream, the specialty at this eating establishment is hand-carved turkey and ham sandwiches that are really tasty. Limited table service is available.

Universal Studios Classic Monster Café—Salads, pizza, and other lunch items are served here.

Special Events

Throughout the year, Universal Studios Florida hosts popular themed events. For example, during the month of October, Universal Studios Florida hosts Halloween Horror Nights (targeted primarily to teenagers). On July 4th and New Year's Eve, Universal Studios Florida presents a gala fireworks spectacular, combining pyrotechnics with lasers and synchronized music. Every spring (early February through late March), there's also a Mardi Gras celebration, and for the Christmas holidays, you can expect to see the park decked out with festive décor.

CHAPTER 16

Universal Escape's Islands of Adventure

THE ISLANDS OF ADVENTURE THEME PARK OFFERS traditional amusement park thrill rides, spread out over a series of themed areas. These themes encompass every aspect of the park, from the rides, shows, and attractions to the architecture, the landscaping, and the music you'll hear in the background. The result is a truly immersive adventure.

Park Overview

Islands of Adventure is a 100-acre park designed to be a theme park for the new millennium. Many of the rides and attractions are truly state-of-the-art and offer full entertainment experiences, not just basic rides. For example, even the roller coasters have a story line.

When visiting Islands of Adventure, be prepared for a full day (and evening) of walking, so wear comfortable shoes. If you want to experience the rides that involve getting wet, seriously consider bringing along a change of clothes and storing it in a locker. Ride all of the water-based rides in a row and then change into dry clothes before continuing your day.

For more information about Islands of Adventure, be sure to check out the park's Web site at *www.usf.com* before you leave home. You can also make reservations and purchase admission tickets online in order to save time once you arrive at the park.

Layout of the Park

From the Port of Entry, which is the main entrance to Islands of Adventure (accessed by walking through CityWalk), all of the themed islands surround a large lake. Moving counterclockwise, once you enter into the park is Seuss Landing, a 10-acre area designed specifically for young people (and those who are young at heart). This is really the only kid-oriented area within this park. The other "islands" are more suited to kids over the age of nine, teens, and adults. The Lost Continent is the next island of adventure and features rides, shows, and attractions for teens and adults alike.

As guests continue their island-hopping adventure, Jurassic Park is next. Based on the movies, this area features the Jurassic Park River Adventure along with an assortment of other dinosaur-themed rides and attractions suitable for people of all ages. Comic strips come alive within Toon Lagoon, where characters like Popeye, Dudley Do-Right, and Beetle Bailey are the basis for a handful of whimsical rides, shows, and attractions.

Finally, for comic book fans of all ages, Marvel Super Hero Island is where you'll find two of the park's most popular thrill rides, The Incredible Hulk Coaster and Doctor Doom's Fearfall.

▐█▌ TRAVEL TIP

To avoid the longest lines, the best times to visit Islands of Adventure are during the winter (January through March), the month of May, or in the fall (September through mid-December). These periods offer the mildest weather and allow you to avoid peak tourist traffic.

By combining thrill rides with family-oriented entertainment, shops, restaurants, and attractions, Islands of Adventure offers something for everyone in a not-so-traditional theme park atmosphere. Visiting Islands of Adventure offers a very different (but equally exciting) experience than anything The Walt Disney World Resort has to offer.

The Rating System

Not all of the rides, shows, and attractions at Islands of Adventure are suitable or designed for everyone. To help you choose which rides and attractions are most worth seeing during your visit to Islands of Adventure, this book offers star-based ratings for each ride and attraction, based on the age group each will most appeal to. Each ride and attraction has earned between one and three stars.

★ = Rides and attractions that earned just one star aren't worth waiting for and could be skipped, especially if your time within the theme park is limited.

★★ = Rides and attractions that earned two stars are good, but they don't fall into the "must-see" category.

★★★ = The rides and attractions that earned three stars are definitely worth seeing and should not be missed.

N.S. = This denotes rides and attractions that are "Not Suitable" for a specific age group.

Restrictions

Islands of Adventure contains multiple adult-oriented thrill rides, plus separate rides and attractions designed specifically for young kids. Certain rides and attractions have height restrictions. For example, people under 54 inches tall are not permitted to ride Dueling Dragons or the Incredible Hulk Coaster. Those under 52 inches tall cannot ride Doctor Doom's Fearfall, and those under 48 inches tall won't be allowed to experience Popeye and Bluto's Bilge-Rat Barges. Visitors must be over 42 inches tall to experience Dudley Do-Right's Ripsaw Falls and over 40 inches tall to experience Jurassic Park River Ride and the Amazing Adventures of Spider-Man. Finally, children must be at least 36 inches tall to ride the Pteranodon Flyers.

Due to the turbulent nature of the above-mentioned rides, expectant mothers and people with certain physical disabilities or limitations should not experience these rides either. For additional information about special accommodations for people with physical disabilities, contact the Guest Services office located near the main entrance of the park.

≡FAST FACT

The hours of operation for Universal Studios Islands of Adventure vary by season. The park typically opens at 9:00 A.M. and remains open until between 6:00 P.M. and 8:00 P.M. For the hours of operation during your planned visit, call ☎(407) 363-8000.

Port of Entry

Upon passing through CityWalk, you'll find yourself at Port of Entry, the main entrance to Islands of Adventure. This area contains a handful of shops, a package pickup station, plus a few snack areas. Port of Entry is an ideal meeting spot if you and the people you're traveling with happen to become separated. In the Port of Entry, you'll also find restrooms, lockers, ATMs, public telephones, the lost and found, and Guest Services. Stroller and wheelchair rentals are also available here.

Shopping
The shops you'll find in the Port of Entry area include:

De Foto's Expedition Photography—Film, camera supplies, batteries, and anything else you'll need to take vacation pictures can be found here. As you enter into Islands of Adventure, professional photographers will be on hand, snapping pictures and welcoming guests. If you choose to purchase the picture taken of you and your family, you can pick it up at this location.

Island Market and Export—Candy, gourmet foods, and gift baskets are among the edible offerings sold here.

Ocean Trader Market—Carver and loom artists sell their crafts.

Port Provisions—T-shirts, caps, rain ponchos, and souvenirs are sold here.

Silk Road Clothiers—Travel wear, leather bags, jewelry, gifts, and souvenirs are sold at this shop. Any of your purchases made within the park can also be delivered to this location (near the entrance/exit of Islands of Adventure).

📑 TRAVEL TIP

Once you've explored some of the shops located within the Port of Entry, it's time to travel toward the various islands. You'll probably want to travel to the right if you're with young kids, or to the left if you're traveling with teens and/or adults. You can also climb aboard the Island Skipper Tour boat and experience a sea voyage that takes you directly to Jurassic Park.

Dining

Throughout the park, you'll find a wide range of dining options, including several full-service restaurants, many snack shops, and countless food kiosks. Pizza, burgers, hot dogs, and chicken dishes are among the main entrees offered.

Confisco Grille (and **Backwater Bar**) is a full-service restaurant featuring personal pizzas, pasta, fresh seafood, grilled meats, specialty burgers, and fresh desserts. Reservations are accepted. Get autographs and photos with some of your favorite Universal Studios Islands of Adventure characters during the **Confisco Grille Character Lunch**. There's no extra charge—just the normal cost of your menu selections. The Confisco Grille is open every Monday through Friday from noon until 2:00 A.M.

Other dining options within the Port of Entry area include: **Arctic Express** (featuring fruit-topped funnel cakes, Belgian waffles, waffle-cone sundaes), **Croissant Moon Baker** (fresh-baked pastries and desserts, coffee, cappuccino, espresso, latte, beer, wine, and soda), and **Spice Island Sausages** (grilled Italian sausage sandwiches, jumbo hot dogs, corn dogs, fresh-cut French fries, beer, wine, and soda).

Seuss Landing

For kids (and those who are young at heart), there's Seuss Landing. This colorful area offers rides, shows, and attractions based on some of Dr. Seuss's famous and beloved characters and children's books. This entire area is designed to make visitors feel as if they've stepped into the pages of a Dr. Seuss story. All of the buildings and surroundings are painted in pastel colors.

Costumed characters taken from the pages of Dr. Seuss's popular books can be seen roaming around this area of the park and are available for pictures and autographs. Weather permitting, there's also the *Seuss Street Show*, a live music show presented several times daily. This show is suitable for children ages twelve and under. Shows typically begin midmorning and continue every hour or two throughout the afternoon. For exact show times, refer to the free *Adventure Guide* given to all visitors entering the park.

⊕ HOT SPOT

The Green Eggs & Ham Café serves an array of meal and snack items, but the specialty of the house is green eggs and ham. This is a fun place for a family with young children to eat breakfast, lunch, or an early dinner. It's also ideal for a midday snack. Hamburgers and chicken fingers are among the other main entrees available.

Caro-Seuss-el

Ages 2–4:	★★★
Ages 5–10:	★★★
Ages 11–15:	★★
Ages 16–Adult:	★★
Senior Citizens:	★★

This is no ordinary merry-go-round. It features the colors, characters, and music that Dr. Seuss made famous. Ride around in circles on the back of a popular character. Some of the characters move up and down, while other are stationary on the turning merry-go-round.

The Once-Ler's House

This interactive area comes straight from the pages of one of Dr. Seuss's popular stories. Listen on the Whisper-ma-phone as the Once-ler tells you the story of the Lorax. Guests can also stand on the stone podium where, by the seat of his pants, the Lorax lifted himself through a hole in the clouds.

One Fish, Two Fish, Red Fish, Blue Fish

Ages 2–4:	★★★
Ages 5–10:	★★★
Ages 11–15:	★★
Ages 16–Adult:	★
Senior Citizens:	★

Steer your flying fish up, down, around and around as you avoid shooting water. This ride has its own catchy theme song that will certainly put even the most serious adults in a light-hearted, childlike mood. If you're traveling with young kids, this is one ride that shouldn't be missed. Riders can fly 15 feet into the air as they travel in the Seussian fish vehicle. Topping off the center pedestal of the ride is an 18-foot-tall sculpture of the star-belly fish featured in the Dr. Seuss book *One Fish Two Fish Red Fish Blue Fish*.

✔ This is a must-see attraction.

The Cat in the Hat

Ages 2–4:	★★★
Ages 5–10:	★★★
Ages 11–15:	★★★
Ages 16–Adult:	★★★
Senior Citizens:	★★★

Thanks to Animatronics, the pages of Dr. Seuss's most famous book, *The Cat in the Hat,* come to life. Visitors ride in moving vehicles that take them through scenes lifted directly from the storybook. The scenes, however, are depicted in 3D using life-size characters and colorful sets. This ride is lighthearted and recommended for people of all ages. Although it's not a thrill ride, it's definitely one of the most impressive, original, and imaginative attractions within Islands of Adventure.

✔ This is a must-see attraction.

⊕ HOT SPOT

For a more elaborate, sit-down meal in a theme-oriented dining area, kids will enjoy chowing down on fried chicken, lasagna, spaghetti, and pizza at Circus McGurkus Café Stoopendous. Special kids' meals are available.

If I Ran the Zoo

Ages 2–4:	★★
Ages 5–10:	★★★
Ages 11–15:	★★
Ages 16–Adult:	N.S.
Senior Citizens:	N.S.

This is an interactive play area that tells the story of Gerald McGrew and his quest to create a totally different zoo of strange and unusual animals. This attraction is divided into three distinct areas: Hedges, Water, and New Zoo.

✔ This is a must-see attraction.

Shopping with Seuss

The shops within Seuss Landing include:

Cats, Hats & Things—All kinds of clothing, gifts, and toys based on *The Cat in the Hat* can be purchased here. As you exit the Cat in the Hat ride, you'll find yourself within this colorful shop.

Dr. Seuss's All the Books You Can Read—This bookshop offers a complete library of Dr. Seuss books, videocassettes, CDs, and computer software.

Mulberry Street Store—Merchandise featuring all of your favorite Dr. Seuss characters can be found here.

Picture This!—Purchase a unique photo of yourself (or your children) within the pages of a popular Dr. Seuss story.

Snookers & Snookers Sweet Candy Cookers—A large selection of candy will satisfy your sweet tooth, while the gifts sold here make excellent souvenirs.

⊕ HOT SPOT

At the Hop on Pop food kiosk, guests can create their own sundae on a stick. Banana splits and ice cream served in waffle cones are also available. If you're really thirsty and don't want soda, check out Moose Juice Goose Juice, a drink kiosk that serves juices, fruit cups, and other beverages.

The Lost Continent

This area of Islands of Adventure houses one of the most thrilling roller coasters in Orlando—the Dueling Dragons. Out of all the areas within Islands of Adventure, the Lost Continent is the smallest. It'll appeal mainly to people in their teen or early-adult years looking for the thrill of a roller coaster ride they won't soon forget.

Poseidon's Fury: Escape from the Lost City

Ages 2–4:	N.S.
Ages 5–10:	★
Ages 11–15:	★★
Ages 16–Adult:	★★
Senior Citizens:	★★

Explore the relics of a once-glorious civilization as you tour the ruins of a mysterious lost city. This city isn't totally dead, however. After eons, something may have survived. You'll find out what when Poseidon himself opens a portal to the underseas through a 42-foot swirling vortex of water. This is the gateway to Atlantis! During your adventure, Zeus suddenly appears and challenges Poseidon on your behalf. Watch out, or you could get caught in the deadly battle between the gods! This is a walk-through attraction that features live actors and many stunning special effects. Young children might find it scary.

Dueling Dragons

Ages 2–4:	N.S.
Ages 5–10:	N.S.
Ages 11–15:	★★★
Ages 16–Adult:	★★★
Senior Citizens:	N.S.

You'll soar up to 125 feet in the air and travel at speeds of 55 miles per hour on one of two distinct, yet simultaneously running tracks that put you perilously close to collision. At one point, the two tracks bring riders within a foot of each other. No matter which track you experience, this is an inverted coaster, so your legs will be dangling freely.

Dueling Dragons is a thrill ride in every sense of the term, so if you don't like high-speed and turbulent roller coasters, you'd best skip it. Since this is one of the most popular attractions within the park, expect a long line. It's best to check out this coaster first thing in the morning or during peak mealtimes. The coaster has a capacity of 3,264 riders per hour, so while the line may seem long, it moves constantly. It's a favorite among thrill seekers!

✔ This is a must-see attraction.

FAST FACT

According to the coaster's designers, the tracks of Dueling Dragons feature one Immelmann, a 70-degree inclined loop, two vertical loops, one cobra roll, one 45-degree inclined loop, one "zero g" roll, a flat spin, and two interlocked flat rolls. This is the world's first inverted dueling coaster.

The Eighth Voyage of Sinbad

Ages 2–4:	N.S.
Ages 5–10:	★
Ages 11–15:	★★
Ages 16–Adult:	★★
Senior Citizens:	★★

This is a live-action stunt show presented several times throughout each day, typically every two hours in the afternoon. During peak vacation times, the show is presented more frequently. Check the *Adventure Guide* (available free of charge at the ticket window) for exact show times. The show itself features fifty pyrotechnic effects, including a 10-foot-tall circle of flames.

The Flying Unicorn

Ages 2–4:	N.S.
Ages 5–10:	★★★
Ages 11–15:	★★★
Ages 16–Adult:	★
Senior Citizens:	★

This non-thrill ride offers a gentle, yet exciting ride through an enchanted forest. The ride simulates flying on a unicorn and is cute and rather kid-oriented.

Dine with the Gods

Within the Lost Continent, you'll find several places to grab a bite to eat. Several of these places offer indoor seating, which provides an excellent opportunity to get out of the sun, sit down, and take a break.

The Enchanted Oak Tavern (and Alchemy Bar)—Within this "buffeteria," hickory-smoked barbecue chicken and ribs, roasted corn on the cob, chicken salad, kids' meals, and soda are served. The adjoining bar features fifty brands of bottled beers.

Fire-Eater's Grill—Sausages are served in a roll or on a stick. Grab an order of fresh fries to round out the meal. Soda, beer, and wine are also served.

Frozen Desert—Soft-serve ice cream and sundaes are guaranteed to cool you down on a hot day. Fresh fruit cups, cookies, and an assortment of candy items are also available.

Mythos Restaurant—This is a full-service restaurant. Menu items include appetizers, fresh seafood, grilled meats, entree salads, gourmet wood-oven pizzas, pasta, and desserts. There's also a full bar and an extensive wine menu. Reservations are accepted.

Oasis Coolers—If you're in the mood for a snack or refreshing drink while on the go, check out this food kiosk for lemonade, soda, nachos, pretzels, and fruit cups.

═FAST FACT

If you return home and wish you had purchased an item you saw at any of the shops within Islands of Adventure, you can order merchandise by phone. Call ☎(407) 363-8320.

Shopping for Treasures

Souvenirs are plentiful within the Lost Continent. Here's a sampling of what treasures you'll encounter:

The Coin Mint—Choose from one of several dozen designs and watch as your selected design gets minted on a metal coin right before your eyes. This is a personalized and rather unique souvenir you can actually watch being made.

The Dragon's Keep—If you survive the coaster, you might want to pick up a Dueling Dragons T-shirt or souvenir. Dragons are the theme behind the merchandise sold here.

Garlands—Handmade silk garlands and satin garters will make any woman feel like a princess.

Metal Smith—Bronze and copper items are available here. There's also a selection of handcrafted pottery.

Shop of Wonders—Silks, copper, brass, woven rugs, travel bags, leather, and cotton goods are among the offerings at this shop. There's also an extensive jewelry selection.

Treasures of Poseidon—Themed merchandise from the Poseidon's Fury: Escape from the Lost City attraction is sold here.

⊕ HOT SPOT

If you want to know what your future holds, visit with the psychic who's on duty within the Shop of Wonders area.

Jurassic Park

Steven Spielberg's motion pictures come to life within this area of Islands of Adventure. If you thought dinosaurs were extinct, think again! This area offers activities and attractions for young kids, and more thrill-oriented rides for teens and adults—all with a dinosaur theme. The state-of-the-art Animatronic creatures look and act extremely real, which adds to the overall ambiance of this area. This is the largest of the areas within the Islands of Adventure theme park.

Camp Jurassic

Ages 2–4:	★
Ages 5–10:	★★★
Ages 11–15:	★★★
Ages 16–Adult:	N.S.
Senior Citizens:	N.S.

Kids can make their way through this prehistoric playground/maze that offers volcanoes and cascading waterfalls. The play area is filled with secret caves and an amber mine to explore. Visitors can also climb along dinosaur capture-nets, ride down slides, and cross suspension bridges. This play area is a self-paced attraction for kids only. Parents can watch from nearby, but will be too large to fit in some parts of this play area.

As a parent, if you're looking to rest your feet, let your kids roam freely in this area while you park yourself at a nearby bench and act as a spectator. Needless to say, never leave your child unattended within this or any other area of a theme park.

Pteranodon Flyers

Ages 2–4:	N.S.
Ages 5–10:	★★
Ages 11–15:	★★
Ages 16–Adult:	★
Senior Citizens:	★

Riders will feel like they've been grabbed by a flying pteranodon as they soar through the air and take an all-too-quick tour of the Jurassic Park area. This ride is most suitable for kids.

💼 TRAVEL TIP

While kids will enjoy this swing ride around Jurassic Park, the wait is typically extremely long, but the ride itself is rather short. Unless you happen to be visiting Jurassic Park on an unusually quiet day, you probably don't want to spend too much time waiting to experience Pteranodon Flyers.

Jurassic Park River Adventure

Ages 2–4:	N.S.
Ages 5–10:	★★
Ages 11–15:	★★★
Ages 16–Adult:	★★★
Senior Citizens:	★

Pass through the grand gates of this prehistoric theme park (just like in the movie) and travel within a riverboat as you see firsthand the scientific marvels that brought dinosaurs back to roam the earth.

While the initial part of your river journey will be quiet, peaceful, and rather beautiful, things don't always go as planned. In fact, you'll soon discover deadly 'raptors and venomous spitters that don't appreciate your visiting their territory. As if that weren't bad enough, a raging T-Rex has gotten loose, and this creature is hungry.

Just when you think you're safe, grab on to your personal belongings and prepare for an 85-foot plunge into total darkness for the conclusion of your adventure. This exciting and somewhat scary ride ultimately ends with a splash, so be prepared to get wet. (Also, be sure to protect your valuables, such as cameras and camcorders, from the water.)

✔ This is a must-see attraction.

═FAST FACT

Over 1.5 million gallons of water are used to create this manmade river ride that ends with a splash!

Jurassic Park Discovery Center

Ages 2–4:	N.S.
Ages 5–10:	★★
Ages 11–15:	★★★
Ages 16–Adult:	★★
Senior Citizens:	★★

Within the hands-on interactive exhibits and displays that make up this attraction, you can examine the massive fossilized remains of a T-Rex. Visitors can also join the activity in the nursery, where you might see a velociraptor hatching from its egg. Visitors along this self-paced walking tour can see how dinosaurs were brought back to life and how they're being raised within Jurassic Park.

Triceratops Encounter

Ages 2–4:	N.S.
Ages 5–10:	★★
Ages 11–15:	★★
Ages 16–Adult:	★★
Senior Citizens:	★★

Thanks to the latest in Audio-Animatronic technology, an extremely lifelike (not to mention life-size) triceratops is part of this unique interactive attraction. This 24-foot-long and 10-foot-tall beast is friendly and outgoing. As guests visit, this creature will snort, blink, flinch, and even make sounds. Visitors are allowed to pet the triceratops and take pictures. (If this creature were really alive, it would weigh more than two full-size elephants.)

▐ TRAVEL TIP

While Triceratops Encounter is somewhat entertaining, if you're pressed for time or there's a long wait, skip it in favor of the more popular and exciting rides and attractions that Islands of Adventure has to offer.

Dining with the Dinos

If encountering dinosaurs makes you hungry, there are several snack shops and dining areas within Jurassic Park that will help you quench your hunger or thirst.

The Burger Digs—The name says it all. Burgers and chicken sandwiches are among this dining area's primary offerings.

Pizza Predattoria—Personal pan pizzas, sandwiches, salads, dessert items, along with soda, beer, and wine are served.

Thunder Falls Terrace—Rotisserie chicken, baby back ribs, beef kabobs, and roasted corn are among the entrees available here.

The Watering Hole—For adult visitors, an assortment of alcoholic beverages is served, including coolers, margaritas, and rum runners.

Bring Home a Dino-Size Souvenir

Dinosaurs don't make the best pets, but you can pick up a wide range of dinosaur-themed gifts and souvenirs at these shops located within Jurassic Park:

Camp Jurassic Outpost—Youth survival gear and *Jurassic Park*-themed merchandise are among the offerings.

Dinostore—If it has to do with dinos, you'll find it here. Toys, books, plush toys, and plenty of educational (and not so educational) souvenirs are available—all with a dinosaur theme.

Jurassic Outfitters—After experiencing Jurassic Park River Adventure, you can see the look on your own face (and take it home with you) because your photo gets taken as you experience that massive drop at the end of the ride. This personalized souvenir is available for purchase at this shop. Here, you'll also find a wide range of Jurassic Park and Islands of Adventure souvenirs.

Toon Lagoon

Take your favorite comic strip characters, add some water, and you have the makings of some lighthearted fun that's suitable for the entire family. All of the rides in this area are family-oriented and aren't really considered thrill rides (with the possible exception of Dudley Do-Right's Ripsaw Falls, which ends in a mighty splash).

Keep in mind, many of the rides and attractions within Toon Lagoon are water-based, so be prepared to get wet (and possibly soaked).

Dudley Do-Right's Ripsaw Falls

Ages 2–4:	N.S.
Ages 5–10:	★★
Ages 11–15:	★★★
Ages 16–Adult:	★★★
Senior Citizens:	★

Based on *Rocky and Bullwinkle,* the popular cartoon from the 1960s, this water-flume ride takes guests on a wild and wet adventure around a 400,000 gallon lagoon. This ride ends with a major splash, so be prepared to get wet. Also, be sure to protect your camera, camcorder, and other valuables from the water when you experience this ride.

⊕ HOT SPOT

On the bridge that overlooks Dudley Do-Right's Ripsaw Falls, passersby have a chance to squirt water at those brave enough to experience this water flume firsthand.

Popeye & Bluto's Bilge-Rat Barges

Ages 2–4:	N.S.
Ages 5–10:	★★★
Ages 11–15:	★★★
Ages 16–Adult:	★★★
Senior Citizens:	★★

This wet and wild water raft ride has its turbulent moments, but overall it's suitable for people of all ages who don't mind getting wet. Twelve people at a time ride in specially designed rafts that travel along the manmade river at about 16 feet per second. If you're carrying valuables or other items you want to keep dry, consider putting them in lockers or within the center (watertight) compartment of the raft before the ride begins.

While this is a fun-filled and rather exciting ride, if the weather is chilly or you don't want to get drenched, consider skipping this attraction. It does, however, offer an awesome way to cool off on a hot and sunny day. As if the water along the ride weren't enough, people on land (exploring Popeye's boat) have a chance to squirt water at those aboard the rafts.

Me Ship, The Olive

Ages 2–4:	N.S.
Ages 5–10:	★★★
Ages 11–15:	★★★
Ages 16–Adult:	★
Senior Citizens:	N.S.

Popeye the Sailor Man invites guests (primarily younger ones) to climb aboard his three-story boat and partake in a fun-filled exploration. From bow to stern, the boat is loaded with interactive activities and things to do. There are water cannons to shoot, whistles to blow, organs to play, bells to clang, and plenty of things to crawl and climb through. If you're traveling with young kids, this will be a fun-filled stop.

Pandemonium Cartoon Circus

Within this amphitheater, live shows and special events are held throughout the day. To find out what live shows are being presented during your visit, check the *Adventure Guide* booklet offered at all ticket windows.

💼 TRAVEL TIP

Along the street that winds through Toon Lagoon, be on the lookout for comic strip captions hanging overhead. Find an appropriate message and have the person or people you're traveling with stand under these signs for a funny photo opportunity.

Dine with Your Favorite Toons

Kick back, relax, read a comic strip, and have some food. The following are the dining options available within Toon Lagoon. If you're looking for a more formal, sit-down meal, consider one of the full-service restaurants located within CityWalk.

Blondie's Home of the Dagwood—This kitchen-style deli offers a 3-foot-long Dagwood sandwich, chicken noodle soup, jumbo smoked turkey sandwiches, kosher deli dogs, veggie sandwiches, kids' meals, chef salads, hi-top apple pie, soda, beer, and wine.

Cathy's Ice Cream—Hot fudge sundaes, waffle-cone sundaes, and soda are what's served here. If you're looking for a cool snack, this is the place to visit.

Comic Strip Café—This buffeteria offers American, Mexican, Italian, and Chinese fast food. Soda, beer, and wine are available for toon-loving adults.

Wimpy's—If you're looking for a place to break for lunch, Wimpy's offers charbroiled burgers and cheeseburgers, jumbo hot dogs, spinach salad, kids' meals, fries, soda, beer, and wine.

Shopping in Toon Lagoon

For those who love reading the Sunday comics or have a special affinity for a specific comic strip character, chances are you'll find a souvenir at one of these shops located within Toon Lagoon:

Gasoline Alley—Comic strip and Islands of Adventure–themed souvenirs are sold here.

Photo Funnies—One-of-a-kind, personalized souvenirs are created while you wait. Photo Funnies allows guests to have their picture taken and then incorporated into a comic strip that costars some of their favorite characters.

Toon Extra—A selection of clothing, accessories, gifts, and souvenirs, all with a toon theme are sold here. You can also pick up personalized gifts and limited-edition collectibles featuring Betty Boop, Popeye, and Beetle Bailey. Some of these items will appeal more to adults and collectors than to kids.

Toon Toys—Nostalgic toys and novelty gifts from sipper straws to plush toys, costumes to candy, activity sets to stationery are what you'll find at this shop. Adults more than kids will find Toon Toys a fun place to visit.

WossaMotta U—Fans of Dudley Do-Right and Rocky and Bullwinkle will find a selection of merchandise including clothing, accessories, watches, backpacks, totes, activity sets, rubber stamps, glassware, and collectibles featuring these and other popular characters.

Marvel Super Hero Island

Rounding out Islands of Adventure is an area designed for teens, young adults, and Marvel comic book fans of all ages. This entire area focuses on characters and themes from Marvel comics, so don't be surprised if you run into the X-Men, Spider-Man, the Incredible Hulk, or other characters as you explore this area.

The main rides within Marvel Super Hero Island are considered thrill rides and aren't suitable for young kids or many senior citizens. If there's a comic book collector in your family, you'll definitely want to check out some of the shops within this area and take a look at the collectibles offered.

The Amazing Adventures of Spider-Man

Ages 2–4:	N.S.
Ages 5–10:	★★★
Ages 11–15:	★★★
Ages 16–Adult:	★★★
Senior Citizens:	★★★

The Amazing Adventures of Spider-Man combines moving vehicles with filmed 3D action and special effects, resulting in a visually stunning attraction/ride that most visitors want to experience multiple times. Upon boarding, guests get a tour of the *Daily Bugle* (the newspaper where Peter

Parker, a.k.a. Spider-Man, works). It's a typical day for Peter until he discovers that evil villains, including Doctor Octopus, are using an antigravity gun to steal the Statue of Liberty. This is where the action heats up. You, along with Spider-Man, experience an action-packed adventure worthy of any super hero.

✔ This is a must-see attraction.

═FAST FACT

> While this ride is somewhat turbulent, most of the thrill-ride elements are created using visual special effects. This ride isn't suitable for toddlers, but everyone else will enjoy it. Expect a wait to experience this ride, but it's well worth it.

Doctor Doom's Fearfall

Ages 2–4:	N.S.
Ages 5–10:	N.S.
Ages 11–15:	★★★
Ages 16–Adult:	★★★
Senior Citizens:	N.S.

What goes up, must come down. That's the premise behind this free-fall ride that takes guests up a 200-foot tower and then drops them.

✔ This is a must-see attraction.

Incredible Hulk Coaster

Ages 2–4:	N.S.
Ages 5–10:	N.S.
Ages 11–15:	★★★
Ages 16–Adult:	★★★
Senior Citizens:	N.S.

Perhaps the most popular ride in all of the Islands of Adventure, this roller coaster allows riders to experience the same thrust as the pilot of a real-life U.S. Air Force F-16 fighter attack jet experiences. The ride starts with a blast (from zero to 40 miles per hour in less than two seconds) and continues with a series of loops, twists, turns, and flips. The ride lasts only two minutes and fifteen seconds, but is one that won't soon be forgotten.

As with any thrill ride, this one isn't suitable for young children. Be prepared for a long wait because this ride is so popular, but if you're a roller coaster fanatic, it's well worth the wait.

✔ This is a must-see attraction.

═ FAST FACT

The Incredible Hulk Coaster features one cobra roll, one weightless roll, one 360-degree carousel, two loops, one inclined loop, one high-speed carousel, and two flat spins. According to the ride's designers, the track measures 3,800 feet in length and includes two subterranean enclosures, one under water and one under land.

Storm Force Accelatron

Ages 2–4:	N.S.
Ages 5–10:	★
Ages 11–15:	★★★
Ages 16–Adult:	★★★
Senior Citizens:	★

If you thought the Mad Tea Party (Tea Cups) ride at The Magic Kingdom took you for a spin, just wait until you experience this faster-spinning thrill ride. Here, Storm faces Magneto in a ride that features sound and visual effects, plus a whole lot of spinning. It's certainly not for young kids or those who have just eaten.

⊕ HOT SPOT

A selection of the most popular video arcade games is offered at Kingpin's Arcade. Your admission ticket to Islands of Adventure does not include the cost of these arcade games.

Recharge Your Super Powers

You don't have to be a super hero or a notorious villain trying to take over the world to work up an appetite. The following are your dining options within Marvel Super Hero Island:

Café 4—This Italian buffeteria's menu includes minestrone soup, Caesar salads, pizza by the slice, spaghetti, fettuccini, Italian hoagies, sausage sub sandwiches, kids' meals, desserts, soda, beer, wine, espresso, and cappuccino.

Captain America Diner—Charbroiled burgers and cheeseburgers, chicken sandwiches, kids' meals, onion rings, apple pie a la mode, shakes, and soda are among the offerings served here.

Chill—Soft-serve ice cream, sundaes, and other treats are available here.

Cotton Candy—Freshly made cotton candy, snacks, soda, and other items that will satisfy your sweet tooth are available here.

Freeze—Snow cones, snacks, and soda are available from this kiosk located in the heart of Marvel Super Hero Island.

Fruit—Whole fruit, fresh fruit cups, snacks, and juice are served here and give health-conscious visitors an alternative to junk food when they're ready for a snack.

Take the Comics Home with You

Marvel Super Hero Island offers the following shops. Here, you can purchase a wide range of toys, comic books, clothing, and other themed merchandise based on Marvel comic book characters.

Arcade News—Here you'll find Dr. Doom merchandise, much of which isn't available anywhere else.

Comics Shop—As the name suggests, comic books and trading cards, plus other comic book–related items for the casual and serious collector, are available here.

Hulk Photo—For those who experience the Incredible Hulk Coaster and don't think they'll remember the experience without a photo, personalized photos can be purchased near the ride's exit. (Photos of every rider are taken.)

The Marvel Alterniverse Store—Higher-priced collectibles, clothing, jewelry, and other items (all based on Marvel comics) are available at this shop.

Spider-Man Shop—Fans of this popular Marvel super hero will find toys, clothing, and other merchandise all based on Spider-Man.

CHAPTER 17

Universal CityWalk

BY DAY, CITYWALK CONTAINS AN ARRAY OF THEMED, family-oriented dining and shopping experiences, while at night, this area transforms into an adult-oriented party scene, complete with restaurants, cafés, shops, nightclubs, movie theaters, bars, and plenty of live entertainment.

An Overview of CityWalk

Even if you've been to CityWalk at Universal Studios Hollywood, this CityWalk offers a very different nighttime entertainment experience, primarily targeted to adults. During the day, however, people of all ages are invited to experience one of several theme-oriented restaurants located within CityWalk, plus explore the unique shops within this area. During the days, street performers are often on hand (weather permitting), entertaining passersby. CityWalk is a 30-acre entertainment complex unto itself. After 6:00 P.M. there is no charge for parking.

Admission to CityWalk is free; however, there may be a cover or admission charge for the nightclubs and/or for special events. A separate admission is required to see a movie at the Universal Cineplex (a twenty-screen movie theater).

≡FAST FACT

For a flat fee of $8.95 per person, unlimited access to all of CityWalk's clubs and bars is available. For $12, admission to the clubs and bars is included along with one Universal Cineplex movie ticket.

The Restaurants

The restaurants within CityWalk typically serve both lunch and dinner; however, many are open late and are ideal for late-night snacks or meals (after visiting a club or seeing a movie). If you're traveling with children or underaged teens, arrange for babysitting services at your hotel so that the adults you're traveling with can enjoy the nightlife offered at CityWalk.

The Hard Rock Café

This is the world's largest Hard Rock Café. It offers seating for 2,200 people and often features live entertainment by top-name artists. Of course, this Hard Rock Café also offers an extensive rock memorabilia collection. The dining room is open from 11:00 A.M. to midnight daily. Don't forget to drop into the gift shop for official Hard Rock Café Orlando merchandise.

The Hard Rock Café Live arena offers seating for 2,500 and live entertainment nightly. There is a cover charge to see the Hard Rock Live house band. The ticket prices vary for national acts that perform at this venue (primarily on the weekends).

While dining, be sure to explore the multilevel dining room and check out the over 1,000 pieces of music memorabilia. For more information, visit the Hard Rock Café Web site at *www.hard rock.com.* For dining reservations at this or any CityWalk restaurant, call (407) 363-8000.

Jimmy Buffett's Margaritaville

This is a family-oriented restaurant by day, but at night, adults will enjoy the three full-service bars. The menu offers a combination of Key West and Caribbean-style foods, known as Floribbean cuisine. Fruits, vegetables, and seafood are the various entrees' main ingredients. Open from 11:00 A.M. to 2:00 A.M. daily. There's a $3.25 cover charge after 10:00 P.M. Live musical performances begin at 10:00 P.M. For reservations and live entertainment information, call ✆(407) 224-2155.

Emeril's Restaurant Orlando

You've seen Emeril Lagasse on TV's Food Network as the host of *Emeril Live*. Now, this world-renowned chef has a permanent home in Orlando, where New Orleans Creole-based cuisine is served. The wine cellar houses over 12,000 selections. Lunch is served daily from 11:30 A.M. to 2:00 P.M. Dinner begins at 5:30 P.M. and is served until 10:00 P.M. (Sunday through Thursday) and until 11:00 P.M. (Fridays and Saturdays). Within the restaurant is a gift shop that sells Emeril's New Orleans Cooking and Louisiana Real & Rustic cookbooks, plus his own line of spices and plates.

The restaurant also houses a cigar bar containing a wall-sized humidor. The dining room seats 250 people. This restaurant appeals mainly to adults.

📖 TRAVEL TIP

While the food is top-notch, the prices at this award-winning restaurant are rather steep. Due to the restaurant's popularity (and Emeril's huge fan base), reservations are an absolute must to avoid a several-hour wait. Call ✆(407) 224-2424.

Bob Marley—A Tribute to Freedom

Set in a Jamaican atmosphere, this one-of-a-kind restaurant celebrates the music, style, and philosophy of Bob Marley. The venue is part museum (featuring over 100 photographs and portraits of Marley), part restaurant, and part nightclub.

On the menu, you'll find Jamaican jerk chicken and roasted plantains. Live reggae music is presented nightly. The full-service bar offers island drinks and Red Stripe beer. Dinner is served nightly (Mondays through Fridays), between 5:00 P.M. and 1:30 A.M. On weekends, the restaurant is open 11:00 A.M. to 1:30 A.M. There's a $4.25 cover charge after 8:00 P.M. to enter the bar. Live musical performances begin at 8:00 P.M. This restaurant/bar will appeal mainly to adults. To learn more about this restaurant, visit its Web site at ✑*www.bobmarley.com*. The dining room offers an adult-oriented atmosphere.

NBA City

NBA City is a colorful, basketball-themed restaurant endorsed and licensed by the National Basketball Association. This is a joint venture between the Hard Rock Café and the NBA/WNBA, so you know it offers a hip place to eat for basketball fans of all ages. The menu offers a wide range of entrees from burgers to sandwiches. Open from 11:00 A.M. to 2:00 A.M., this is definitely a family-oriented restaurant that also contains a gift shop that sells official NBA and WNBA merchandise.

Patamoré

This open-air marketplace café environment offers authentic Italian cuisine served a la carte or family style. Open from 8:00 A.M. to midnight (marketplace area) and 5:00 P.M. to midnight (restaurant area), pizzas, grilled chicken, and steaks, plus pasta, pastries, and sandwiches are served. Full bar service is available.

The Motown Café

Music and memorabilia from top Motown artists are what you'll hear and see throughout this unique restaurant. Get a behind-the-scenes look at the Supremes, the Temptations, and other music legends as you enjoy slow-cooked American cuisine and live entertainment. An in-house singing group performs many of Motown's classic hits live on stage every twenty minutes.

This restaurant will definitely appeal more to adults with an appreciation for Motown's music and history. Open Sundays through Thursdays between 5:00 P.M. and midnight, and Fridays and Saturdays between 5:00 P.M. and 2:00 A.M. There's a $5.25 per-person cover charge to visit the bar after 9:00 P.M.

⊕ HOT SPOT

To learn more about this restaurant, visit the official Motown Web site at ✑*www.motown.com.*

The NASCAR Café

No matter how old you are, if you're a NASCAR racing fan, you'll appreciate this themed restaurant. It's jam-packed with NASCAR memorabilia that's displayed throughout the dining room and all public areas. In addition, there are full-size stock cars on display, plus video monitors showing NASCAR racing highlights.

Open from 10:00 A.M. to 10:00 P.M., in addition to the dining room, this restaurant offers an arcade area and a gift shop. Like the Hard Rock Café and NBA City, this is a fun, family-oriented restaurant that tends to get crowded during lunchtime and early evenings (for dinner).

Pat O'Brien's

Modeled after the famous New Orleans watering hole, Pat O'Brien's is suitable for adults, over the legal drinking age. Every evening, guests are entertained by dueling pianos and sing-alongs. A full-service bar is offered. Dining hours are between 11:00 A.M. and 1:00 A.M. daily in the main bar and courtyard. Guests must be over the age of twenty-one to enter after 7:00 P.M. There's a small cover charge to enter the dueling piano bar, which is open (and features live music) between 6:00 P.M. and 2:00 A.M.

The Latin Quarter

This area offers food and entertainment inspired by twenty-one Latin American nations. Dining and dancing are offered late into the night as guests are entertained by music from Central America,

South America, Mexico, and the Caribbean. Open from 11:00 A.M. to 1:30 A.M. There's a small cover charge after 10:00 P.M.

═FAST FACT

In addition to the themed restaurants, CityWalk contains a unique assortment of shops. Whether you're looking for something to do for an hour or an entire evening, chances are you'll be pleased with what's offered at CityWalk.

The Universal Cineplex

After a day of roller coasters, rides, and shows, perhaps you'll want to kick back and enjoy one of Hollywood's latest blockbuster films. The Universal Cineplex within CityWalk features twenty screens, all offering stadium seating, cutting-edge projection equipment, state-of-the-art sound systems, and air conditioning. For show times and movie listings, call ✆(407) 354-3374.

On bad-weather days and evenings, or when a hit movie first opens, expect larger-than-normal crowds here. The good news is that when a blockbuster film first opens, it'll typically be shown on multiple screens to accommodate the larger crowds.

CityJazz

This jazz center features ongoing live performances (nightly) in a nightclub setting. It's also the home of the Down Beat Jazz Hall of Fame, which was established in 1952 and features such distinguished jazz luminaries as Louis Armstrong, Ella Fitzgerald, and Dave Brubeck.

Over 500 pieces of memorabilia are on display. A light menu is served daily between 8:30 P.M. and 1:00 A.M. The Down Beat Jazz Hall of Fame museum is open from 3:00 P.M. to 6:00 P.M. There's a small cover charge after 8:30 P.M. (which includes the live entertainment).

The Groove

This dance club offers state-of-the art lighting and sound, plus a full-service bar. If you're an adult looking to dance the night away, this should be your destination for the evening. The dancing begins nightly at 9:00 P.M. and goes until 2:00 A.M. There's a small per-person cover charge. All guests must be twenty-one or older.

CityWalk Shopping

Throughout the day and into the night, a handful of unique shops are available within CityWalk. Shop here for souvenirs, collectibles, and a wide range of unusual merchandise. Shops include:

All-Star Collectibles—Autographed sports memorabilia and other collectibles are on display and can be purchased.

Cartooniversal—Check out the wide assortment of character apparel and souvenirs.

Cigarz at CityWalk—Here, cigar aficionados can find an unparalleled assortment of cigars and accessories, plus a knowledgeable staff.

Dapy—Novelty items for kids and adults are available. This is a chain store found in many malls.

Elegant Illusions—Inexpensive replicas of fine jewelry are sold here.

Endangered Species Store—A wide range of merchandise, toys, and clothing based on wild animals and the rain forest are sold here. This is a fun place to shop, especially with children.

Fossil—Fine leather goods, watches, apparel, and sunglasses are what's ticking at this shop.

Fresh Produce—Men's, women's and children's apparel, all in festive colors, can be found here.

Glow!—This shop sells items that glow in the dark, reflect, and/or illuminate.

Quiet Flight Surf Shop—Surf and beach wear from well-known labels and designers is sold here.

Silver—This jewelry shop offers a wide range of merchandise created from sterling silver. The prices are reasonable and the selection is impressive for this type of shop.

Starbucks—That's right, you can get that all-important caffeine boost at a full-service Starbucks, located in the heart of CityWalk. It's a great place to stop in the morning, or anytime throughout the day or night when you want a cup of gourmet coffee.

The Universal Studios Store—If you didn't pick up a souvenir at Universal Studios Florida or Islands of Adventure, you'll find a large selection of merchandise, clothing, and toys here.

CHAPTER 18

SeaWorld and Discovery Cove

LOCATED JUST MILES AWAY FROM THE WDW RESORT and the Universal Orlando Resort is another extremely popular, family-oriented theme park—SeaWorld Orlando. In the past few years, this park has undergone a massive redesign and expansion. It now offers a full day's worth of activities, rides, and shows suitable for everyone.

Park Overview

While Disney's Animal Kingdom offers guests an up-close look at land-based animals living in their natural habitats, SeaWorld offers a look at sea creatures and combines that experience with rides, shows, and other attractions. In addition, a second theme park, called Discovery Cove, offers an even more personalized look at some of the ocean's most amazing creatures, including dolphins.

SeaWorld is a 200-acre park that's open year-round, from 9:00 A.M. to 7:00 P.M. (with extended hours during the summer months and holiday periods). To truly see the majority of what SeaWorld has to offer, you'll need at least eight hours. If you haven't visited this park in a while and you have an extra day in your travel itinerary, it's well worth experiencing, especially if you're traveling with kids and teens.

Both SeaWorld and Discovery Cove are owned and operated by Anheuser-Busch. For more information about these two theme parks, call ☎(800) 4-ADVENTURE or ☎(407) 351-3600. You can also visit the SeaWorld Web site at ✐*www.seaworld.com*.

═FAST FACT

Like any theme park or tourist attraction, gift shops, snack shops, and restaurants are all in abundance throughout the SeaWorld park. Guest services such as wheelchair rentals, locker rentals, kennels, first aid, ATMs, and a foreign currency exchange are all available within the park.

Special Tours

In addition to the exciting rides, shows, and attractions that bring guests closer to understanding the mysteries of the ocean and the exotic creatures that live within the sea, SeaWorld offers a series of highly educational tours and programs, including:

Marine Mammal Keeper Experience—This eight-hour program allows guests to experience the thrill of working alongside marine mammal experts at SeaWorld. Guests will bottle-feed orphaned manatees, interact with seals and walrus, plus get a close-up look at other creatures of the sea. Priced at $389 per person, this experience is open to people over the age of thirteen. The program begins at 6:30 A.M. and includes lunch.

Sharks Deep Dive—This unique experience takes place within the Shark Encounter attraction. Participants don SeaWorld wetsuits and either snorkel or scuba dive in an authentic shark cage during their close encounter. The cage traverses through a 125-foot-long underwater habitat teeming with an array of more than fifty sharks. This is a two-hour program that's priced at $150 per person (for scuba diving) and $125 per person (for snorkeling). This price does not include park admission.

Trainer for a Day—This seven-hour program allows guests to work with SeaWorld's expert animal trainers as they interact with a wide range of animals, including killer whales, sea lions, and dolphins. Priced at $389 per person, this experience is open to people over the age of thirteen. It includes lunch, a "Trainer for a Day" T-shirt, a waterproof disposable camera, and a seven-day pass to SeaWorld.

Whale Swim Adventure—Come face-to-face with false killer whales and interact with these unique creatures. Four guests at a time suit up in SeaWorld wetsuits and enter the water with the whales during this two-hour program. The program includes lunch and is priced at $200 per person.

For more information about these tours and special programs, call ☎(800) 406-2244 and use option #5, or ☎(407) 363-2380.

Admission

Like all theme parks, there is an admission fee for SeaWorld and a separate admission fee for Discovery Cove. A one-day admission ticket to SeaWorld is priced at $51.95 (adults) and $42.95 (kids ages three to nine). Discounts are available to senior citizens, military personnel, AAA members, Florida residents, and guests with disabilities. You can also save 10 percent off the ticket prices by prepurchasing your tickets online at ✐*www.seaworld.com.*

An annual passport for SeaWorld is priced at $84.95 (adults) and $74.95 (kids and senior citizens). Other annual passports that offer admission to SeaWorld as well as Busch Gardens are available, as are discounted two-year passports.

Admission to Discovery Cove, which includes admission to SeaWorld for seven consecutive days, is priced at $229 (adults); however, various discounted package deals are available if you're also interested in participating in the Trainer for a Day program, for example. Call ☎(877) 4-DISCOVERY for additional information. There's also a Dolphin Lover's Family Sleepover program, priced at $329 per person.

If you're staying in the Orlando area for several days and want to see more than the Disney theme parks, you can save money by purchasing the Orlando FlexTicket. This one ticket offers unlimited admission to four or five non-Disney theme parks, including SeaWorld, Universal Studios Florida, Islands of Adventure, Busch Gardens, and Wet 'N Wild, over a fourteen-day period. Admission to Discovery Cove is not included. For more information, call ✆(800) 224-3838.

≡FAST FACT

SeaWorld charges a daily parking fee of $7 per car or $8 per RV or camper. If you're staying at a non-Disney hotel, consider utilizing shuttle bus service to the SeaWorld theme park. Ask your hotel's front desk attendant or concierge for details.

Getting to SeaWorld

SeaWorld is located at the intersection of Interstate 4 (I-4) and the Beeline Expressway (approximately ten minutes south of downtown Orlando and fifteen minutes from the Orlando International Airport).

The easiest way to reach SeaWorld (from the airport, The WDW Resort, or Universal Orlando Resort) is via car; however, taxi service and shuttle buses are available.

The Rating System

To help you choose which rides and attractions are most worth seeing while visiting SeaWorld, this book offers star-based ratings for each ride and attraction, based on the age group each will most appeal to. Each ride and attraction has earned between one and three stars.

★   = Rides and attractions that earned just one star aren't
        worth waiting for and could be skipped, especially if your
        time within the theme park is limited.

★★   = Rides and attractions that earned two stars are good, but
        they don't fall into the "must-see" category.

★★★   = The rides and attractions that earned three stars are
        definitely worth seeing and should not be missed.

N.S. = This denotes rides and attractions that are "Not Suitable"
        for a specific age group.

SeaWorld Highlights

Ages 2–4:	★★
Ages 5–10:	★★★
Ages 11–15:	★★★
Ages 16–Adult:	★★★
Senior Citizens:	★★★

SeaWorld offers a wide range of rides, shows, and attractions, most of which cater to a family audience. Perhaps the most popular show at this theme park is the **Shamu Adventure,** a fun-filled live show starring killer whales interacting with their trainers. The nighttime version of this show, **Shamu Rocks America,** features SeaWorld's trainers and whales performing with rock music in the background.

🧳 TRAVEL TIP

The Shamu Rocks America show is typically presented right before the park closes every evening. Exiting this show can take up to forty minutes, plus you'll have to deal with heavy crowds. The show, however, is fabulous.

Check with the park's ticket office or customer relations desk for daily show times. Shows are presented on a weather-permitting basis. Be sure to arrive at least fifteen to thirty minutes early to the show in order to ensure admission and good seats, especially during peak vacation periods. For kids especially, there's a section of seats within Shamu Stadium that guarantees audience members will get splashed by the performing whales. To learn more about Shamu and SeaWorld's killer whales, visit the Shamu Web site at ✍*www.shamu.com.*

✔ This is a must-see attraction.

Kraken

Ages 2–4:	N.S.
Ages 5–10:	N.S.
Ages 11–15:	★★
Ages 16–Adult:	★★★
Senior Citizens:	N.S.

This is the new flagship roller coaster at SeaWorld. It's also the tallest, fastest, longest, and only floorless roller coaster in Orlando. It will take you to the height of a fifteen-story building and turn you upside down seven times, all at speeds reaching 65 miles per hour.

Kraken is named after a legendary sea monster—a massive, mythological underwater beast. As you experience this coaster, your feet will dangle as you sit on open-air, pedestal-like seats with nothing around you except shoulder restraints. There's no one to hold on to, nothing in front of you, and nothing below you. There's only sky above and the wind in your face.

✔ This is a must-see attraction.

Clyde and Seamore Take Pirate Island

Ages 2–4:	★
Ages 5–10:	★★
Ages 11–15:	★★★
Ages 16–Adult:	★★
Senior Citizens:	★★

Sea lions, otters, and walrus perform with trainers in this rather lighthearted "adventure" designed for kids and teens. While the story line is a bit childish, this show features a cast of well-trained sea lions interacting with their trainers and the audience.

Journey to Atlantis

Ages 2–4:	N.S.
Ages 5–10:	N.S.
Ages 11–15:	★★★
Ages 16–Adult:	★★★
Senior Citizens:	★

As you kick off your adventure to the lost city of Atlantis, you'll be traveling on water and high-speed rails. Evil spirits will try to keep you from your destination, but your bravery and sheer guts will keep you one step ahead. Along your journey, you never know what's around the next corner or the next drop. Oh, and there are drops. In fact, one drop is 60 feet long and goes nearly straight down. Journey to Atlantis is a thrill ride that nicely combines special effects, the excitement of a roller coaster, and the thrills of a turbulent water ride.

Shamu's Happy Harbor

Ages 2–4:	★★★
Ages 5–10:	★★★
Ages 11–15:	N.S.
Ages 16–Adult:	N.S.
Senior Citizens:	N.S.

For young kids, this is a freestyle play area filled with giant pink flamingos and palm trees. Young guests are encouraged to run, jump, and climb as they explore four stories of nets, shoot through tunnels, cool down in a splashy water maze, and slip down nine slippery slides.

Pets Ahoy!

Ages 2–4:	★★★
Ages 5–10:	★★★
Ages 11–15:	★★
Ages 16–Adult:	★★
Senior Citizens:	★★

This is a fun-filled and funny live show starring a cast of trained dogs, cats, birds, rats, potbellied pigs, and other animals performing a series of entertaining skits. Nearly all of the cast members were rescued from local animal shelters. Kids in particular will enjoy this show; however, it's definitely suitable for the entire family.

Odyssea

Ages 2–4:	N.S.
Ages 5–10:	★
Ages 11–15:	★★★
Ages 16–Adult:	★★★
Senior Citizens:	★★★

Acrobatics, athleticism, modern dance, and special effects are used to create a fun-filled but nontraditional circus (sort of like *Cirque du Soleil*). The thirty-minute show comprises several specialty circus acts, featuring performers from around the world.

Shark Encounter

Ages 2–4:	★★
Ages 5–10:	★★
Ages 11–15:	★★
Ages 16–Adult:	★★
Senior Citizens:	★★

Travel through the world's largest underwater acrylic tunnel and find yourself just inches away from dangerous predators like eels, barracuda, venomous fish, and more than fifty sharks. This is a large and beautiful coral reef habitat.

Key West Dolphin Fest

Ages 2–4:	N.S.
Ages 5–10:	★★★
Ages 11–15:	★★★
Ages 16–Adult:	★★★
Senior Citizens:	★★★

Guests have a chance to see Atlantic bottlenose dolphins perform live with their trainers in an entertaining, family-oriented show. SeaWorld also offers a pool area where guests can see, feed, and pet dolphins. In addition, be sure to check out the Dolphin Nursery, a chance to see newborn dolphins with their moms.

✔ This is a must-see attraction.

═FAST FACT

At SeaWorld, more than 200 programs designed for various age groups are offered year-round and include day camps, resident camps, sleepovers, family camps, teacher camps, and group programs. To learn more about the various SeaWorld Adventure Camp programs, call (866) GO-TO-CAMP or ☎(800) 406-2244.

Wild Arctic

Ages 2–4:	N.S.
Ages 5–10:	★
Ages 11–15:	★★★
Ages 16–Adult:	★★★
Senior Citizens:	★★

This motion-simulator-based thrill ride takes guests on a helicopter journey to the frozen north for an Arctic exploration that's filled with surprises. The photography and overall realism is highly impressive. You're about to preview a part of the world that few see firsthand.

Manatees: The Last Generation?

Ages 2–4:	★★
Ages 5–10:	★★
Ages 11–15:	★★★
Ages 16–Adult:	★★★
Senior Citizens:	★★★

This exhibit allows guests to see Florida manatees up close and learn about the dangers this species is currently facing. It's both educational and entertaining, like all of the shows and exhibits at SeaWorld that involve live animals.

Pacific Point Preserve

Ages 2–4:	N.S.
Ages 5–10:	★★★
Ages 11–15:	★★★
Ages 16–Adult:	★★
Senior Citizens:	★★

Sea lions and fur seals living in a 2.5-acre naturalistic environment that replicates the rocky northern Pacific coast are the stars of this exhibit. Young people, in particular, will enjoy this zoo-like attraction.

Getting Hungry?

SeaWorld offers many restaurants, ranging from full-service to cafeteria style. For families looking for an entertaining dinner show, the nightly Makahiki Luau Dinner and Show features traditional music, song, dance, and food from the islands of Hawaii. Reservations are required. Call ✆(800) 327-2420. The luau is performed nightly at the Seafire Inn and is priced at $37.95 (adults) and $27.95 (kids).

When it comes to dining and shopping, one of the newest areas of SeaWorld is The Waterfront. This five-acre nautical neighborhood (located in the heart of SeaWorld) offers a selection of dining and shopping options, plus live music and street performers throughout the day.

▐█▌ TRAVEL TIP

In addition to watching the Shamu Adventure or Shamu Rocks America shows, you can dine with Shamu and the whale trainers. A buffet-style meal is offered and is located poolside. Reservations are required. Call ✆(800) 327-2420.

Kids and SeaWorld

Since SeaWorld combines fun with wildlife education, the theme park's animal trainers offer these suggestions to parents regarding how to enhance a child's experience while visiting this theme park:

- At the end of each day, encourage your kids to draw pictures or write short stories about the favorite parts of their day at SeaWorld.
- Take lots of pictures, with a focus on your kids interacting with the various animals. Later, spend time reviewing the photos (or video) with your kids.
- Throughout your vacation, keep a "memory bag" close by. A "memory bag" can be a purse, pocket, or a backpack pouch reserved for holding fun keepsakes that your kids collect (or purchase).
- While the trip is still fresh in their minds, ask your children what they learned during their trip and what they would like to do next time.

══FAST FACT

There are a handful of other activities and exhibits at SeaWorld. For example, the Penguin Encounter is an exhibit featuring penguins, while the Rico & Roza's Musical Feaste offers a twenty-five-minute musical revue celebrating food, family, and fun. The Clydesdale Hamlet is the home to SeaWorld's famous Budweiser Clydesdale horses. Guests can pet the horses and have photos taken with them.

Discovery Cove

Located adjacent to SeaWorld is Discovery Cove, which opened in summer 2000. This truly unique theme park re-creates an exotic tropical island, complete with sandy beaches. Unlike most theme parks, however, only a limited number of visitors are granted admission each day to Discovery Cove. Advanced reservations are definitely required.

Instead of rides, shows, and attractions, Discovery Cove offers a one-on-one, up-close, and hands-on look at marine wildlife, including dolphins.

The park is staffed by a team of highly trained and knowledgeable animal trainers and caregivers who work directly with guests to provide an extremely personalized experience that includes interacting one-on-one with dolphins and other sea creatures. This park is designed for guests over the age of six. Younger children will be limited in terms of what activities they can participate in.

Discovery Cove offers snorkeling in a manmade coral reef, lagoon, and tropical river; the chance to swim and interact with dolphins; and a lovely manmade beach. Best of all, this park is open to only 800 to 1,000 people per day, so there are never any long lines or crowds.

Visiting Discovery Cove is an all-day experience (with lunch included). The package includes:

- A reserved dolphin swim experience.
- Unlimited access to snorkeling in the coral reef.
- Unlimited access to wade and swim in the ray pool.
- Unlimited access to the free-flight bird aviary, the resort pool, and the tropical river.
- A freshly prepared meal for lunch.
- Use of a mask, snorkel, swim vest, towels, lockers, and other amenities.
- All-day self-parking.
- A seven-day pass to SeaWorld Orlando.

Anyone who has ever thought about swimming or interacting with dolphins, or who wants to try snorkeling in a 100 percent safe and supervised environment, will definitely enjoy this experience.

The only drawback to this park is that the souvenir photographs taken of guests by the on-staff professional photographer are rather expensive, yet this is a special personalized keepsake that virtually all guests wind up purchasing.

For more information about Discovery Cove, call (877) 4-DIS-COVERY or visit the park's Web site at *www.discoverycove.com*.

FAST FACT

Discovery Cove is home to Atlantic bottlenose dolphins, stingrays, over 10,000 tropical fish, barracuda, sharks, and more than 300 exotic birds.

CHAPTER 19

Exploring Greater Orlando

IF YOU CHOOSE TO EXPLORE MORE OF THE NEARBY Greater Orlando area, you'll find literally hundreds of other family-oriented activities that offer more than another theme park experience. This chapter will highlight some of the non–theme park activities you'll find at resort hotels and throughout Orlando.

Resort Hotel Activities

If you're staying at one of The WDW Resort hotels, each hotel offers activities that range from swimming and boat rentals to biking, shopping, and tennis. Health clubs and full-service day spas are also offered at several of The WDW Resort hotels (as well as independent resort hotels, such as the nearby Wyndam Palace Resort).

Golf

The WDW Resort offers ninety-nine holes of what Disney calls the world's greatest golf. The resort offers five championship eighteen-hole courses and a nine-hole walking course.

GOLF COURSES ON WALT DISNEY WORLD RESORT			
Eagle Pines	Par 72/6,772 yards	Rating: 72.3	Slope: 131
Lake Buena Vista	Par 72/6,820 yards	Rating: 72.7	Slope: 128
Magnolia	Par 72/7,190 yards	Rating: 73.9	Slope: 133
Oak Trail	Par 36/2,913 yards	N/A	N/A
Osprey Ridge	Par 72/7,101 yards	Rating: 73.9	Slope: 135
Palm	Par 72/6,957 yards	Rating: 73.0	Slope: 133

In addition to the golf courses, The WDW Resort contains three full-service pro shops, four driving ranges, and four practice putting greens. If you don't feel like packing up your own clubs and bringing them with you to Orlando, all Disney courses rent Callaway golf clubs and FootJoy shoes. Private golf instruction from Disney's PGA Professional staff is available by appointment, but you'll want to schedule your lessons as far in advance as possible. Keep in mind, proper golf attire is required on all of Disney's golf courses. Shirts with collars and Bermuda-length shorts are part of the dress code.

WDW Resort guests can reserve tee times up to ninety days in advance, and day guests can reserve up to thirty days in advance by calling ✆(407) WDW-GOLF (939-4653). All reservations must be guaranteed with a major credit card.

For more information about the golfing opportunities available at The WDW Resort and for current rates, call ✆(407) WDW-GOLF, or visit the special Web site at ✐*www.golf.disneyworld.com.* Special golf vacation packages are also offered throughout the year. Call ✆(407) 939-7677 for travel package information. January through April is the busiest golfing season at Disney.

Miniature Golf

If mini-golf is more your thing, there are several miniature golf courses on WDW Resort property. For example, there's the family-oriented Fantasia Gardens Miniature Golf and Garden Pavilions, which offers two whimsical eighteen-hole miniature golf courses and a 22,000-square-foot outdoor meeting facility located near Epcot and the Disney-MGM Studios.

≡FAST FACT

Complimentary taxi vouchers (through Yellow Cab) are provided for Walt Disney World Resort guests who are coming to play golf at one of Disney's golf courses. The valet/concierge desk or Bell Services will summon a cab for you. The Pro Shop at the golf course will assist you in returning to your resort.

Calling All Sports Fans!

In addition to the ESPN Club and ESPN Store at Disney's BoardWalk, The WDW Resort also offers the Disney's Wide World of Sports complex, which hosts all sorts of professional and amateur sporting events throughout the year and is the permanent training location for the Harlem Globetrotters. Tickets to the "premium" sporting events that take place at this complex can be obtained by calling TicketMaster at ✆(407) 839-3900.

Disney's Wide World of Sports is a 200-acre complex that contains sports fields, baseball diamonds, tracks, tennis courts, basketball courts, and a 7,500-seat baseball stadium, designed to accommodate professional teams and amateurs alike in more than thirty different sports.

A flat one-price daily admission gives guests access to watch as many "nonpremium" events as they'd like throughout the day and tour the complex. For ticket prices and admission information, see Chapter 3.

To reach Disney's Wide World of Sports, take the WDW bus service, or by car, take I-4 to The Magic Kingdom exit (#25), then follow signs. Parking is free. The D-Sports Shop located in the complex sells a wide range of official NBA, NFL, MLB, and NHL merchandise and clothing. There are also several other sports-oriented shops that sell equipment, apparel, memorabilia, and souvenirs.

⊕ HOT SPOT

The NFL Experience is an exciting attraction for football fans of all ages. This interactive football playground allows fans to kick the ball through uprights, throw footballs at targets, and test their speed in the 40-yard dash.

Drive a Race Car

Champion driver Richard Petty has teamed up with Disney to offer the Richard Petty Driving Experience at the Walt Disney World Speedway. Now you can experience what it's like to drive an actual two-seat stock car around a professional track at speeds of up to 145 miles per hour.

The basic Riding-Along Experience ($89 to $125) allows you to be in the passenger seat of a two-seat stock car as a professional driver takes you for three laps around the track. The Rookie Experience ($349 to $499) puts you in the driver's seat for eight laps around the one-mile tri-oval track, in a car that can reach 125 miles per hour. This is a three-hour program. The upgraded King's Experience ($749 to $1,199) offers sixteen laps of driving divided into two eight-lap sessions. The Experience of a Lifetime ($1,199 to $1,249) allows you to participate in a thirty-lap program (which is divided into three ten-lap sessions). You'll receive professional instruction designed to teach you the basics of racing.

The Walt Disney World Speedway is open to spectators, who can watch nonprofessional races, free of charge, between 9:00 A.M. and 5:00 P.M. daily (weather permitting). For more information about the **Richard Petty Driving Experience**, call ☎(800) BE-PETTY or visit the Web site at ✐*www.1800bepetty.com.*

Tennis Anyone?

Disney's Wide World of Sports complex offers eleven clay courts, plus there are over twenty-five additional courts located at the various WDW Resort hotels. Disney's Racquet Club at the Contemporary Resort offers six courts, plus a pro shop and private instruction. Court time can be reserved between 8:00 A.M. and 8:00 P.M. daily. Some lighted courts are available and are open until 9:00 P.M.

Other court locations include: Disney's Grand Floridian Resort & Spa (two clay courts), Disney's Fort Wilderness Campground (two hard courts), Disney's Yacht Club Resort and Disney's Beach Club Resort (two hard courts), Disney's Old Key West Resort (three hard courts) and Disney's Saratoga Springs Resort & Spa. All are lighted for night play.

For the best court times, you'll have to plan ahead. Reservations are taken up to one year in advance for the courts at Disney's Racquet Club, as well as at many of the other WDW Resort hotel locations. For many of the courts, the rental fee is $15 per hour; however, some of them are free of charge.

For more information about Disney's Racquet Club and where you can play tennis at The WDW Resort, call ✆(407) 824-3578. For information about any of the tennis courts at The WDW Resort, call ✆(407) WDW-PLAY.

≡FAST FACT

Private tennis lessons, with a U.S. Tennis Association–certified instructor, are available at Disney's Racquet Club for $50 per hour. To play against a pro, without receiving instruction, costs $45 per hour. Racquets and ball machines can both be rented for an additional fee.

Row, Row, Row Your Boat

At various locations throughout The WDW Resort, you can rent various types of boats by the half hour or by the hour. Renting a boat is a wonderful and relatively inexpensive way to spend a morning or afternoon enjoying the outdoors, without dealing with crowds at one of the Disney theme parks.

Boats available for rent include canoes, canopy boats, pedal boats, pontoon boats, sailboats, and speedboats. You can also go parasailing or waterskiing. Many of these boating activities can be done from the various hotels located along the Seven Seas Lagoon, Crescent Lake, or Buena Vista Lagoon. To rent any of the boats at The WDW Resort, you must be a guest at any WDW Resort hotel and have a valid driver's license or passport. No privately owned boats are allowed to be used anywhere on WDW property. Some restrictions apply in regard to minors renting boats. Check with any WDW Resort hotel for details or to reserve a boat.

There's Even Bass Fishing

Back in the mid-1960s, Bay Lake, which is located on Disney property, was stocked with 70,000 bass. Well, those fish have multiplied, making for a wonderful fishing opportunity. If you want to partake in the fishing activities, you must sign up for one of the Fishing Excursions that take place throughout the day. Reservations are required. Call ✆(407) 828-2204 (**Downtown Disney Fishing Excursion**), ✆(407) 934-5409 (**The Fishing Hole**), or ✆(407) 824-2621 (**WDW Golf & Recreation Reservations**).

All fish that are caught must be released. Fishing equipment is provided. The price for a two-hour Fishing Excursion ranges from about $50 to $70 per person. Up to five people can participate in each excursion. The cost of a five-person tour is $160, with a departure in early morning, midmorning, or afternoon.

Other Activities at The WDW Resort

Some of the other activities you can participate in at The WDW Resort include:

- Basketball
- Biking
- Dancing (at the night clubs at Pleasure Island or Disney's BoardWalk)
- Day spa treatments (massages, body wraps, etc.)
- Fitness/health clubs
- Hiking
- Horseback riding

- Jogging
- Playgrounds
- Rock climbing
- Shopping
- Swimming
- Video arcades
- Volleyball

🧳 TRAVEL TIP

For information about these activities, many of which are free of charge, call 📞(407) WDW-PLAY, or speak with a Disney cast member at whichever WDW Resort hotel you're staying at during your vacation. Equipment needed to participate in the above activities is provided (or can be rented).

The Town of Celebration

When Walt Disney first began designing Disneyland and later The Walt Disney World Resort, he dreamed of creating an actual town. Well, in 1996, Walt's dream became a reality when the town of Celebration, Florida, was officially founded. The first phase of this massive construction project included 350 residences, two office buildings, fourteen businesses in the town center, a 150-bed medical center, a school, a teaching academy, and a golf course (which is open to the public). After the completion of this first phase, additional phases were subsequently built, transforming this into a community.

While Celebration is a private residential community, tourists are invited to the downtown area to explore the unique shops and restaurants, and to take in the atmosphere of this storybook-like community. Yes, there's even upbeat music piped into the streets through hidden speakers as you walk through the downtown area.

There are several restaurants and shopping opportunities in Celebration. There's also a full-service bank and a post office located in the downtown area, as well as an AMC movie theater, live entertainment in the streets, and paddleboat and sailboat rentals on the lake that's adjacent to downtown Celebration.

Celebration, Florida, covers 4,900 acres and is surrounded by 4,700 acres of protected greenbelt near the intersection of I-4 and U.S. 192 (about a ten-minute drive from The WDW Resort). Located just outside of Celebration is Orlando's largest indoor shopping mall.

💼 TRAVEL TIP

If you're interested in possibly purchasing some real estate in Celebration and making this town your home, be sure to visit the Celebration Preview Center (open 10:00 A.M. to 6:00 P.M. daily). It's located in the heart of downtown Celebration. To reach Celebration Realty, call ✆(407) 566-4663.

Tourist Information

When you arrive in Orlando, visit any tourist information center or the front desk of virtually any hotel, and you'll be able to pick up brochures or additional information about the various attractions in the Orlando area, many of which are conveniently located just minutes (by car) from The WDW Resort or Universal Studios Florida. Special savings coupons are available for many of these attractions in the Orlando edition of the Entertainment Book or from the various tourist books available free of charge from hotels and tourist information desks.

The Official Visitor Center (located at 8723 International Drive, Suite 101, at the corner of International Drive and Austrian Court), is one place you can pick up discount tickets for many of Orlando's top attractions. Call ✆(407) 363-5872 for more information.

See Orlando is a complimentary quarterly publication from SEE Florida Magazines, Inc. This full-color publication includes ads and information about tourist attractions, plus offers dozens of money-saving coupons for the attractions and nearby restaurants. You can pick up this publication at many hotels and tourist information offices, as well as at the Information Desk located at the Orlando International Airport.

Orlando-Area Activities

Located in the Orlando, Kissimmee, and Lake Buena Vista area, in between The WDW Resort and Universal Studios Florida, there are literally dozens of smaller, independent attractions designed to appeal to tourists of all ages. There are water parks, animal parks (both zoos and shows), unique shopping opportunities, dinner shows, theatrical performances, theme restaurants, fine-dining restaurants, family-oriented (inexpensive) restaurants, boat rides, helicopter tours, and all sorts of other ways to spend a few hours or an entire day having nonstop fun in Florida's sun.

▐▙ TRAVEL TIP

If the weather's bad and you're looking for indoor activities, or you have an afternoon or evening free that you'd like to spend outside of a theme park, consider taking a drive along International Drive in Orlando. In addition to finding literally hundreds of restaurants and stores, you'll also find many popular tourist attractions and activities suitable for the entire family.

The following are just a few of the many Orlando-area attractions designed for families that are available outside of The WDW Resort (many of which are located along International Drive). These attractions are listed in alphabetical order. Call each attraction directly for driving directions and admission prices.

Air Florida Charter, Inc., ✆(407) 888-4114—Aerial sightseeing flights that include a bird's-eye viewing of The WDW Resort, SeaWorld, and Universal Studios Florida are offered. All tours are narrated and provide excellent photo opportunities.

Arabian Nights, ✆(800) 553-6116—This family-oriented dinner show features a cast of over fifty of the world's most famous horses in an indoor twenty-five-act equestrian show. Reservations are required.

Balloons by Renee, ✆(407) 422-3529—Hot-air balloon rides at sunrise are offered.

Belz Factory Outlet World, ✆(407) 354-0126—This shopping center features 170 outlet shops in one location. Save up to 75 percent off of retail prices.

Boggy Creek Airboat Rides, ✆(407) 344-9550, *⊘www.bcair boats.com*—Explore some of Florida's wetlands with a professional guide, while traveling at speeds of up to 45 miles per hour. You might even see alligators in their natural habitat.

Busch Gardens, ✆(888) 800-5447, *⊘www.buschgardens.com*— Located in Tampa, Florida (about a sixty-minute drive from The WDW Resort), this is an entirely different theme park experience that features some of the best thrill rides you'll find anywhere on the East Coast. Busch Gardens also features a world-famous wildlife animal park and a water park.

Cinemark USA, Inc., ✆(407) 351-3117, *⊘www.cinemark.com*—In the Orlando area, moviegoers have a selection of state-of-the-art theaters to choose from. Watching a movie is a relatively inexpensive yet entertaining activity.

Colonial Lanes (Bowling), ✆(407) 894-0361—This bowling alley, located at 400 North Primrose in Orlando, features thirty-two Brunswick lanes and a game room. It's open daily between 9:00 A.M. and midnight.

Dolly Parton's Dixie Stampede Dinner & Show, (866) 443-4943, ✆(407) 238-4455, *⊘www.dixiestampede.com*—You'll enjoy a delicious rotisserie chicken dinner as you watch this fun-filled musical extravaganza, produced by Dolly Parton. Relive the splendor of the Old South as you watch cowboys on horses perform stunts and see a stampede of buffalos. This $28 million production is colorful, action-packed, patriotic, and fun for the whole family. The custom-designed theater/dining room is located just a few minutes from SeaWorld and is adjacent to the Orlando Premium Outlets mall. Shows are presented nightly at 6:30 P.M. and 8:30 P.M. Admission: $43.99 (adults) and $28.99 (kids).

Fighter Pilots USA, ✆(800) 568-6748, ✑*www.fighterpilotsusa.com*—Experience an air combat mission with an F-16 fighter pilot in a Merchetti fighter trainer. No experience is necessary.

The Florida Mall, ✆(407) 851-6255, ✑*www.simon.com*—This is the largest indoor mall in the Orlando area. What you'll find here are more than 200 specialty stores, five department stores, and restaurants.

Gatorland, ✆(407) 855-5496, ✆(800) 393-JAWS, ✑*www.gatorland.com*—See live alligator wrestling, along with many alligators up close. This zoo-like attraction also features all sorts of exotic snakes and a special kids' area/petting zoo.

Golf—If you have a passion for golf, there are dozens of public and members-only golf courses throughout the Orlando area. For a complete listing of golf courses, driving ranges, and pro shops, check the Greater Orlando Yellow Pages, found at most public telephones and within the majority of hotel rooms.

Green Meadows Petting Farm, ✆(407) 846-0770, ✑*www.greenmeadowsfarm.com*—Designed with kids in mind, this petting zoo allows young people to get close to the animals. Visitors can interact with ostriches, ducks, potbellied pigs, peacocks, sheep, cows, donkeys, an American bison, and other farm animals.

Jungleland Zoo, ✆(407) 396-1012, ✑*www.thejunglelandzoo.com*—See hundreds of rare and exotic animals (over 500 in all). Several live animal shows are also presented throughout the day. This outdoor zoo is located at 4580 West Irlo Bronson Highway in Kissimmee.

KartWorld, ✎(407) 396-4800—Take a few laps in a high-powered go-kart. The track at this driving facility is almost one mile long. The cost is $3.75 per lap. Bumper boats and other activities can also be experienced here for an additional fee.

Kissimmee Billie Swamp Safari, ✎(800) 949-6101—The Seminole Tribe of Florida invites guests to their reservation for a fun-filled day of air boat rides, swamp buggy eco-tours, reptile and alligator exhibits, hiking tours, and other family-oriented activities.

Mall at Millenia, ✎(407) 363-3555, ✎*www.mallatmillenia.com*— This is the newest and most prestigious indoor mall in the Orlando area. It features dozens of upscale stores and restaurants. The mall is open Monday through Saturday, between 10 A.M. and 9:30 P.M., and on Sundays, between 11 A.M. and 7 P.M. It's located right off of exit 78 of I-4 at 4200 Conroy Road in Orlando.

Medieval Times Dinner and Tournament, ✎(800) 229-8300, ✎(407) 396-1518, ✎*www.medievaltimes.com*—This dinner show transports guests back to the medieval era, a time when knights were revered as heroes. While guests enjoy a multicourse feast, eaten without benefit of utensils, a cast of 100 knights on horseback (and other costumed characters) participate in an interactive show that kids and teens in particular will enjoy. The show includes authentic jousting matches, hand-to-hand combat, and a rather lighthearted storyline. Price (including dinner): $44.95 (adults) and $29.95 (kids).

Orlando Science Center, ✎(407) 514-2000, ✎(888) OSC-4FUN, ✎*www.osc.org*—If you're looking for an educational and fun indoor activity to experience with your kids, visit Orlando's Science Center, which offers many fully interactive exhibits, plus a planetarium and laser shows.

Ripley's Believe It or Not! Museum, ☎(407) 363-4418, ✐*www.ripleysorlando.com*—See, hear, and experience a museum full of the strange, wacky, and totally outrageous. Admission: $15.95 (adults) and $10.95 (kids). This attraction is located at 8201 International Drive in Orlando.

Skull Kingdom, ☎(407) 354-1564, ✐*www.skullkingdom.com*—This "haunted family attraction" is a fun-filled haunted mansion, complete with live actors and special effects. A magic dinner show is presented nightly for an additional admission fee.

Skycoaster, ☎(407) 397-2509, ✐*www.adventuresinflorida.net/Skycoaster.htm*—Most people have heard of bungee jumping and sky diving; Skycoaster is a spin-off of these sports. It allows brave riders to soar through the air at speeds of up to 70 miles per hour while strapped into a harness that's held by a giant rubber band and that swings freely from a tall tower. This attraction is located in nearby Kissimmee, Florida. Prices start at $37 per flight. Visit the Web site for a $5-off discount coupon.

Skyventure, ☎(407) 903-1150, ☎(800) SKY-FUN1, ✐*www.skyventure.com*—This is a skydiving wind tunnel that allows non experienced and experienced skydivers alike to experience the thrill of skydiving without jumping out of a plane. Instead, riders fly on a 120-mile-per-hour column of air.

Splendid China, ☎(800) 244-6226, ✐*www.floridasplendidchina.com*—This attraction features over sixty detailed replicas of China's famous landmarks, as well as a live animal show featuring tigers. There's also "The Mysterious Kingdom of the Orient" acrobatic show presented every evening, as well as shops and dining opportunities. Admission: $28.88 (adults) and $18.18 (kids). AAA members and senior citizens receive a 10 percent discount.

Titanic: Ship of Dreams, ☎(407) 248-1166 ext: 3103, ✐*www.titanicshipofdreams.com*—This museum is designed primarily for teens and adults. The exhibit features over 200 priceless artifacts from the

Titanic as well as multimedia documentaries and interactive exhibits that retell the story of this ill-fated cruise ship.

Water Mania, &(407) 396-2626, *www.watermania-florida.com*— Fans of water parks will enjoy the various fun-filled water slides and water-based attractions at this park.

Wet 'N Wild, &(407) 351-1800, *www.wetnwild.com*—This water park features all sorts of water slides, pools, and fun-filled activities for the entire family. Wet 'N Wild also offers a huge video arcade. If you'll be visiting Wet 'N Wild and the Universal Orlando Resort theme parks, save money by purchasing an Orlando FlexTicket. (See Chapter 14 for more information.)

WonderWorks, &(407) 351-8800, *www.wonderworksonline.com*— This high-tech arcade and entertainment center offers a variety of cutting-edge arcade games, virtual reality attractions, and motion-simulator rides. Also featured is what WonderWorks calls the world's largest Laser Tag Arena and a virtual reality attraction that allows guests to "create" their own virtual roller coaster and then ride it. It's located at 9067 International Drive in Orlando. (Look for the upside-down building!) A magic dinner show is presented nightly (for an additional admission fee). Visit the Web site for a discounted admission coupon.

World of Orchids, &(407) 396-1887—If you enjoy gardening, flowers, and nature, World of Orchids offers the largest permanent indoor display of flowering orchids, as well as exotic fish, birds, African chameleons, and more.

Kennedy Space Center and Florida's Space Coast

Located about 35 miles east of The WDW Resort is Florida's Space Coast region, which features three of Florida's top ten beaches (according to *Southern Living* magazine). In addition to the beaches, this area features incredible shopping, museums, and water sport activities for the entire family. Plus, you can visit the world-famous Kennedy Space Center (a fun and educational experience unto itself).

If you have a rental car, taking a day trip to Florida's Space Coast can be an exciting break from the theme parks. To reach this area by car from Orlando, take the Bee Line Expressway East to A1A. For additional information about Florida's Space Coast region, call the Office of Tourism at ✆(800) 93-OCEAN or point your Web browser to ✑*www.Space-Coast.com*.

Kennedy Space Center

From the early days of America's space program, the Kennedy Space Center has played a pivotal role. Through the Mercury, Gemini, and Apollo space shuttle programs, the NASA mission control and launch facility has captured the world's attention.

Home of the legendary Launch Control Center, where NASA engineers have guided launches since the Apollo program of the early 1960s, Kennedy Space Center boasts the Vehicle Assembly Building, which is one of the largest buildings in the world, plus the space shuttle launch pad.

🧳 TRAVEL TIP

In addition to the lovely beaches and the Kennedy Space Center, some of the awesome family-oriented activities and attractions available within the Space Coast area include: Cocoa Beach Pier (✆321-783-7549), Ron Jon Surf Shop (✆321-799-8888), the Brevard Zoo (✆321-254-WILD), the Air Force Space and Missile Museum (✆321-499-4444), The U.S. Space Camp Florida (✆800-63-SPACE), the U.S. Astronaut Hall of Fame (✆321-269-6100), and Island Boat Rides (✆321-544-3490).

The Kennedy Space Center offers about a day's worth of activities, tours, and fun for all ages. There's also an IMAX theater showing the 3D movie *Space Station*, which takes viewers on a visually stunning journey to the space station located 220 miles above the earth.

The Kennedy Space Center is very different from your typical museum, plus it offers an experience that's far different from what you'd get at nearby theme parks. You'll find many hands-on exhibits that are designed to be inspirational, educational, and fun at the same time. There's also a Spaceflight Simulator that guests can experience firsthand, and special programs like the Astronaut Training Experience. Another special treat offered here is the Lunch with an Astronaut program. For an additional fee, kids and teens can experience a once-in-a-lifetime chance to have a three-course lunch with a real-life astronaut. Guests have the opportunity to ask questions and have their photo taken with the astronaut. Price: $29.95 (adults) and $19.95 (kids). Reservations are required.

For additional information about Kennedy Space Center, call ✆(321) 499-4444 or visit ✑*www.KennedySpaceCenter.com*. The visitor's center is open daily from 9 A.M. until dusk. Admission prices vary, based on the tours, exhibits, live shows, and activities you'd like to experience. The Maximum Access Admission Ticket is priced at $33 (adults) and $23 (kids) and includes the Kennedy Space Center Tour, IMAX films, admission to the Astronaut Hall of Fame, and all attractions and exhibits.

🧳 TRAVEL TIP

Looking for some out-of-this-world gifts and souvenirs? Be sure to visit the Space Shop at Kennedy Space Center. It's the largest retail store in the world that's devoted to space-themed merchandise. You can also order merchandise by phone at ✆(800) 621-9826.

CHAPTER 20

Planning Your Itinerary

IT'S A WISE IDEA TO DO A BIT OF PREPLANNING IN order to help ensure you make the most of your vacation and stay within your allocated budget. After all, unless you'll be staying in Orlando for a long period of time, it's impossible to see and do everything. Thus, you need to make decisions about how you'll spend your time.

Plan Accordingly

As you plan your itinerary, make sure to obtain input from everyone you'll be traveling with. Also, leave plenty of flexibility in each day's schedule. Allow ample time to explore and enjoy experiences as they happen, without worrying too much about staying on a timetable and getting to the next preplanned activity. In most cases, creating an itinerary with plans down to the hour or minute might make you more organized, but it will also create a tremendous level of stress during your vacation as you run around trying to stick to your schedule. Be sure to leave time in your schedule for travel between destinations, meals, and rest/relaxation.

For the purposes of preplanning your itinerary and visiting theme parks, it's best to divide your day into three chunks of time:

morning, afternoon, and evening/nighttime. Use the following Travel Itinerary worksheets to help preplan your itinerary, keeping in mind that you'll most likely be altering this itinerary once you arrive in Orlando and start actually experiencing your vacation. Use these worksheets to guide you in scheduling the things you believe you (and your family) will most enjoy based on the time you have available.

Airline Information

Departing date:
Departing time:
Airline:
Flight number(s)/connecting cities:
Departing airport:
Arriving airport:
Arrival time:
Seat assignment(s):

Returning date (to go home):
Departing time:
Airline:
Flight number(s)/connecting cities:
Departing airport:
Arrival time (to home city):
Seat assignment(s):

Travel agency used:
Travel agent/airline phone number(s):

Parking lot name/number at airport:
Location/aisle:

Airport Ground Transportation Information

Getting to the airport:

Taxi/limo service name:
Phone number:
Reservation number:
Pickup date/time:
Pickup location:

Getting home from the airport:

Taxi/limo service name:
Phone number:
Reservation number:
Pickup date/time:
Pickup location:

Rental Car Information

Rental car company:
Confirmation number:
Daily rate:
Pickup location:
Rental car company phone number:
Type of car reserved:

Accommodation Information

Hotel/resort name:
Phone number:
Reservation number:
Check-in date:
Check-out date:
Type of accommodations reserved:

DAY 1

Date:
Day of week:

Morning Activities

Time	Location	Activity	Description

Breakfast restaurant:
Reservation time:
Restaurant phone number:

Afternoon Activities

Time	Location	Activity	Description

Lunch restaurant:
Reservation time:
Restaurant phone number:

DAY 1

Evening/Nighttime Activities

Time	Location	Activity	Description

Dinner restaurant:

Reservation time:

Restaurant phone number:

Notes

DAY 2

Date:

Day of week:

Morning Activities

Time	Location	Activity	Description

Breakfast restaurant:

Reservation time:

Restaurant phone number:

Afternoon Activities

Time	Location	Activity	Description

Lunch restaurant:

Reservation time:

Restaurant phone number:

DAY 2

Evening/Nighttime Activities

Time	Location	Activity	Description

Dinner restaurant:

Reservation time:

Restaurant phone number:

Notes

DAY 3

Date:

Day of week:

Morning Activities

Time	Location	Activity	Description

Breakfast restaurant:

Reservation time:

Restaurant phone number:

Afternoon Activities

Time	Location	Activity	Description

Lunch restaurant:

Reservation time:

Restaurant phone number:

DAY 3

Evening/Nighttime Activities

Time	Location	Activity	Description

Dinner restaurant:

Reservation time:

Restaurant phone number:

Notes

DAY 4

Date:
Day of week:

Morning Activities

Time	Location	Activity	Description

Breakfast restaurant:
Reservation time:
Restaurant phone number:

Afternoon Activities

Time	Location	Activity	Description

Lunch restaurant:
Reservation time:
Restaurant phone number:

DAY 4

Evening/Nighttime Activities

Time	Location	Activity	Description

Dinner restaurant:

Reservation time:

Restaurant phone number:

Notes

DAY 5

Date:
Day of week:

Morning Activities

Time	Location	Activity	Description

Breakfast restaurant:
Reservation time:
Restaurant phone number:

Afternoon Activities

Time	Location	Activity	Description

Lunch restaurant:
Reservation time:
Restaurant phone number:

DAY 5

Evening/Nighttime Activities

Time	Location	Activity	Description

Dinner restaurant:

Reservation time:

Restaurant phone number:

Notes

DAY 6

Date:
Day of week:

Morning Activities

Time	Location	Activity	Description

Breakfast restaurant:
Reservation time:
Restaurant phone number:

Afternoon Activities

Time	Location	Activity	Description

Lunch restaurant:
Reservation time:
Restaurant phone number:

DAY 6

Evening/Nighttime Activities

Time	Location	Activity	Description

Dinner restaurant:

Reservation time:

Restaurant phone number:

Notes

DAY 7

Date:
Day of week:

Morning Activities

Time	Location	Activity	Description

Breakfast restaurant:
Reservation time:
Restaurant phone number:

Afternoon Activities

Time	Location	Activity	Description

Lunch restaurant:
Reservation time:
Restaurant phone number:

DAY 7

Evening/Nighttime Activities

Time	Location	Activity	Description

Dinner restaurant:

Reservation time:

Restaurant phone number:

Notes

DAY 8

Date:
Day of week:

Morning Activities

Time	Location	Activity	Description

Breakfast restaurant:
Reservation time:
Restaurant phone number:

Afternoon Activities

Time	Location	Activity	Description

Lunch restaurant:
Reservation time:
Restaurant phone number:

DAY 8

Evening/Nighttime Activities

Time	Location	Activity	Description

Dinner restaurant:

Reservation time:

Restaurant phone number:

Notes

DAY 9

Date:
Day of week:

Morning Activities

Time	Location	Activity	Description

Breakfast restaurant:
Reservation time:
Restaurant phone number:

Afternoon Activities

Time	Location	Activity	Description

Lunch restaurant:
Reservation time:
Restaurant phone number:

DAY 9

Evening/Nighttime Activities

Time	Location	Activity	Description

Dinner restaurant:

Reservation time:

Restaurant phone number:

Notes

DAY 10

Date:
Day of week:

Morning Activities

Time	Location	Activity	Description

Breakfast restaurant:
Reservation time:
Restaurant phone number:

Afternoon Activities

Time	Location	Activity	Description

Lunch restaurant:
Reservation time:
Restaurant phone number:

DAY 10

Evening/Nighttime Activities

Time	Location	Activity	Description

Dinner restaurant:

Reservation time:

Restaurant phone number:

Notes

DAY 11

Date:
Day of week:

Morning Activities

Time	Location	Activity	Description

Breakfast restaurant:
Reservation time:
Restaurant phone number:

Afternoon Activities

Time	Location	Activity	Description

Lunch restaurant:
Reservation time:
Restaurant phone number:

DAY 11

Evening/Nighttime Activities

Time	Location	Activity	Description

Dinner restaurant:

Reservation time:

Restaurant phone number:

Notes

Important Phone Numbers

The following are many of the phone numbers listed within this book that will help you learn more about the various theme parks and other activities within the Greater Orlando area.

AAA Travel Department: ☎(800) 222-7448
AARP: ☎(800) 424-3410
AeroMexico: ☎(800) 237-6639
Air Canada: ☎(800) 247-2262
Air Florida Charter, Inc.: ☎(407) 888-4114
Air Force Space and Missile Museum: ☎(321) 499-4444
AirJamaica: ☎(800) 523-5585
AirTran Airways: ☎(800) AIR-TRAN
AirTransat: ☎(877) 872-6728
Alamo Car Rental: ☎(800) 327-9633
Alaska Airlines: ☎(800) 252-7522
American Airlines: ☎(800) 433-7300
American Eagle: ☎(800) 422-7300
American Express Travel: ☎(800) 346-3607
AmericaWest Airlines: ☎(800) 235-9292
Amtrak: ☎(800) USA-RAIL
ANA Airlines: ☎(800) 235-9262

Arabian Nights: ✆(800) 553-6116

ATA Airlines: ✆(800) 225-2995

Avis Car Rental: ✆(800) 831-2847

Bahamasair: ✆(800) 222-4262

Balloons by Renee: ✆(407) 422-3529

Belz Factory Outlet World: ✆(407) 354-0126

Boggy Creek Airboat Rides: ✆(407) 344-9550

Brevard Zoo: ✆(321) 254-WILD

British Airways: ✆(800) AIR-WAYS

Budget Car Rental: ✆(800) 527-0700

Busch Gardens: (888) 800-5447

Cap'N Jack's Marina: ✆(407) 828-2204

Caribe Royale Resort Suites & Villas: ✆(800) 823-8300

Celebration Health Hospital: ✆(407) 303-4000

Celebration Hotel: ✆(888) 499-3800

Celebration Realty: ✆(407) 566-4663

Centra Care (Walk-In Medical Facility): ✆(407) 239-7777

Central Reservation Service: ✆(800) 548-3311

Champion Air: ✆(800) 225-5658

Check-In Reservation Services: ✆(800) 237-1033

Cinemark USA, Inc.: ✆(407) 351-3117

Cirque du Soleil Show & Ticket Info: ✆(407) 939-7600

CityWalk Special Event Hotline: ✆(407) 224-5500

Cocoa Beach Pier: ✆(321) 783-7549

Colonial Lanes (Bowling): ✆(407) 894-0361

ConJet Airlines: ✆(800) 809-7777

Continental Airlines: ✆(800) 523-3273

Copa Airlines: ✆(800) 359-2672

Del Frisco's Steak House: ✆(407) 645-4443

Delta Airlines/Delta Express: ✆(800) 221-1212

Destinations Travel Service: ✆(407) 859-3501

Discovery Cove (SeaWorld): ✆(800) 4-ADVENTURE

Disney Catalog (Mail Order): ✆(800) 237-5751

Disney Credit Card: ✆(877) 252-6576

Disney Cruise Lines: ✆(888) DCL-2500

Disney Restaurant Advance "Priority Seating" Reservations:
✆(800) WDW-DINE

Disney Souvenir Merchandise: ✆(407) 363-6200

Disney Special Activities / VIP Tours: ✆(407) 560-4033

Disney Theme Park Operating Hours: ✆(407) 824-4321

Disney Tour Information: ✆(407) 939-8687

Disney World Reservations & Information: ✆(407) W-DISNEY

Disney's All-Star Movies Resort: ✆(407) 939-7000

Disney's All-Star Music Resort: ✆(407) 939-6000

Disney's All-Star Sports Resort: ✆(407) 939-5000

Disney's Animal Kingdom Lodge: ✆(407) 934-7639

Disney's Beach Club Resort: ✆(407) 934-8000

Disney's BoardWalk Information: ✆(407) 939-5100

Disney's BoardWalk Resort: ✆(407) 939-5100

Disney's BoardWalk Villas: ✆(407) 939-6200

Disney's Caribbean Beach Resort: ✆(407) 934-3400

Disney's Contemporary Resort: ✆(407) 824-1000

Disney's Coronado Springs Resort: ✆(407) 939-1000

Disney's Fort Wilderness Resort & Campground: ✆(407) 824-2900

Disney's Grand Floridian Resort and Spa: ✆(407) 824-3000

Disney's Kids' Nite Out (Babysitting): ✆(407) 828-0920

Disney's Old Key West Resort: ✆(407) 827-7700

Disney's Polynesian Resort: ✆(407) 824-2000

Disney's Pop Culture Resort ✆(407) W-DISNEY

Disney's Port Orleans Resort—French Quarter Resort: ✆(407) 934-5000

Disney's Port Orleans Riverside Resort: ✆(407) 934-6000

Disney's Racquet Club (Tennis): ✆(407) 824-3578

Disney's Saratoga Springs Resort & Spa: ✆(407) W-DISNEY

Disney's Swan / Dolphin Resort: ✆(407) 934-4000

Disney's Vacation Club (Time-Share): ✆(800) 500-3990

Disney's Wilderness Lodge: ✆(407) 824-3200

Disney's Yacht Club Resort: ✆(407) 934-7000

Doctors-On-Call: ✆(407) 399-3627

Dollar Car Rental: ✆(800) 800-4000

Dolly Parton's Dixie Stampede Dinner & Show: ✆(866) 443-4943

Dolphins in Depth / DiveQuest Info: ✆(407) WDW-TOUR

Downtown Disney/Pleasure Island Info: ✆(407) 934-7781

Dream Cars Unlimited Car Rental: ✆(866) 624-6396

Econo Car: ✆(800) 665-9001

El Al Airlines: ✆(800) 223-6700

Enterprise Car Rental: ✆(800) RENT-A-CAR

Entertainment Books: ✆(800) 933-2605

Eventures Unlimited, Inc.: ✆(800) 356-7891

E-Z Car Rental: ✆(407) 352-3131

Fighter Pilots USA: ✆(800) 568-6748

Florida's Space Coast Office of Tourism: ✆(800) 93-OCEAN

Frontier Airlines: ✆(800) 432-1359

Gatorland: ✆(407) 855-5496

Green Meadows Petting Farm: ✆(407) 846-0770

Greyhound: ✆(800) 229-9424

Hard Rock Hotel: (888) 322-5541

Hertz Car Rental: ✆(800) 654-3131

Hertz Gold Club Reservations: ✆(800) CAR-GOLD

Hilton Grand Vacations Club: ✆(407) 238-2600

Hotel Reservations Network: ✆(800) 511-5321

House of Blues Concert Info: ✆(407) 934-2222

Ibera Airlines: ✆(800) 772-4642

Icelander Airlines: ✆(800) 223-5500

Island Boat Rides: ✆(321) 544-3490

Islands of Adventure Guest Services: ✆(407) 224-4233

JetBlue Airlines: ✆(800) 538-2583

Jungleland Zoo: ✆(407) 396-1012

KartWorld: ✆(407) 396-4800

Kennedy Space Center: ✆(321) 499-4444

Kissimmee Billie Swamp Safari: ✆(800) 949-6101

Kissimmee–St. Cloud Convention & Visitors Bureau: ✆(407) 847-5000

LTU Airlines: ✆(800) 888-0200

Mall at Millenia: ✆(407) 363-3555

Martinair Airlines: ✆(800) 627-8462

Mears Transportation: ✆(407) 423-5566

Medieval Times Dinner and Tournament: ☎(800) 229-8300

Mexicana Airlines: ☎(800) 531-7921

Midwest Airlines: ☎(800) 452-2022

National Car Rental: ☎(800) 227-7368

Northwest Airlines/KLM: ☎(800) 225-2525

Official Visitor Center: ☎(407) 363-5872

Orlando Science Center: ☎(407) 514-2000

Orlando/Orange County Convention & Visitors Bureau: ☎(407) 363-5871

Payless Car Rental: ☎(800) PAY-LESS

Portofino Bay Hotel: ☎(888) 322-5541

Ripley's Believe It or Not! Museum: ☎(407) 363-4418

Ron Jon Surf Shop: ☎(321) 799-8888

Royal Pacific Resort: ☎(407) 503-3000

Sandlake Hospital: ☎(407) 351-8500

Saudia Airlines: ☎(800) 472-8342

SeaWorld Adventure Camp: ☎(866) GO-TO-CAMP

SeaWorld Tours & Programs: ☎(407) 363-2380

SeaWorld General Information: ☎(800) 4-ADVENTURE

Shades of Green on Walt Disney World Resort: ☎(407) 824-3600

Sheraton/Vistana Resort: ☎(407) 239-3100

Skull Kingdom: ☎(407) 354-1564

Skycoaster: ☎(407) 397-2509

Skyventure: ☎(407) 903-1150

Song Airlines: ☎(800) 359-7664

Southwest Airlines: ☎(800) 435-9792

Spirit Airlines: ☎(800) 772-7117

Splendid China: ☎(800) 244-6226

Summerfield Suites: ☎(800) 830-4964

SunTrust Bank: ☎(407) 237-4141

The Florida Mall: ☎(407) 851-6255

Thrifty Car Rental: ☎(800) 367-2277

TicketMaster: ☎(407) 839-3900

Titanic: Ship of Dreams: ☎(407) 248-1166 ext: 3103

U.S. Astronaut Hall of Fame: ☎(321) 269-6100

U.S. Space Camp Florida: ✆(800) 63-SPACE

United Airlines: ✆(800) 241-6522

Universal Cineplex Movie Listings: ✆(407) 354-5998

Universal Orlando Resort Guest Services: ✆(407) 363-8000

Universal Orlando Resort Reservations: ✆(888) U-ESCAPE

Universal Orlando Resort Vacation Package Information:
✆(800) 711-0080

Universal Studios Florida Lost & Found: ✆(407) 224-4244

Universal Studios Merchandise Sales & Information: ✆(407) 363-8320

Universal Studios Studio Audience Info: ✆(407) 224-4233 Option #5

Universal Studios Vacations: ✆(800) 711-0080

Universal Studios VIP Tours: ✆(407) 363-8295

US Airways: ✆(800) 428-4322

US Airways Vacation Packages: ✆(800) 455-0123

Vanguard Airlines: ✆(800) 826-4827

Varig Brazil Airlines: ✆(800) 468-2744

Virgin Atlantic Airlines: ✆(800) 862-8621

Walgreens Pharmacy: ✆(800) 289-2273

Walt Disney Travel Company: ✆(407) 939-7675

Walt Disney World Guest Information: ✆(407) 824-4321

Water Mania: ✆(407) 396-2626

WDW Golf Info & Reservations: ✆(407) WDW-GOLF

WDW Speedway: ✆(800) BE-PETTY

Weather Forecast Info (Orlando Area): ✆(407) 824-4104

Wet 'N Wild: ✆(407) 351-1800

WonderWorks: ✆(407) 351-8800

World of Orchids: ✆(407) 396-1887

Yellow Cab Co. (Taxi): ✆(407) 699-9999

Zoom Airlines: ✆(866) 359-9666

Attraction Selection Worksheet

The following is a worksheet that will help you choose which rides, shows, and attractions you and the people you're traveling with will want to experience once you arrive at each of the Disney theme parks. Place a checkmark in the appropriate column next to each listed ride, show, and attraction.

The Magic Kingdom

Rides, shows, and attractions listed in alphabetical order.

1=Must see   2=Experience if time permits
3=Already experienced   4=No interest

Attraction Name	1	2	3	4
Astro Orbiter	☐	☐	☐	☐
Barnstormer at Goofy's Wiseacre Farm, The	☐	☐	☐	☐
Big Thunder Mountain Railroad	☐	☐	☐	☐
Buzz Lightyear's Space Ranger Spin	☐	☐	☐	☐
Cinderella's Castle	☐	☐	☐	☐
Cinderella's Golden Carrousel	☐	☐	☐	☐
Cinderella's Surprise Celebration	☐	☐	☐	☐
Country Bear Jamboree	☐	☐	☐	☐
Davy Crockett Keel Boats	☐	☐	☐	☐
Disney Railroad	☐	☐	☐	☐
Donald's Boat	☐	☐	☐	☐
Dumbo the Flying Elephant	☐	☐	☐	☐
Enchanted Tiki Room— Under New Management	☐	☐	☐	☐
Frontierland Shootin' Arcade	☐	☐	☐	☐
Goofy's Country Dancin' Jamboree	☐	☐	☐	☐
Hall of Presidents, The	☐	☐	☐	☐
Haunted Mansion, The	☐	☐	☐	☐
It's a Small World	☐	☐	☐	☐
Jungle Cruise, The	☐	☐	☐	☐
Liberty Square Riverboat	☐	☐	☐	☐
Mad Tea Party (a.k.a. The Teacups)	☐	☐	☐	☐
Main Street Cinema	☐	☐	☐	☐
Many Adventures of Winnie the Pooh, The	☐	☐	☐	☐
Mickey's Country House and Judge's Tent	☐	☐	☐	☐
Mickey's PhilharMagic	☐	☐	☐	☐
Mickey's Toontown Fair	☐	☐	☐	☐

Attraction Name	1	2	3	4
Minnie's Country House	☐	☐	☐	☐
Peter Pan's Flight	☐	☐	☐	☐
Pirates of the Caribbean	☐	☐	☐	☐
Share a Dream Come True Parade (Afternoon Character Parade)	☐	☐	☐	☐
Snow White's Scary Adventures	☐	☐	☐	☐
Space Mountain	☐	☐	☐	☐
SpectroMagic Parade	☐	☐	☐	☐
Splash Mountain	☐	☐	☐	☐
Stitch's Great Escape	☐	☐	☐	☐
Swiss Family Treehouse	☐	☐	☐	☐
The Magic Carpets of Aladdin	☐	☐	☐	☐
Timekeeper, The	☐	☐	☐	☐
Tom Sawyer Island	☐	☐	☐	☐
Tomorrowland Indy Speedway	☐	☐	☐	☐
Tomorrowland Transit Authority	☐	☐	☐	☐
Toon Park	☐	☐	☐	☐
Toontown Fair Hall of Fame	☐	☐	☐	☐
Walt Disney's Carousel of Progress	☐	☐	☐	☐
Wishes (Evening Fireworks Show)	☐	☐	☐	☐
Other:	☐	☐	☐	☐
Other:	☐	☐	☐	☐
Other:	☐	☐	☐	☐
Other:	☐	☐	☐	☐
Other:	☐	☐	☐	☐
Other:	☐	☐	☐	☐
Other:	☐	☐	☐	☐
Other:	☐	☐	☐	☐
Other:	☐	☐	☐	☐
Other:	☐	☐	☐	☐
Other:	☐	☐	☐	☐
Other:	☐	☐	☐	☐
Other:	☐	☐	☐	☐
Other:	☐	☐	☐	☐

Epcot

Rides, shows, and attractions listed in alphabetical order.

1=Must see	2=Experience if time permits
3=Already experienced	4=No interest

Attraction Name	1	2	3	4
Body Wars	☐	☐	☐	☐
Cranium Command	☐	☐	☐	☐
Honey, I Shrunk the Audience	☐	☐	☐	☐
Imagination!	☐	☐	☐	☐
Innoventions	☐	☐	☐	☐
Leave a Legacy	☐	☐	☐	☐
Mission: SPACE	☐	☐	☐	☐
Soarin' over California	☐	☐	☐	☐
Spaceship Earth	☐	☐	☐	☐
Test Track	☐	☐	☐	☐
The Land	☐	☐	☐	☐
The Living Seas	☐	☐	☐	☐
The Making of Me	☐	☐	☐	☐
Universe of Energy	☐	☐	☐	☐
Wonders of Life	☐	☐	☐	☐
Other:	☐	☐	☐	☐
Other:	☐	☐	☐	☐
Other:	☐	☐	☐	☐

The World Showcase at Epcot

Rides, shows, and attractions listed in alphabetical order.

| 1=Must see | 2=Experience if time permits |
| 3=Already experienced | 4=No interest |

Attraction Name	1	2	3	4
American Adventure	☐	☐	☐	☐
Canada	☐	☐	☐	☐
China	☐	☐	☐	☐
France	☐	☐	☐	☐
Germany	☐	☐	☐	☐
IllumiNations: Reflections of Earth	☐	☐	☐	☐
Italy	☐	☐	☐	☐
Japan	☐	☐	☐	☐
Mexico	☐	☐	☐	☐
Morocco	☐	☐	☐	☐
Norway	☐	☐	☐	☐
Tapestry of Dreams Parade	☐	☐	☐	☐
United Kingdom	☐	☐	☐	☐
Other:	☐	☐	☐	☐
Other:	☐	☐	☐	☐
Other:	☐	☐	☐	☐

The Disney-MGM Studios

Rides, shows, and attractions listed in alphabetical order.

1=Must see   2=Experience if time permits
3=Already experienced   4=No interest

Attraction Name	1	2	3	4
Beauty and the Beast	☐	☐	☐	☐
Disney Stars and Motor Cars Parade	☐	☐	☐	☐
Disney-MGM Studios Backlot Tour, The	☐	☐	☐	☐
Fantasmic!	☐	☐	☐	☐
Great Movie Ride, The	☐	☐	☐	☐
"Honey, I Shrunk the Kids" Movie Set Adventure	☐	☐	☐	☐
Indiana Jones Epic Stunt Spectacular	☐	☐	☐	☐
Jim Henson's Muppet Vision 3D	☐	☐	☐	☐
Magic of Disney Animation, The	☐	☐	☐	☐
Mickey's Sorcerer's Hat	☐	☐	☐	☐
Osborne Family Spectacle of Lights, The	☐	☐	☐	☐
Playhouse Disney—Live on Stage!	☐	☐	☐	☐
Radio Disney Studios	☐	☐	☐	☐
Rock 'n' Roller Coaster Starring Aerosmith	☐	☐	☐	☐
Sorcery in the Sky Fireworks Spectacular	☐	☐	☐	☐
Sounds Dangerous: Starring Drew Carey	☐	☐	☐	☐
Star Tours	☐	☐	☐	☐
Stunt Show Spectacular	☐	☐	☐	☐
Twilight Zone: Tower of Terror 4, The	☐	☐	☐	☐
Voyage of the Little Mermaid	☐	☐	☐	☐
Walt Disney: One Man's Dream	☐	☐	☐	☐
Who Wants to Be a Millionaire—Play It!	☐	☐	☐	☐
Other:	☐	☐	☐	☐
Other:	☐	☐	☐	☐
Other:	☐	☐	☐	☐
Other:	☐	☐	☐	☐

Disney's Animal Kingdom

Rides, shows, and attractions listed in alphabetical order.

1=Must see   2=Experience if time permits
3=Already experienced   4=No interest

Attraction Name	1	2	3	4
Affection Section	☐	☐	☐	☐
Boneyard, The	☐	☐	☐	☐
Conservation Station, The	☐	☐	☐	☐
Cretaceous Trail	☐	☐	☐	☐
DINOSAUR	☐	☐	☐	☐
Discovery Island	☐	☐	☐	☐
Expedition EVEREST	☐	☐	☐	☐
Festival of the Lion King	☐	☐	☐	☐
Flights of Wonder at Caravan Stage	☐	☐	☐	☐
Fossil Fun Games	☐	☐	☐	☐
It's Tough to Be a Bug!	☐	☐	☐	☐
Kali River Rapids: A Whitewater Adventure	☐	☐	☐	☐
Kilimanjaro Safaris	☐	☐	☐	☐
Look Backstage!	☐	☐	☐	☐
Maharajah Jungle Trek	☐	☐	☐	☐
Mickey's Jammin' Jungle Parade	☐	☐	☐	☐
Oasis, The	☐	☐	☐	☐
Pangani Forest Exploration Trail	☐	☐	☐	☐
Pocahontas and Her Forest Friends	☐	☐	☐	☐
Primeval Whirl	☐	☐	☐	☐
Rafiki's Planet Watch	☐	☐	☐	☐
Tarzan Rocks!	☐	☐	☐	☐
Tree of Life, The	☐	☐	☐	☐
TriceraTop Spin	☐	☐	☐	☐
Wildlife Express to Conservation Station	☐	☐	☐	☐
Other:	☐	☐	☐	☐
Other:	☐	☐	☐	☐

Index

Everything® You Need for a Family Vacation to Remember

The Everything® Family Guide to Hawaii
ISBN 10: 1-59337-054-7
ISBN 13: 978-1-59337-054-1
$14.95

The Everything® Family Guide to New York City, 2nd Ed.
ISBN 10: 1-59337-136-5
ISBN 13: 978-1-59337-136-4
$14.95

The Everything® Family Guide to Washington D.C., 3rd Ed.
ISBN 10: 1-59869-287-9
ISBN 13: 978-1-59869-287-7
$14.95

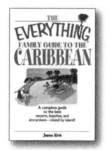

The Everything® Family Guide to the Caribbean
ISBN 10: 1-59337-427-5
ISBN 13: 978-1-59337-427-3
$14.95

The Everything® Family Guide to Cruise Vacations
ISBN 10: 1-59337-428-3
ISBN 13: 978-1-59337-428-0
$14.95

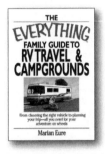